No One Can Stop the Rain

A Chronicle of Two Foreign Aid Workers during the Angolan Civil War

Karin Moorhouse & Wei Cheng

INSOMNIAC PRESS

Library and Archives Canada Cataloguing in Publication

Moorhouse, Karin, 1961-
No one can stop the rain : a chronicle of two foreign aid workers during the Angolan Civil War / Karin Moorhouse and Wei Cheng.

Includes bibliographical references and index.
ISBN 1-894663-90-X

1. Moorhouse, Karin, 1961- 2. Cheng, Wei, 1958- 3. Angola--History--Civil War, 1975-2002--Civilian relief. 4. Doctors Without Borders (Association). 5. Angola--History--Civil War, 1975-2002--Personal narratives, Australian. 6. Volunteers--Australia--Biography. 7. Volunteers--Angola--Biography. I. Cheng, Wei, 1958- II. Title.

DT1424.M66A3 2005   967.304   C2005-900248-4

The publisher gratefully acknowledges the support of the Canada Council, the Ontario Arts Council and the Department of Canadian Heritage through the Book Publishing Industry Development Program.

Printed and bound in Canada

Insomniac Press
192 Spadina Avenue, Suite 403
Toronto, Ontario, Canada, M5T 2C2
www.insomniacpress.com

THE CANADA COUNCIL | LE CONSEIL DES ARTS
FOR THE ARTS | DU CANADA
SINCE 1957 | DEPUIS 1957

ONTARIO ARTS COUNCIL
CONSEIL DES ARTS DE L'ONTARIO

No One Can Stop the Rain

A Chronicle of Two Foreign Aid Workers during the Angolan Civil War

To the people of Angola,
especially Manuel Vitangui, who lost his life while trying to
save the lives of others.
(Kuito, November 25, 2000)

Wei and Manuel Vitangui, just weeks before his death.
Kuito, October 7, 2000

A portion of the proceeds from the sale of this book will be donated to Médecins Sans Frontières.

Special thanks to our friend Lincoln Siliakus,
who dedicated months of his own valuable time to
edit and refine the first manuscript.

Contents

"Being unwanted, unloved, uncared for, forgotten by everybody, I think that is a much greater hunger, a much greater poverty than the person who has nothing to eat"

Mother Teresa (1910 – 1997)

Foreword

I am proud to write the foreword to *No One Can Stop the Rain* not only because it is a moving and significant work in its own right, but also because I believe that it belongs in a new genre of writing about the human condition.

The book tells the story of two Médecins Sans Frontières volunteers—Wei, a surgeon, and his wife, Karin, a marketing executive, who left their well-paid careers for a year to work in Angola, Africa, during the end of the thirty-year civil war there.

This is a new, world phenomena—young people in privileged western situations giving part of their lives to those who are experiencing mass suffering. This was once the way of the religiously-committed—priests and nuns, for example—and of unusual, often eccentric, people who gave up their lives to work among lepers or other outcast groups.

This new movement of people from all walks of life leaving that life for a time to help other humans outside their own community and their nation-state, often at risk to themselves, is a fascinating development in internationalism. It could even been seen as the humanist side of globalization, something which is usually viewed only as an economic matter.

This book is a fine expression of this new phenomenon and this new life-story genre—one, I suspect, of many such books by those who go out to help—each telling strikingly individual stories of this special involvement in the human condition.

The experiences that Wei and Karin had are not those of a journalist or a scholar or a diplomat or a traveller. These are experiences which can come only through deep and singular, often agonizing, involvement in the lives of others and within another community.

I suspect that the old travellers' tales will now fade in the face of this *engaged* genre of interracial and international experience with its hitherto unavailable insights which, in this case, inspire a narrative that has a sense of urgency which comes only from such engagement.

I am writing this in the week after the tragic Asian tsunami of 2004, where we have seen forms of internationalist volunteer action making an unprecedented appearance and at the same time, presenting to the world, a clearer picture of the multi-faced nature of the Non-Governmental Organizations (NGOs) with a dramatic clarity. In Indonesia alone there are nearly 100 NGOs in action.

The rise of NGOs such as Médecins Sans Frontières is itself a story of positive human innovation and a new creative form of diplomacy and this story, too, is partly told in this book.

In my own research on the League of Nations—the forerunner of the UN—I was interested to discover back then in the 1930s the first tentative signs of the emergence of what we now know as the NGO.

The first glimmer of such a movement came around the doomed World Disarmament Conference of 1932, which was convened by the League of Nations after seven years of planning, and now is all but forgotten. The nation-states of the world—including the US and the USSR—met to adopt a plan to disarm the world. The aim of the conference was to reduce the armed forces of all countries to a level compatible with national safety, ultimately to the level of police forces.

For the first time at an international conference (itself an innovation of the 1920s) citizen organizations from around the world were granted a morning to present their petitions to a conference plenary session and were given the time to speak as 'ordinary people' to the diplomats and statesmen at the conference.

What we now know as NGOs were then designated as the International Organization Tribune at the conference, and in the 1930s a non-governmental body called the Federation of International Organizations was established in Geneva.

In many ways, this book and the experiences it recounts of the work of Médecins Sans Frontières has its historical linkage back to those days.

I was struck by something Karin e-mailed to me about the book. She wrote of the emotional roller-coaster one rides when integrating into new surroundings. "We never write about it specifically in our book, but if you take a retrospective, helicopter view of our stories, written largely while we were in Angola, you see us move through a series of typical emotions. Joining MSF was something we always said we would do 'one day.' Yet from this idealistic juncture, when the decision to go was finally made, we were suddenly overcome by fear: fear of the unknown—worse than the reality itself. On arrival we moved into a state of heightened awareness—one of shock and awe at strange, new conditions. Before long we were emotionally overwhelmed as we settled in and tried to make a home for ourselves with death everywhere. However, by drawing strength from those we observed around us, we soon moved into the middle phase, that of normalization, when we started to take things in our strides; settle into a new rhythm; and accept new standards of existence. This was quickly followed by something we called 'desensitization', when everything became so normal that we didn't even bat an eyelid. And finally we arrived at a condition of love—we felt so much a part of the place that we didn't want to leave; almost losing perspective on the inherent dangers. This was the last stage of integration before we were confronted with the final turmoil—the counter-shock one experiences when returning home."

I thought this a precise and believable summing up of the emotional demands of such a commitment.

Karin and Wei worked through the NGO, Médecins Sans Frontières, an international humanitarian aid organization that has provided emergency medical assistance to populations in danger in more than eighty countries since its establishment in 1971. MSF frequently finds itself involved in situations of war and conflict; refugees and displaced people; natural or man-made disasters, and long-term assistance programs. In countries where health structures are insufficient or even non-existent MSF collaborates with local authorities to provide medical assistance. MSF works in the rehabilitation of hospitals and dispensaries, vaccination programs, and water and sanitation projects.

MSF also seeks to raise awareness of crisis situations; MSF acts as a witness and will speak out, either in private or in public, about the plight of populations in danger for whom MSF works.

This book fulfils this part of the MSF mission — to bear witness.

Karin says of their book that it is based on e-mail correspondence and diary notes—a chronicle of their journey to Kuito. The remnants of a provincial capital, at the heart of the country, the city had the unenviable reputation of being one of the world's most heavily mined cities...a vast humanitarian citadel...of victims of landmines and war, the malnourished and the displaced...and that it also captures the ordinary life of both residents and field volunteers in this dire situation.

This book then is one of the first of many personal accounts we will see of work coming out of this world movement, the implications of which are still unchartered and unforeseeable, but which could be of significant diplomatic importance.

The book bears witness to a new form of awakening of the human spirit.

— Frank Moorhouse
  Sydney, January 2005

Frank Moorhouse is the author of **Grand Days** *and* **Dark Palace***, two historical novels which are set against the background of the rise and fall of the League of Nations in the 1920s and 1930s after it struggled to prevent World War II. A former Woodrow Wilson Scholar and Senior Fulbright Fellow, he has written and lectured on international organizations and the future of international cooperation. Karin Moorhouse is his niece.*

Introduction

Karin writes...

In early 2000, when Wei and I left our comfortable life in Hong Kong to volunteer for Médecins Sans Frontières (MSF) we barely knew where to find Kuito, Angola on the map. Although we had wanted a posting in Africa, we only had vague notions of the complex problems that faced that particular nation that could have been Africa's richest. Angola was ruled by Portugal for 475 years until 1975 and, at the time of our arrival, had been wracked by civil war for over three decades. It was Africa's longest running conflict. After heavy fighting resumed once more in the early nineties, nearly one million people lost their lives.

We were assigned to Kuito, the remnants of a provincial capital at the heart of the country. With its unenviable reputation of being one of the world's most heavily mined cities, Kuito was also home to over one hundred thousand displaced people who had been uprooted by war, starved, brutalized, and forgotten. Kuito was a tormented town, where a cruel past collided with perpetual uncertainty. It was also a vast humanitarian citadel—a refuge where people went in search of life's basics: food, shelter, security, and medical care.

This is a chronicle of our encounters as MSF volunteers. These stories remain embedded in our minds and vividly illustrate the widening chasm that exists between our modern society and the less privileged world. Years of war and neglect had driven the standard of living for the majority of Angolans back to the Stone Age. Yet this huge humanitarian crisis was closer than one might like to imagine—geographically, closer to Europe than Sydney is to Hong Kong.

Yet, how do you write a book like this without falling into that omnipresent trap, where images morph into the wallpaper of today's television-fed society? We have all seen them before: conflict in Africa, vivid sensational images of emaciated children, poverty and death that are the ugly the face of any war. These are real people after all. The problem is this: our minds are highly self-protective. While misery is an unavoidable reality of Angola, pictures like this easily numb us into a state of low-level consciousness about what is happening in Africa today. The irony is, having been there and discovered things for ourselves, we now know those images are very real. But what this imagery fails to capture is a perspective of "normal" life in a desperate situation. In writing, we hope to fill some of these voids.

During our time in Angola, eleven wars were being fought in Africa, affecting half the countries on the continent and twenty percent of the population.[1] This astonishing statistic begs to question another phenomenon—our tendency to heap the problems of African nations together into one ill-defined basket. Doubtlessly, we do this to make our fatigue seem justified. It makes it easier to cast Africa off into the furthest reaches of our minds. We find discreet comfort in its apparent irrelevance to our everyday life. However, war-weary and deprived, Angolans wished for nothing more than lasting peace and the chance to get on with their lives. They had endured a civil war that had lurched on unabated for over thirty years. The majority had never experienced something as simple as peace.

Our observations come from the rather unusual perspective of an Australian-Chinese couple and are rooted in our own cross-cultural experiences. Over the years, we have often cringed at ill-informed Western interpretations of Chinese culture and Chinese views of Western morés. We know too well that the process of real social integration is both slow and laboured and were therefore acutely aware of our limitations as foreigners in Angola. Wei and I lived in Kuito for less than a year—a short time in which to cope with the demands of a new language, a new culture, and new jobs. While we did all we could to keep abreast of current affairs and the differing aspects of Angolan society, our story is little more than a narrative of a journey to a new land and our work amongst the people of Kuito. In addition, we were aid workers for the first time. In this context, all we did was bear witness to a world that churned on around us.

Our portrait of Kuito was largely written during our time there in the form of e-mails sent to family and friends. We needed this: writing was therapy, helping us process events that took us to the very edge of words. So much happened that we simply felt obliged to record it in the form of photos and the best words we could muster. But our correspondence quickly became more than that—these e-mails generated strong interest as our friends and family stayed compassionately engaged in what was happening in this little-known corner of the world. It was also they who encouraged us to share our experiences with a larger audience through this book.

The first part of this book emerged from the series of descriptive e-mails written mainly by Wei as a means of reassuring a fretting wife of his safety. Once I arrived, eight weeks later, the task of writing fell largely to me, as Wei's increased workload made it hard for him to settle in front of a computer. Many of the passages read much as they were intended—as e-mails to family or friends. We combined these with historical perspectives, diary notes, unfinished letters, thoughts, and stories that were, frankly, too difficult to share with anyone at the time. Collectively they paint a picture of life as it unfolded around us; a life that touched us to the core. On reflection, they also capture a little of what life is like for aid workers in any of today's trouble spots and may provide some insight to others who, like us, have always said they will volunteer "one day."

Above all, we hope this book pays sufficient tribute to ordinary Angolans and their remarkable ability to endure human misery. These inspirational people opened us up to the unexpected: something that went well beyond the media imagery, something we learned can be repeatedly terrorized, but never obliterated. In the face of untold adversity, we found an enduring human spirit. The sheer resilience of Angola's forgotten rural population was constantly exhibited in a steadfast will to survive: to plod on, to see the dawning of the next day, or the next hour. That was both inspiring and humbling.

Since leaving Angola, this protracted war has finally ended, but it should never be assumed that the plight of its people can now be cast aside.

Angolan flag flies over the remnants of residential Kuito.

Chapter 1
The Busyness Trap

Karin continues...

Until joining MSF, we were just regular Hong Kongers, largely preoccupied with our own stress-pressed lives. By invitation, we attended the occasional charity ball, but these fancy black-tie events were oxymorons for us. Engrossed entirely in our careers, we never seemed to find time to do anything more charitable than pull out a chequebook.

We were often asked what possessed us to uproot everything and join MSF. We had our pat answers, like: "It was a life goal," or "It fulfilled a need to do something more meaningful." And whilst all of that is true, these answers come across as rather trite to us now. Moreover, since Wei and I met in early 1981, a volunteer project like this was something we had always talked about. In fact, it was as students at the University of New South Wales in Sydney that the idea of volunteering was born. As if proving the circular nature of history, Afghanistan dominated world news back then. The early eighties was the era of the Mujahedeen, part of the history of the Cold War in which the Soviet Union was the invader and the US was backing the other side—the side that spawned Osama bin Laden and Al-Qaeda. But all that is another story.

Then, as now, MSF was working in Afghanistan helping civilians caught in the crossfire.[2] I have distinct recollections that our interest was ignited by something as simple as a television documentary about a relatively new organization called Doctors Without Borders (MSF). Idealistic as we were in our youth, the work of the volunteers captivated us. From the comforts of the student lounge, we soon found ourselves confronting the idea that we too should make a more constructive commitment to humanity at some point in our lives. It seemed like an easy thing to say. Statements of idealism and social consciousness ride high on a university campus. It is simple to commit to something in the distance, but I am sure we never thought that it would take us some twenty years to do it and that we would actually realize it together.

From that idealistic juncture, life took a fairly predictable path. We graduated from university—Wei became a doctor, and I joined the ranks of young executives bustling towards a marketing career. After a long courtship, we wed in 1988 and left Australia for Hong Kong where Wei trained as a general surgeon and started mind-numbing years of work and study for endless higher qualifications. For the first four years we lived in hospital quarters at Caritas Medical Centre in Sham Shui Po, at that time a suburb still to bene-fit from the urban renewal program. I worked for a leading dairy company in Kwun Tong's industrial heartland and for years com-muted between these two run-down parts of town. Industrial Kowloon was our world. And although I learned to love Sham Shui Po, it was the closest I had come to living in an urban slum.

By the early 1990s, the influx of Vietnamese Boat People had reached a crisis point and the refugee camp in Sham Shui Po had become everyday headlines. With city camps over-burdened and overflowing, dissenting voices grew, opposing the sanctuary Hong Kong offered. We followed the issue with compassion and cringed when we passed the iron huts on Cheung Sha Wan Road that stifled so many dreams of freedom. We watched kids suffer intolerably humid nights, whiling away the hours by staring out through the barbed wire to the streets below. They were unwanted prisoners in the middle of a city that was poised for an unparalleled period of prosperity. Because Caritas was the nearest hospital for the Sham Shui Po camp, we came in contact from time to time with volunteers from MSF. Humbled by their great work in our very own backyard, Wei and I soon reaffirmed our pledge to volunteer for MSF. Even so, it still took us a further decade to do it.

By that time, Hong Kong had been reunited with China, and the refugee camps were all but gone. The Dragon Centre, a shopping mall that married shimmering glass with a quirky theme park, had replaced the iron and barbed wire. We too had moved on. Wei was a pediatric surgeon at Queen Mary Hospital and an assistant profes-sor with the University of Hong Kong. I had moved through the ranks to become a senior executive for Nestlé. I often wonder where all those years went…recollections occluded by the timeless blurry cycle of work and sleep. Our intentions never waned, but we became caught up in life and careers, so it wasn't until the last day of 1999—the momentous end of a century—when we finally made our move.

Many endorsed our decision to follow our hearts, but it was a real shock to others, especially Wei's family. By then, we had moved to the south side of the island, had a beautiful sea-view apartment, and had everything the doubters thought we could ever want. Others delicately alluded to a mid-life crisis. I don't remember any crisis as such; our pledge just morphed into a steely determination. And with age comes a growing self-realization that the great mindless rush up the career ladder leaves its own casualties in its wake. Little by little our conundrum took on something of Socrates' warning: The unexamined life is not worth living.[3] And like a deck of cards being slowly reshuffled, our priorities started to shift. What once seemed important gradually became less so. Our need to do something more meaningful and live true to our word took to the foreground of our minds.

Chapter 2
Resolution

Karin writes…

We left our jobs at the end of March 2000, but as it was to be months before we would be assigned a mission, we took advantage of the time to take a real holiday—our first in ages. It was an ideal opportunity to do things that our careers had always prevented. We spent the first week at home sleeping more than we had in years, before packing up the apartment and putting our life into storage. We used these carefree months to visit friends and family dispersed throughout Asia and Europe, and it wasn't long before we headed to my sister's place, near the sparkling waters of the Bosphorus. Istanbul became our temporary home base for short trips and excursions to neighbouring countries. There we rested, and for the first time in a long while we lived a simple life as a couple. From Turkey we also flew to the headquarters of MSF Belgium for interviews and to attend preparatory training for new volunteers.

In June, when Wei was attending one such course, I stayed with friends in Paris, whiling away the relaxing hours before he joined me. I was wandering leisurely around a department store in a chic suburb when Wei phoned me to explain the proposal. I could tell from his animated voice that he was excited. In his mind, he had probably already decided. I was on the lower ground floor of the store, midway down an aisle among the shelves of stuffed toys, of all things. In an effort to block out the surrounding noise, I pressed my mobile phone engagingly to my ear, finger in the other.

"An-go-la? Civil war…in An-go-la?" I stammered, not knowing whether I was hearing correctly and half-buying a moment to gauge my own reaction. Wei's enthusiasm was not dampened by my hesitation. "Yes, Angola, and with positions for both of us!"

He stalled, bracing himself for my reaction to the next part of the equation.

"But there is a slight problem," he explained gently. "We cannot go together. They want me there in August, but your job won't start until the end of September. That's only about eight weeks later."

I felt momentarily relieved, as if he had fed me the very reason I needed to reject the whole proposal. After all, we had come this far on the overriding premise that this was something we would do together.

"But what about the project in Chad?" I enthused. Prior to leaving Hong Kong, MSF had proposed a mission in southern Chad. We had spent time researching this country and were in many ways mentally prepared for the prospect of life in that dry sub-Saharan country, further north.

As if already charged with the ammunition he needed, Wei rattled off a short précis of the project in Angola and Kuito, where we'd be stationed. He explained that he thought his skills as a surgeon could be put to better use there. The position in Chad was for a physician-surgeon and Wei didn't feel ideally suited. Delighted with the prospect of something for both of us, he was already sold. He coddled me encouragingly, as the implications of war surgery raced through my mind. He was seeking my spontaneous approval, yet I sensed I was being presented with a fait accompli.

"An eight week gap? Isn't there time to discuss things this weekend...here in Paris?" I blurted, feeling somewhat left out. Still struggling to hear and lost in my own whirlpool of concern, I felt my anxiety intensify. Angola? Civil war? Without me?

What does a practical Aussie girl do when faced with that sort of dilemma? Get down to it! Wei arrived in Paris a few days later. We threw ourselves into research and had some really good chats about it. Our first impressions of the country were gleaned from the government Web site, which boasted a host of gentrified topics: art, culture, and music. As a keen chef, I was enthralled by the section entitled "The Cuisine of Angola," where I first learned of the national dish, maize *funge*. Angola's façade appeared to be that of a progressive nation that placed business, economics, and development as high priorities. The Web site's so-called virtual tours of Luanda's tourist attractions, steeped in a Portuguese past, were strangely reassuring. But, as we were to learn, Angolans could not eat tourist attractions and tourists were thin on the ground.

For a more level-headed view, we searched the *Lonely Planet* travel guide, only to be confounded by their lack of coverage on the country—little more than a disquieting warning about Angola's bleak outlook. The guide suggested that reading its pages would be safer than visiting the country. No more comforting was Robert

Young Pelton's armchair guidebook, *The World's Most Dangerous Places*,[4] described as "a look at the places where many fear to tread." We found Angola listed amongst his top ten, along with the likes of Afghanistan, Chechnya, and Colombia.

Wei and I continued to talk about Angola at length and contacted people who had volunteered before us. To our surprise, they spoke lovingly of a great project and warm people. Slowly our initial state of ignorant anxiety evolved into a better-informed view. In a peculiar mix of abject fear and exhilaration, our decision became one of resolute commitment. We decided to go to Kuito.

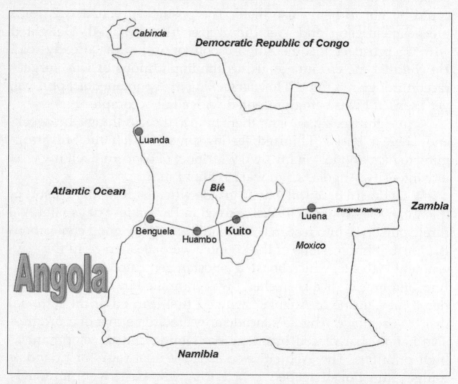

Map of Angola, southwest Africa. Kuito, the capital of Bié province, lies at the heart of the country, along the Benguela Railway.

Chapter 3
Into the Unknown

Wei writes...

As I packed my bags in Istanbul I was overcome by a sense of adventure pitted against fear of the unknown. It was a hot July day with a sunny blue sky that would fill anyone with optimism. We had long been resolved to join MSF, but our decision to leave the comforts of Hong Kong had not been an easy one. We had literally thought about it for years. After all, why would one abandon a comfortable cocoon to opt for lesser certainty? It was as if leaving somehow meant permanent closure on what we had become. These issues, however trivial now, made it easy to procrastinate, and years had slipped by in this way. But these questions loomed as I wrote in my diary:

With sadness I am leaving Istanbul, my fifth "hometown." After sixteen years in Beijing, sixteen in Hong Kong, nine in Sydney, and a year in London, it is my feelings for Istanbul that make it qualify for entry onto my special list. In a short space of time I have grown to love this city: its rich culture, history, and the warm hospitality of its people. These past months have been so special, but today I feel flat, pensive, and more than a little worried. Where am I going? Why? I am hoping this experience will benefit me greatly as a person. Yet, I have no doubt it will be humbling—destined to make me think even harder about life and its true meaning.

As I look back at those words I wrote, I had no idea about the testing experiences we were going to face. What was compelling us to jump into a civil war in Africa? While growing up, I never even imagined so much as leaving China. I often think back to my childhood during the Cultural Revolution, when I had to recite Mao's teachings. I memorized them all and remember many to this day. Yet, I recall one of Mao's essays with clarity; one that made a deep and lasting impression, and I remember reflecting on it as I wrote those parting words in Istanbul. It was Mao's eulogy to Henry Norman Bethune (1890–1938), a Canadian surgeon and true humanitarian worker. In 1938, during the Japanese invasion of China, he worked tirelessly and selflessly alongside the Chinese to provide medical aid until he fatefully cut his finger with a scalpel. The wound became infected and he died of septicemia in a remote, war-torn area of Hebei province in central China. Bethune remained my childhood hero, and I suspect that in some small way it was his example that inspired me to volunteer for MSF.

How could I have imagined back then that so many years later I would make a pilgrimage to his hometown of Gravenhurst, Ontario, and that today I am a medical researcher at his alma mater, the University of Toronto? One of life's wonderful coincidences, I guess.

Wei as a Little Red Guard during the Cultural Revolution in China, 1968.

Chapter 4
Casa Quatro

Wei writes...

I was finally in Angola, the middle of sub-Saharan Africa, having flown in from Paris overnight. I did not sleep well. The dishevelled fellow next to me exuded an overwhelming odour of stale alcohol, which did little to alleviate the usual discomforts. Roused from a jet-lagged stupor, I scrambled down the steps of the plane and into the terminal. Through my bleary eyes, Luanda's airport seemed no more sophisticated than a bus terminal. Three dour-faced officers one-finger typed our personal data, taking an hour to clear the planeload. I eventually got through, however, and was greeted by a colleague who took me directly to head office. I filled out a few forms before being rushed back to the airport once more. It was August 11, 2000, and I was on my way to Kuito.

Even if half its seats had been removed for cargo, the plane was comfortable enough. Two South African pilots welcomed us warmly aboard the twin-prop. They explained the need to fly as high as possible and warned us not to worry about the corkscrew flight path they would perform on landing. Only when they were over the airstrip, would they start their spiralling descent—a precautionary measure to reduce the risk of being shot down. One of my companions casually leaned over and explained that two United Nations (UN) planes had suffered that exact fate about eighteen months prior. UN flight 806 was shot down on December 31, 1998, followed by another in January 1999, killing all twenty-two people on-board. Perhaps her comments weren't intended to cause alarm, as she proceeded to reassure me that battle for Kuito had ended months before. We continued our flight in quiet contemplation.

We flew first to the southern coastal town of Benguela, a town that is supposedly quite beautiful, although I couldn't see much. The pilots told us that they had to complete an assignment there as the airport staff had turned off the runway lights and gone home the previous night before they could deliver their payload. Meanwhile, I had time to get to know my new colleagues: a young nurse called

Anne-Sophie and a Congolese doctor called Génevière, who was accompanying me from the Luanda office, to show me the ropes.

The flight to Kuito usually took an hour or so, up over the escarpment across the plateau, but our detour to Benguela made it last a lot longer. At about 12° south of the equator, Kuito is the capital of Bié, a large province at the heart of the country. Bié is also where one of the country's most important rivers, the Rio Kwanza, rises. I fought my exhaustion by taking advantage of the low altitude to take photographs, and, when Kuito finally came into view, I was fascinated to see my new home from the air—a flat town spread out over a dry ochre plain.

The airstrip proved to be every bit as coarse as the jokes about it and the legendary potholes provided a bumpy welcome. The runway had already been written up in a UN report as the main stumbling block to the humanitarian effort in the region. Long-promised repairs were as elusive as ever. All supplies for MSF and the United Nations World Food Programme (WFP) depended entirely on airfreight and any attempt at maintenance closed the runway for large parts of the day.

We finally landed at the *Aeroporto de Kuito* at about 4 p.m., and I was rushed through the hand-over on the tarmac with the departing surgeon. He was taking the same plane on its return, as he had been waiting weeks for my arrival. I had been delayed by the usual visa problems. My induction was therefore little more than rapid immersion therapy: a jet-lagged twenty-minute briefing on the tarmac about the patients and staff who awaited me at the hospital. And that was it! I was officially in charge.

My bags had already been loaded into the back of a Land Cruiser, so we drove off as soon as the plane took to the sky. I was feeling weary, but was keen to see my new surroundings. My first impressions were of a hot, listless town with a dozing main street, but I was in awe as we toured the devastation en route. In more prosperous times Kuito must have been a pretty town, but now every façade had been peppered with mortar spray—without exception. While much of the rubble had been cleared, the buildings were but husks of their former glory. Shot-up tenements complemented mortar-pitted pavements. Quaint bungalows were faded and decaying. In stark contrast to Hong Kong, the tallest building was just seven stories high and that too was destroyed. The day was strangely tranquil, yet we cruised around a backdrop that resonated a violent past. Downtown Beirut is perhaps the only other city I have seen from which to draw a parallel, but even there the damage was no longer so all-embracing and restoration was taking place. It was only as I squinted to temper the bright light, that I could imagine shadows of old Portugal—exfoliating pink stucco contrasted the white window frames of the bruised civic buildings. Tree-lined streets connoted a sense of pride: the city was tidy, if not dusty. Someone then leaned over to explain that there was no running water, little electricity, nothing of the functioning life we usually took for granted, although by then I was hardly surprised. Since transportation was near impossible without a proper road network, glass was also rare. Many windows remained completely open to the elements; the rest were either bricked-up, covered with corrugated iron, or straw mats. And everywhere I looked women and children were lugging heavy liquid loads atop their heads.

The driver pulled up sharply outside a tidy bungalow and started to unload my bags into what I surmised was home: *Casa Quatro* (House 4). During the tour of the city ruins I had been bracing myself for the worst, but the house was infinitely better than I had imagined and on entering I felt instantly comfortable. I was shown to my bedroom and dropped my bags. It had unpolished floors, a wardrobe, and a simple table. At a glance it was a little austere, but I was happy enough and too tired to care. It wasn't late, but by now my head was spinning, so after a light snack I turned in. With details of my hand-over drifting confusingly around in my head, I fell into a deep slumber for almost twelve hours. Occasionally I woke to the sporadic sound of gunshots, but rose refreshed and ready to face my first day.

After breakfast, I radioed for a driver who arrived within minutes to collect me. He rounded the corner and promptly deposited me at the hospital. *Casa Quatro* was barely two minutes from work. The Provincial Hospital of Bié was a government facility, ostensibly managed by MINSA, Ministry of Health of Angola. The buildings had sustained extensive damage at the height of the conflict, but MSF had helped to rehabilitate them and now worked in partnership with MINSA to keep the hospital running. MSF provided most of the drugs and equipment and all of the doctors, while the government provided nursing and administrative staff.

The pungent aroma of antiseptic—masking something infinitely worse—overwhelmed me as I entered the corridors. I took a few steps into the wards and stopped dead, staring at beds crammed into every conceivable space. The rooms were cavernous, greying, and packed to bursting point. One particularly shabby ward in the basement housed over sixty patients: men, women, and children, all together. I quickly tallied that I had well over one hundred patients under my care, making it impossible to provide adequate attention to all. Feeling sufficiently depressed, I braced myself for the condition of the operating theatre.

I was first rushed through an introduction to the department heads and, with barely a moment's notice, faced my first patient. He was a middle-aged man who had been suffering from a strangulated hernia for over a week. His bowel had become gangrenous and had turned into an abscess. This had subsequently ruptured, but I could hardly blame the nurse who had diagnosed it as a simple abscess. I was taken aback, having never seen such a late presentation. I did a laparotomy, bowel resection, and primary anastomosis, which involved cutting out the dead and infected gut and rejoining the remainder. It wasn't the most elegant piece of surgery, but facilities in the operating theatre were rudimentary. It became immediately obvious there was no ventilator, no monitoring equipment, and no shadowless lights, and the training of most of the staff was far from adequate. I quickly observed that scrubbing for an operation meant simply washing your hands with soap. Everyone walked into the theatre in their street shoes. Although grappling to cope with these new conditions, the operation went quite smoothly, I thought. From that first day, I was grateful for the assistance of four male nurses, whom I was to train as surgical assistants: Eduardo Elambo Kayangula (Eduardo), Mario de Jesus Setumba (Jesus), Malaquias Wana Jila (Malaquias), and Antonio Jacinto Bento (Bento). Their invaluable skills helped me cope with the large volume of common procedures and monitor the progress of post-operative patients in the wards.

The next patient was typical of what I was to face for the rest of my stay. The young man had stepped on a landmine about two or three weeks before. He had been carried to us from a village some eighty kilometres away. When I cut open his blackened dressing, the foul smell was so noisome that I retched. The sight of maggots working their way out of the wound took my breath away. I had no option but to amputate the dead limb—a disfiguring operation—repugnant to even the most jaded surgeon. I assisted Eduardo in the

Chapter 5
Oil or Diamonds?

Karin writes…

Until its abrupt end in February 2002, Angola's civil war had been consistently rated at the top of the world's most under-reported humanitarian crises.[5] It had been effectively forgotten by the outside world. In the years just prior to the end of the conflict, the Angolan government had been trying hard to foster a process of normalization within the international arena. It endeavoured to present the country as orderly and peaceful, as a means to attract much needed foreign investment and raise the government's credibility and standing in the world at large. In reality, Angola's political situation had oscillated between periods of tenuous peace and all-out war.

On one side was the MPLA (Popular Movement for the Liberation of Angola) that makes up the government to this day. The MPLA has ruled since independence in 1975. President dos Santos and a small clique of families form the ruling-elite. Most are apparently fabulously rich now. On the other side was UNITA (National Union for the Total Independence of Angola), headed by Jonas Savimbi. He was once a charismatic leader of the Ovimbundu people from the central highlands—the area around Kuito. Although a professed Maoist, Savimbi continually manipulated his political façade as it suited him. He reached an almost cult status, running a tightly-controlled military machine over which he wielded absolute power.

Until the collapse of the Soviet Union, Angola's war was essentially a Cold War proxy-conflict. The former Soviet Union armed the MPLA and thousands of Cuban troops fought there. Some Western powers—notably apartheid South Africa and the US—aided Savimbi's attempt to undermine the leftist-leaning government. The tables turned at the end of the Cold War. By then the government had officially abandoned its Marxist-Leninist ideals. The US, South Africa, and much of the rest of the world ended their support for the various warring factions. A UN-brokered peace accord led to a ceasefire and multi-party elections in September 1992. The MPLA amputation. I am glad it was he, rather than I, who ultimately cut off the patient's leg. It fell with a dull thud into the scrap bucket. I felt a sense of revulsion that clung to the roof of my mouth for hours.

That evening, a motley bunch of volunteers from various continents shared a laugh and a beer at *Casa Quatro*. I felt I needed it after my very basic initiation to amputation that day. After they left, I felt compelled to write—to record the stories of the patients I had treated on my first day; as if it would somehow cleanse my mind of the grievous bodily harm inflicted on fellow man. I wrote to Karin and imagined I was retelling the stories to her in person. I found thoughts of her so comforting.

Remains of provincial government buildings and the city centre, Kuito. World Food Programme storage tents in the distance.

emerged with the majority of parliamentary seats, but failed to achieve an outright majority with just 49.6 percent of the votes. Savimbi rejected the results as fraudulent, refused to participate in the government, and plunged the country back into a deadly escalation of the conflict.

This was never a religious or tribal war. Although the leaders of the opposing camps drew base support from the differing clans, ethnic differences could not account for the motives of either side. Nor was the war being fought across ideological lines, but had become single-mindedly focused on control of Angola's bountiful resources. The government (MPLA) commanded vast offshore oil reserves, while UNITA dominated the diamond-rich interior. Much of the revenue generated was used to fuel the war-machine.

A second UN-brokered peace effort led to the Lusaka Protocol in 1995, but, by 1998, this accord had failed and full-scale war resumed. By early 1999, the UN finally withdrew the remainder of its peacekeeping forces, and Angola was left to lurch on alone. UNITA, on the defensive in rural Angola, became increasingly isolated. UN sanctions stifled its efforts, enabling the government to strengthen military initiatives, funded by growing oil wealth. By then, most Angolans no longer understood the reason for the protracted war that had rampaged on around them for a lifetime. Neglected and unable to influence events, they bore the full brunt of both sides' pursuit for absolute power.

While we were not to know it at the time, our stay in central Angola occurred when the civil war was in its final throes. The government, in pursuit of the last vestiges of Savimbi's army, had forged into the country's interior. After a long, bloody battle, they captured Kuito and pushed into the surrounding countryside. While general insecurity prevailed beyond the city limits, we were effectively parked in a sanctuary—a safe haven held hostage to the final battles of Angola's thirty-year war.

Remnants of UN peacekeeping efforts, Kuito. The truck carries a license plate of the failed MONUA mission (UN Mission of Observers in Angola) that withdrew in February 1999.

Chapter 6
Daily Life

Wei writes...

My first moment to relax came ten days after my arrival. I sat in the backyard and wrote home, describing daily life. Surprisingly, I really liked my domestic surroundings. *Casa Quatro* was a small bungalow, painted pink. The backyard was deep and shady and the guards tended a thriving vegetable garden. A small central courtyard was filled with plants and flowers, which lifted my spirits when imbued with the morning light. To my mind, it was the best of the four MSF residences, and I shared it with several other colleagues before Karin arrived. It was one of the few houses in the street to have undergone some renovation. The flat roof was still covered with plastic sheeting, held down with rocks, and there were yellow watermarks on the ceiling, a telltale sign of what would happen when the rainy season began. However, none of this seemed to matter.

In those early days I made a point of sticking to all the team rules and protocols. I wore T-shirts emblazoned with MSF logos so people would quickly understand what a Chinese man was doing wandering the streets of Kuito. At night we could only move around in an MSF vehicle and I carried my walkie-talkie everywhere. Mario Piriquito, the radio operator, would check our locations each evening. He was a theatrical character who carried out this routine in a lyrical DJ-style, lightening the tone of the proceedings. I also befriended our housekeeper, Dona Fatima, who came most days to help with the household chores. Early on we could barely understand each other, but she remained undaunted. An instinctively maternal woman, Dona Fatima laughed warmly as she went about her work, cleaning, washing, and ironing. This was no easy task, requiring skills I was yet to acquire as we had nothing but a concrete scrub-board and hot charcoals to fireup the antique iron.

I tried hard to settle into the new routine and looked for things to help me feel at home. Familiarity came from strange places—muesli with warm, powdered milk quickly became my inspiration at breakfast. We also made espresso in one of those simple pots with two chambers that disappeared when the electric models first appeared. For lunch, we would go to the imaginatively named *Casa Dois* (House 2), to enjoy a hearty meal prepared by our cook, while most evenings we prepared a light snack from cans in the pantry. While I couldn't savour a bottle of Chianti Classico, Castle beer from South Africa was abundant—though warm—in our kerosene fridge.

During my first week we visited a British humanitarian de-mining organization called the HALO Trust. An ex-soldier called Damian was in charge and his thick, Australian accent instantly betrayed his origins. I felt encouraged to find a fellow Aussie in our midst and listened attentively when he briefed us on known mine-fields: where it was safe to move and what to avoid. Through this information and our weekly briefings I rapidly learned about the hazards beyond the security perimeter. Our understanding of the latest developments was based on reports collated with the help of other non-governmental organizations (NGOs). Although information was scant and relied heavily on rumour, even this proved invaluable. The *Polícia Nacional de Angola* (PNA) also gave us snippets of "non-sensitive" information, but we often knew it before they notified us—military activity had a habit of leaving traces on my patients.

Most of the heavy fighting in and around Kuito had already shifted further afield, but we still heard gunshots and skirmishes in the distance. Perhaps the antics of drunken soldiers, perhaps something more serious? One day we heard that seventeen houses had been torched and forty-five villagers shot. From this atrocity I received just one patient, a woman who had been shot in her shoulder. It took her two days to reach us. The official story was that UNITA was responsible, but the tragedy was that she had simply been out foraging for food. In those early days I also treated a lot of gunshot wounds that were not directly related to the fighting and was perplexed when two patients came in, both with gunshot wounds to their feet. As I was trying to work it out, my staff gently explained that one had refused to haul some luggage for the police. The other patient said he had no alcohol to satisfy police demands. The punishment was the same: a bullet to the foot. I was horrified.

But I was most disturbed by landmine mutilation. I still can't describe how distressing it was to see human flesh mangled in this way. I had just amputated the right leg of a woman who stepped on landmine when the driver of an army vehicle arrived on a stretcher without a face and just one eye. His wounds from an anti-tank mine were grotesque. According to Damian, few new landmines were being laid and there was no longer a definitive front line, as the current struggle had degenerated into a state of guerrilla warfare. I had no idea how impervious the government security ring around Kuito was, but guerrilla incursions occurred frequently within and around the perimeter. "Security perimeter" was a bit of a misnomer, as it was little more than a line up to where the landmines had been cleared. There were a couple of army checkpoints on the edges of the city, but beyond this seven-kilometre radius, things were very unstable. This area was also known as the "grey zone" and was beyond the reach of MSF and other aid organizations. There, ordinary people were forced to survive without help or medical care; neglected innocents caught between two warring factions. MSF had previously worked in these UNITA-controlled areas, before things became really unstuck. But then it became just plain dangerous as neither side was willing to guarantee the security of aid workers.

There were consistent reports of the government's *limpeza* campaign (a systematic engagement to "cleanse" an area of guerrillas). As a direct result of this initiative, 17,000 more villagers had been threatened and forced to move to Kuito. There were also regular accounts of suspected UNITA sympathizers being killed. If they stayed at home, these villagers probably had as much chance of being killed by the regular army as by UNITA. Leaving their homes seemed to be their only option. Also worrying was talk about the WFP winding down its food relief operations as early as April, due to lack of support from the international community. That was just eight months away. Many people doubted whether the displaced would have had a chance to grow enough food to be independent by then. Availability of seed and farming implements aside, there were landmines in the fields and ongoing guerrilla incursions. Of course, we all wanted to see them become self-sufficient, but under those conditions it was a lot to expect.

Despite the comforts of *Casa Quatro* and my fresh-faced enthusiasm, I admit to having felt a little uneasy in those first days. A strange disquiet lingered with the calm. I was also beginning to feel a bit isolated, as there was no way of knowing what was going on in the outside world. There were no newspapers or magazines. Ordinary mail took up to two months to reach us, so I yearned for a short-wave radio. On the other hand my digital camera proved invaluable. I bought it the night before we left Hong Kong and took it everywhere in my backpack in order to capture moments of daily life.

Common anti-personnel mines on display at the HALO Trust office, Kuito.

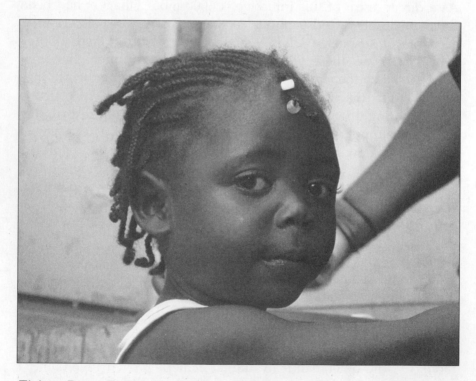

Elvica, Dona Fatima's granddaughter.

Chapter 7
Patient Patients

Wei continues...

The mortality rate of the surgical department was unacceptably high by any standards. Naturally enough, this gnawed at me, but many of its causes were beyond my control. Patients routinely arrived too late, with their conditions in precariously advanced and complicated states. Landmine victims, for example, could take up to eight days to reach our services. By this time, infection had festered and part of the limb would already be dead. Treatment was not helped by the patients' malnutrition and poor general health. Typical patients included landmine victims, who required wound debridement (removing dead skin and muscle), and amputation and bullet injuries that also needed debridement and dressing. Together these made up the largest proportion of the war injuries. Lack of medical care meant I also received patients with very advanced general surgical conditions like strangulated hernias and perforated appendices. However, to my surprise, by far the highest numbers of patients were those suffering from abscesses, caused by poor hygiene and malnutrition—indirect effects of the ongoing war. During the height of the conflict, in 1991 and again in the late 1990s, many Kuito residents fled to the safety of coastal cities like Luanda and Benguela. A wave of displaced people then came to occupy their vacant houses. Successive waves followed, far more than could possibly be accommodated. By the time I arrived, Kuito had a population of 190,000 further expanded by the arrival of about 100,000 internally displaced people from neighbouring areas. These IDPs, as they were inevitably called, camped around the outskirts of the city where they had come in search of security, food, and care. As a result of this population influx, my workload was heavy and growing. I also delivered several babies by emergency Caesarean section and did three in my first ten days. One mother even chose to name her newborn son after me. This practice was not uncommon, but I thought his name—Wei Sangumba—had a nice ring to it. As our profession has become so specialized nowadays, general surgeons rarely experience the pleasure of bringing life into the world. At last this was some truly uplifting work! I relished every moment.

Angola exported 800,000 barrels of oil a day, yet we would regularly run low on fuel for the hospital generator, which was our only source of power. When I arrived, all the operating drapes that were used to cover the patient during surgery had holes, making it difficult to achieve a sterile area. The towel clips we used to hold these drapes were designed for manipulation by two fingers. Yet ours were so rusty we needed two hands to open them. "Não tem," the pidgin Portuguese equivalent of "Méi yŏu (Mandarin for "don't have"), was one of the first phrases I learned. I placed an order for nearly forty surgical items—not fancy Swan-Gans catheters—but basic things like trousers for the operating theatre. Until then, I had a choice of wearing bloodstained trousers or operating naked. The hospital was large enough, yet MSF supplied 98.5 percent of the drugs and equipment, without which there would have been nothing.

At medical school I had learned that during an incision you cut through the various distinct layers that make up the skin: the stratum corneum, the stratum basilica of the epidermis, dermis, subcutaneous fat, and so on. But I soon discovered an additional layer: dirt. Through no fault of their own, my patients arrived in appalling conditions and were rarely washed or prepped for their operation. The plight of the IDPs was particularly desperate. Unable to gain access to simple soap and water, they were characteristically covered from head to toe with dirt, which over time became so encrusted that I had to spend the first five minutes scrubbing the affected area before making an incision.

What's more, in developed countries, doctors seldom encounter worm infestation unless in those intrepid travellers. Yet, worms were a commom occurence and I am not referring to the regular garden variety. Ascaris, or worms, took up residence in the human gut and usually went undetected until the intestine was perforated, for some reason. Easily fifty percent of my patients were infested with worms. If I performed a Caesarean section the chances were that I encountered them in the small intestine; so, too, when I operated to repair an intestine perforated by typhoid. Many malnourished patients had their conditions compounded by the effects of worms, as the parasites competed for the limited nutrition inside their weakened hosts. I vividly remember removing a writhing ball of white worms from an unfortunate patient at the end of the operation list one morning, before wandering despondently over to *Casa Dois* for lunch. I opened the lid of the pot and couldn't believe my luck. Lunch was spaghetti with tomato sauce—it was lukewarm and sticky, all too close to the imagery of the morning and enough to make my spirit quail. I skipped lunch.

There was no shortage of work. Officially there were 250 beds in the hospital, but more than four hundred patients crowded the wards and the staff struggled to keep up with the number of new admissions. So many patients slept on the floor that I had to literally jump between the mattresses when conducting ward rounds. And in the pediatric wards—managed by Monica, an Italian doctor—two or three babies shared one bed. Four young volunteer doctors struggled to cope with this daunting load as there were no Angolan physicians and I was the only surgeon in a province with over one million people. Any doctors they once had left long ago for the safety of Luanda. In fact, before the war, there were only about seven hundred fifty doctors nationwide for a population of 12.5 million and many of these were Cuban or Vietnamese, who had left at the end of the Cold War.

At times it was so heart rending. Monica cried when a child she referred to me with an acute distended abdomen died before we were able to operate. By and large, we were all learning to live with frustrations and disappointments Despite this, morale among the volunteers remained high and the enthusiasm of some local staff kept me hopeful.

Then one night in that last week of August I was called to *Banco de Urgência* (Accident and Emergency department) to treat a girl who had been shot in the right groin. Her parents suspected the bullet was still lodged within and were overwhelmed with worry. However, after a quick look, I discovered that the bullet had exited her body and miraculously damaged neither vessel, nerve, nor bone. She needed little more than a wound dressing. When my translator helped me tell the parents of her lucky escape, their reaction was too moving for words. With tears in their eyes, they poured out their gratitude in Umbundu, the local language, clapping their hands in elation. I had never seen such an overt expression of thanks. I had done nothing for the child except examine her and reassure her parents, but even this was powerful and their joyous response was enormously rewarding.

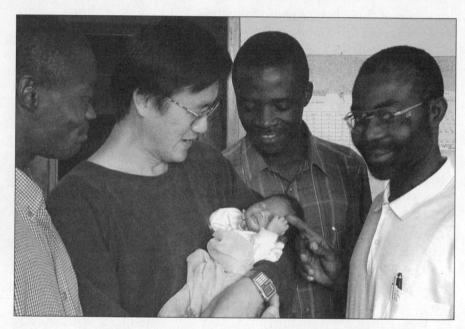

Eduardo, Wei, Malaquias, and Loló with little Wei Sangumba.

Chapter 8
Death's Precipice

Wei continues…

I never even knew her name, but she was probably about twelve years, older perhaps. There was no way of telling, as malnutrition ravages the body, stunts growth, and distorts one's ability to judge age by the usual standards. She was one of the first patients referred to me from the pediatric ward and she had all the telltale signs: protruding ribs and hair tinged the colour of straw. Her sallow, ebony skin contrasted with the bright patterned cloth that was spread out under her. She lay there—motionless—on death's precipice.

That day, Monica had implored me to come quickly. She wanted to know whether there was anything I could do for the child. It was during those weeks when I was still full of that infallible sense of optimism one has on arrival—a belief I could make some sort of difference. With another landmine amputation complete, I slipped out of my theatre greens and pulled on my jeans. I was tired —enthusiastic but worn down by a blur of nights on-call. My sleep had been interrupted at 2 a.m. that morning with another emergency and I had already been at the table for five hours from 7 a.m. But Monica's call sounded urgent so I stepped outside and followed the covered walkway that snaked the hospital's main buildings. As I passed, I greeted the kitchen staff with a faltering: "Bom Dia." They responded warmly, as they stirred cauldrons over the smouldering fire. The sight of the open kitchen with its dirt floor made be balk when I first set eyes upon it, but by then it already felt commonplace. I strode by. On passing the laundry room a muscular woman looked up from her concrete tub with a smile—a soiled blanket in one hand, a coarse piece of soap in the other. Her colleagues gaggled with laughter about something I couldn't understand, so I waved a benign response before bounding up the front steps to the pediatric ward. The foyer was crammed with children and anxious mothers. I filled my lungs with the last of the fresh air and wove my way through the sea of humanity. The wards were dark and airless.

Monica had no clue why the girl wasn't responding to treatment and had been anxious to fill me in on the details: how the girl had been admitted the day before in a perilous state, how she had "died" at night and been revived. A naso-gastric tube was taped lamely to her forehead in a last attempt to decompress her stomach. Perhaps it was operable; perhaps surgery was the answer to the condition Monica felt helpless to diagnose? I examined the child as best I could, but knew instinctively there was little I could do. I could find no reason to operate. I didn't even know what was wrong, except that she was starving and a fulminating infection had invaded her body. The few tests we could conduct had been inconclusive, so what more could I add? I say "tests," but in reality we had to rely on our clinical skills. The laboratory could do no more than match blood types and count blood cells—little comfort given the array of illnesses we faced each day.

Each death encroached on my psyche in some way, but this young patient lingers as a symbol of Angola: a peculiar mix of beauty and tragedy, innocence and horror. She looked as though she had already led such a hard life. Her loveliness had been drained at an age when she should have been so full of dreams. Weeks later, working from a photo, I immortalized her last hours in a sketch: her right hand curled into a limp fist and her left arm splayed across her chest as if calmly yielding to a greater force. It was a drawing that expressed some of the emotion that churned in those first few weeks. She symbolized the life that was being leeched from Angola's soul during the last vestiges of that futile war and man-made famine.

I, too, was born in a famine, and perhaps that is why I was so taken by her. It was China's Great Famine, a period of unfathomable human suffering, which killed an estimated thirty million people. My mother insists that I only survived by the grace of our relatives who sent powdered milk from abroad. But this young patient had no such relatives. That she was malnourished in Angola—a country that could be Africa's richest—heaped insult on her demise. China's Great Famine was also man-made: the calamitous result of policies of the Great Leap Forward and Mao's determination to industrialize rapidly. Through a tragically naïve scheme, Mao urged the peasants to build backyard furnaces to smelt iron to boost the production of steel, an indicator of industrialization. In practice the scheme worked in reverse, forcing the destruction of masses of useful items into masses of poor quality metal. Vast quantities of precious fuel were burned to stoke the ovens and huge quotas were assigned. A bizarre mix of fear and patriotic zeal left no labourers to work the fields. Unsustainable agricultural practices in vogue at the time ensured the crops withered and China starved. And no one wanted to admit it was happening. Like Angola, power struggles took higher priority. Marshall Peng Dehuai tried to alert Mao to the folly, but was denounced and later died in prison. He wrote:

The millet is scattered over the ground.
The leaves of the sweet potato are withered.
The young and old have gone to smelt iron.
To harvest the grain there are children and old women.
How shall we get through the next year?[6]

Angola's famine was also man-made folly. The fields were mined, the men went to fight, the maize withered. Millions of children and women were harangued and displaced. The crops were not planted and tens of thousands of nameless souls never got through the next year.

I hung my sketch of this child in *Casa Quatro*. My feelings were often tinged with anger when I looked at her. How could a nation be left to degenerate to such standards? Modern-day medicine puts all the tools at our disposal. No one flinches when we send a patient for an array of expensive investigative tests to eliminate all manner of possibilities. It is what is expected, what the patient expects. But my days in Kuito were tainted with the frustration of often not knowing what was wrong and not having the tools to find out. And when we could do nothing, our hearts took a battering.

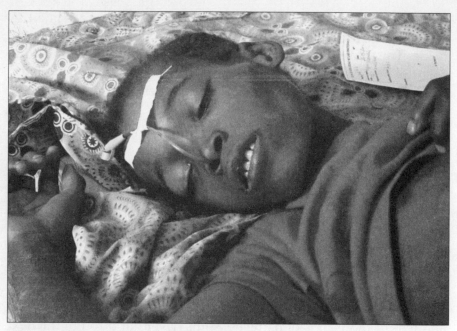

Regrettably, I never knew her name.

Wei's sketch.

Chapter 9
Flattery for Inanities

Wei continues...

Augusto Sapalo Silivondela was my translator. He was an amiable guy with a cheerful disposition. He accompanied me everywhere and was quick to learn my idiosyncrasies. In the first month I also drew support from a group of interpreters who were enlisted to help me during evening emergencies. Without a little of the local tongue, communication was reduced to mere inanities. At first I was totally dependent on translation, not only for the Portuguese but also for the local language, Umbundu. But with Augusto's help, I soon began an intensive schedule of Portuguese lessons. In moments of downtime, he drilled me in the basics in the hope that I would become independent. Before long, I did my first solo consultation over the phone and felt quite proud of myself. My staff seemed to understand. I had been constantly called to the hospital, during the day and night, but on proving I could make myself more or less understood via phone, I no longer had to go to the hospital for every trivial issue.

Ironically, I had learned my first words of Portuguese just months before in Istanbul. We were staying there when we accepted the mission to Angola and Karin's sister was quick to locate a Portuguese teacher. Nathália was a native of Brazil. She and her Turkish husband, Tuğhan, soon became good friends. Through peals of laughter, Nathália coached us intensely in the basics, while the calls to prayer at a neighbouring mosque resonated enchantingly in the background. However, my language progress appeared to slow down in Kuito, but, I admit, I found it an interesting language. The French, Italians, and Spaniards in our team just bluffed their way through with minimal instruction due to the similarity of these Latin languages. Finally the legend that many Europeans speak five languages seemed less mysterious. It also helped that the locals were used to hearing all sorts of bizarre accents and were particularly adept at flattery—"Você fala o Português muito bem!" (You speak Portuguese very well!)—a guarantee that I was anything but fluent.

But when it comes to languages, I have learned that inflated self-confidence and a thick skin are infinitely better than being crippled by inhibitions.

After acquiring the skill to construct basic sentences, I soon moved to establishing a routine and wanted to organize a more comprehensive training program for my assistants who were keen to learn. Their enthusiasm was inspiring, but my language skills slowed the process. Malaquias was a very presentable guy: tall, well spoken, and confident. He was Chockwe, from a group of people who come from further north and speak a different Bantu dialect. Eduardo was smart, affable, and always keen to learn more English. And although it took me a while to know them better, Jesus and Bento exhibited signs of real promise. Both had fun personalities, especially Bento who I soon determined to be our resident comic. He always made people laugh, but I was frustrated by my inability to understand the subtleties of his humour. I was curious to learn more about him, as I was told that he was orphaned at an early age, raised by nuns, and educated in Cuba. The final member of the surgical team was a nurse's aid called Sebastião de Melo (Loló for short). He had apparently remained behind during the height of the city's bombardment to keep the operating theatre going.

One day, while I was attempting to teach them something about resuscitation, we were interrupted by an emergency Caesarean section. I was rapidly becoming an expert in these, having done seven in quick succession, including my first set of twins the night before. Our lesson soon morphed into one about the pros and cons of Caesareans. It was difficult to stick to our training program when all manner of emergencies kept crashing through the door. I pushed my team quite hard and apart from our heavy clinical load, I explained other interesting cases to them. I gave them books and asked them to read up about what they saw and to share their learning the next day. To my great relief, they all proved themselves to be accomplished amputators and were much more experienced than I. But after assisting them with a few, I did one myself and when they saw the stump-wound, they liked it so much that they asked me to demonstrate the improved technique. I am sure they didn't realize that I myself had just studied it in the Red Cross surgical handbook just days before.

I tried hard to make changes to the operating theatre. My first simple step was to introduce the use of slippers. Until then, people had been wearing their street shoes, something I wouldn't even dream of doing at home. I also had the logisticians elevate the water taps so we could scrub our hands more effectively. We raided the MSF storeroom and found new surgical gowns and a load of surgical instruments. Everyone seemed pleased with the improvements, which I hoped would bring back a sense of pride.

Then there was the really thorny issue—punctuality. It quickly became obvious that people had a fairly lax attitude, which was particularly frustrating, especially when caring for the critically ill. Their time frame was very different, but this was probably in part an understandable reaction to the hopeless situation. Lack of incentive to work harder or faster reminded me of the China of old, but with patient care being my overriding responsibility, I felt I had to push things along a little more strenuously.

I admit that entire weeks passed without me realizing what I had been doing, but a visit to the prosthesis factory and rehabilitation centre stood out. Managed by the International Committee of the Red Cross (ICRC), it was located conveniently close to my orthopedic ward. Ricardo, a Colombian and an expert in prosthetic legs, explained how they were made and I was fascinated. As we toured the facility, he demonstrated how they start with a plaster cast of the patient's amputated stump. Next, they heat polypropylene and apply suction to make it adhere to the cast. Once cool, the cast is removed and trimmed to produce a socket for the stump. An artificial foot-and-knee-joint mechanism is connected to the socket to complete the new limb. There was still a problem with this. After being idle and hospitalized for months on end, many patients didn't want to persist with the fitting of a prosthetic leg and intensive physiotherapy. In Kuito, too many limbless people hobbled conspicuously on crutches. I knew the decision for an artificial limb was a personal choice, but I was encouraged to see how close to normal their life could be. Ricardo had his patients demonstrate their basketball skills and it was a convincing display. As a result of that visit, I decided not to discharge amputees until they had visited the centre. Only once they had seen the potential for improved mobility and shared the experience of fellow amputees could they make an informed choice.

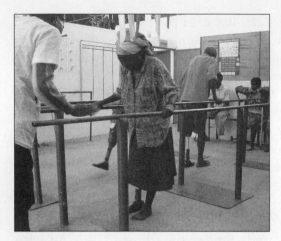

Physiotherapy session at the rehabilitation centre managed by the International Committee for the Red Cross (ICRC).

Prosthetic legs ready for the latest landmine victims.

Chapter 10
Music and Dark Thoughts

Wei writes...

It was a Friday night and I couldn't sleep. Shards of music awoke me from my insect-haunted slumber. Gradually I became conscious of an incessant din, peppered with distant laughter. With further sleep unlikely, I lay there marvelling at how people can be so passionate about *festas* (parties) in the middle of a war. Music seemed to be at the very heart of life: a defiant expression or therapy to soothe the soul. Parties seemed to take on a new meaning and even more so during the days of heavy fighting. According to our Field Coordinator, Sabrina, just about everyone became oblivious to the shelling during the worst days of the war. Going to the disco every week became one of her mechanisms for coping with life. She observed that elsewhere people have long-term career goals and life plans, while in this part of the world people lived for the day. I pondered this, as there was no doubting that life could be brutally short around Kuito.

As I became more familiar with my surroundings, I started to jog in the mornings. The weather was pleasant and I talked João, our house guard, into joining me. Having a sort of bodyguard certainly made me feel safer, although he looked quite amused during our first run. I couldn't decide whether he enjoyed the public display of his international connections or whether it was my puffing and panting that amused him so. We stuck to the main roads close to home, where the streets were flat and lined with trees. João hardly worked up a sweat, barely opening his mouth to breathe. He was certainly fitter than me. On our runs we invariably attracted a large entourage of children who found it highly entertaining to run with us, making me feel like the Pied Piper.

Men singing in unison also woke me on occasion, but it took me some time to realize that the singing came from new army recruits. I came across a small platoon on an early run. They were jogging in formation, chaperoned by soldiers brandishing threatening submachine guns. Their youthful looks disturbed me. Some appeared to be no more than children, yet I doubted that their singing was a spontaneous expression of joy.

One Sunday morning I was also drawn towards music in what I thought was a church. It was early in the morning but the singing was enthralling and the backup instruments fascinated me. As I was soon to discover, the melodious tunes came from a building that wasn't a church at all. It was none other than the local basketball stadium, roofless after past mortar attacks. More than five hundred people were packed into the structure…and what a sight it was! It was an eclectic mix: men with three-piece suits in an array of colours, women with traditional wraparound skirts formed from a length of bright fabric. The ladies looked resplendent with their hair in scarves. Accompanied by guitars and African drums, the harmony was inspirational and the sway of their bodies was choreographed to perfection.

Their talent for dancing and singing starts at an early age and both were undoubtedly the most common forms of artistic expression. Music allays fears and alleviates burdens. It makes grief more tolerable and embellishes an otherwise burdensome existence. Young girls also frequently played a rhythmical clapping game in the streets and, while I wasn't sure of the rules, it was a delight to watch. The leader set the pace by clapping and kicking her legs energetically to the rhythm. Others took turns to join her—clapping in parts or in unison while hopping to the beat. I was totally enthralled by their ability to indulge in such simple pleasures hour after hour. It was like a spontaneous street band, yet the instruments were no more than a pair of hands. Children sang in the street, usually in the cool of the evening. Typically, one led while the others echoed such a tuneful chorus that I often found myself drifting away with their melodies, forgetting the troubles around me.

That week in the operating theatre was once again all about *não tem* as we regularly had unplanned gaps in the operating lists simply because we ran out of simple things like Provodone iodine (sterilizing liquid), sterile surgical gowns, and bandages. My other alarming discovery was that surgery had been rated the lowest priority amongst the hospital's various departments because it had the lowest mortality rate. The "award" for the highest death rate went to pediatrics. Monica said that she lost, on average, two children a day because they arrived too late to be treated effectively. She spent her first two months crying at night—an understandable reaction to daunting conditions. In any case, I didn't like the method of prioritization and met with quite a bit of resistance from the other doctors at the weekly meeting. I had asked for improvements to our intensive care facilities, but the others said it was futile, due to the quality of nursing care. We argued a bit about this, which forced me to think hard about their views. Although they were young, these doctors had already been here for four months or more—a small eternity—and their views had no doubt changed over that short space of time. As the new kid on the block, I couldn't accept the mortality rates and my frustration made me want to do something, even though I knew resources were limited.

Even more depressing was the way my patients seemed to accept their lot, whether it was the loss of a leg, an eye, or whatever. They didn't even seem to bear a grudge and I suspected they felt that complaining would have been of little use. They accepted in silence, not wanting to learn beforehand about the procedure and its inherent risks. I always tried to explain the possible complications in the same way we did back home, but I noted that Augusto often skipped the bit about the possibility of death. On several occasions, he admitted to not having translated that part. "It is not our culture," he told me, gently but firmly, adding a sense of closure to the issue.

How much is life worth? Well, before Angola, my answer was "priceless." But there I saw death everywhere: people dying due to the lack of basic medical care that anywhere else we take for granted, dying from poor hygiene and malnutrition. In theory it seemed easy to come up with a simple formula that a life equalled $1 of clean water, $10 of food, or $100 of medical treatment. After all, that is all it would have taken to save a life in Kuito. Elsewhere in the world we talk so freely of human rights and the right to health care. What rights did these Angolans have? Barely the simple right to survive!

By now, the initial romantic euphoria was over—if, indeed, it ever was that. The realities of poverty, war, and its consequences were starting to sink in. Yet I knew this was the very reason I was there. Life in Kuito was turning out to be very confronting indeed.

In praise of the Lord: Kuito basketball stadium.

Singing in the outdoor church.

Chapter 11
170,000 Needles

Wei writes....

Meningitis (a lethal infection that causes inflammation of the membrane covering the brain) was on the rise, so we started an emergency immunization campaign. We had detected the rise of meningitis through statistics we collected at the MSF health posts. At first, we had a lot of trouble securing government support, but the situation deteriorated so rapidly that we simply had to act. The illness spreads rapidly and often leads to death, especially among children. It can also cause mental retardation, loss of sight, and loss of hearing. We solicited the support of other aid agencies for this major logistical exercise that involved setting up numerous immunization centres around the city and keeping the vaccines cool to prevent them from being rendered ineffective.

As I could never venture far from the hospital, I kept to an indirect role. One morning, though, I rose before dawn to help prepare the vaccines and set up a centre. It was the first time that I had ventured into the camps, so I was keen to join the team. An orange dawn was breaking as we headed eastward. As the grass huts came into view, a barking dog cut through the quiet. The morning haze imbued the harsh surroundings with a certain softness, but the sight was mesmerizing. Row upon row of grass huts were the same monochromatic brown. Bathed in the orange-pink hue of sunrise they took on a surreal, almost picturesque, quality. However, they were the most miserable homes I had ever seen.

Not a soul had stirred as we pulled into the compound and started to unload. We busied ourselves with our assigned tasks. I pitched in to help set up shop, while one of our local staff members roused the villagers into action. With the air of a town crier, he extolled the virtues of immunization and urged mothers to bring their children to the marshalling area. Hundreds of drowsy villagers soon emerged from their huts and came hither from all of directions: children, women, and the elderly. Fascinated by the spectacle, I did what I could before strolling off among the swelling crowd. With my camera in hand I captured what I could of the moment. I love faces: old faces, leathery faces, fresh faces, expressive faces, and there among the dispossessed every face told a story. I snapped photo after photo when suddenly a familiar voice cut through the airwaves. There was an emergency Caesarean waiting for me at the hospital and I had to go. But that day the team immunized 25,000 people: truly meaningful work.

At 5 a.m. the next day, before my operating list started, I stopped off at the immunization centre closest to the hospital to see if I could help. The team had set up in the basketball stadium close to home and I was impressed by their organizational skills from the moment I arrived. In one corner a small group diluted the vaccines with solution and drew up hundreds of syringes. A supporting team made cotton swabs, while another folded sharp boxes for used needles. Others brought order to the swelling crowds using megaphones and formed them into queues demarcated with wooden sticks and tape. The beneficiaries were asked to roll up their sleeves so that two staff members, armed with buckets of water, could clean the dirt off the exposed upper arms, while two nurses vaccinated at lightening speed. At the end of this immunization production line, more women registered the ages of recipients. All in all it was a super-efficient and uplifting experience. Within five days we had immunized over 130,000 people: something very simple that helped an entire community.

By the weekend we still had another 40,000 to go, but, even at an early stage, it was apparent that our quick action had averted an epidemic. Although the team was exhausted, the work was cause for celebration. Weekends were always quite social, often involving a farewell party for a departing team member. *Casa Três* (House 3) was a favoured location and that weekend we hosted a major event. The local staff loved this kind of festivity, for obvious reasons: food, drink, music, dancing, and a chance to let loose. It was free, as the volunteers sponsored parties from our monthly contributions to the food bill, and that night we celebrated our success with great gusto. It was a great way to relax and revel in the spirit of teamwork.

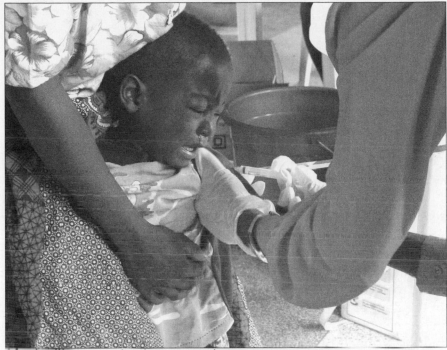

Meningitis immunization campaign.

Queue at a vaccination centre.

Rousing the camp residents for vaccinations.

Chapter 12
Nourishing News

Wei continues…

At times I led a rather mechanical and insular life: work, *Casa Quatro*, and back again, but, with Augusto's help, I ventured out whenever I had a chance. I could never go too far, not only because I was forever needed at the hospital, but also because there weren't really too many places we could go.

At 1,600 metres, Kuito sits in the heart of a plateau. The city is dissected in an east-west direction by the main provincial thorough-fare, although it saw little traffic as the roads were still closed. This same road once defined the front line of the battle to control the city. In the days of heavy fighting government troops had been camped in our neighbourhood and UNITA was on the other side of town. To the east, a small rivulet runs through a gully, which cuts across the main road. There, an abandoned bridge lay unfinished. The road traversed the river and rose steeply up an embankment before continuing eastward towards the Benguela Railway line. The landscape in that direction was dotted with thousands of grass and sod huts. From the hospital compound I could see a few tall trees in the distance and was told they marked the edge of the security perimeter— the end of the de-mined area. They were just a few kilometres away. It was the dry season when I arrived, so everything was toast-brown and dust blew across these flats without interruption. We lived in downtown Kuito: part of the old Portuguese settlement, full of bungalows with gardens. Locals said that decades ago they weren't permitted to live in this part of the city, but that changed when the settlers left, some twenty-five years before. The tree-lined streets provided some shade from the scorching sun, while power lines sagged between leaning poles. On the fringes of town, housing standards deteriorated into the maze of adobe huts and dirt tracks that formed the new suburbia. I was still to explore this part of the city, but I had decided to stick to tarmac roads for the time being.

Although I was quite accustomed to my new routine I still craved news, so the day I bought a newspaper was a major achievement.

There were no newspaper stands or newsagents, in fact, next to nothing and reading matter was highly coveted. Augusto suggested we begin our search at the local radio station. It was a ten-minute walk from the hospital. We registered at the police checkpoint, handed over our identity cards and received a well-worn pass in exchange. We entered a featureless room and sat down to wait. Moments later, a bespectacled fellow came out to greet us. Augusto introduced him as the head of the station. He squeezed my hand enthusiastically, and I sensed his delight at being able to converse in English. We explained our elusive search for a newspaper and he was keen to help. He disappeared and minutes later returned with a dog-eared edition of the previous day's *Jornal de Angola*. Seizing the commercial opportunity, he sold it to me for Kwanza (KZR) 5, about US$0.40, which was equivalent to about half a day's salary for the hospital cleaning lady. I dug into my pockets and gleefully handed over the money before we bid each other farewell like old friends.

Augusto and I headed for the door, as I was excited to read the first news in weeks. I was so eager that I amazed myself with how much Portuguese I could understand by literally guessing my way through. Like any newspaper, it contained an editorial, a sports section, and news of movie stars. I read about the tragedy of the Russian submarine, the *Kursk,* an election boycott by the president of Monte Negro, and Courtney Love's legal problems. The features of the latest Nokia mobile phone and its ability to deliver text messages featured prominently in an advertisement, although I wondered who could afford such technology.

Inspired by my initial success, I went over to buy another paper a few days later, but by the time I arrived it was 5:04 p.m. and the radio station was closed. Some two weeks later, Augusto and I tried again and someone enthusiastically produced another tattered edition. I dug into my pockets once more, but in my excitement I neglected to notice it was exactly the same edition I had bought a fortnight ago—they hadn't received anything since.

We also ventured to the local bookshop, situated on the main street which was just a short walk from home. The shop had twenty metres of near-empty racks, but I purchased two school dictionaries and a simple grammar book. Judging from the stock, the store's museum-piece cash register didn't see much activity. There were no more than three school titles. The shop reminded me of those in Beijing in the 1970s when, as a child, I craved to read, but the shelves were stocked with only a few publications. Everything was banned apart from endless rows of *Quotations of Mao*, *Selected Works of Mao Zedong*, Lenin's *State and Revolution*, and Marx's *Das Kapital*. More often than not, Kuito's bookshop was closed as there was nothing inside.

But, without reading matter, the residents of Kuito loved listening to radios and they were more prevalent than I had expected. Our guards and the nurses carried them around wherever they went, as if radios were fashion accessories. I had already talked to Karin on the satellite phone and asked her to bring us one, but I couldn't stay alive for another month without knowing what was happening around the world. So I went to the market and found a Philibs short-wave radio, an imitation Philips. It bore no indication of the country of origin, although China would have been the obvious bet. It cost me about US$13 and worked well enough to tune in to the *BBC World Service*. After that, I spent most evenings sitting in the court-yard listening to the news. It was a familiar, reassuring voice that became a friend at the end of the day. After the broadcast I would switch it off and listen to the strange quietness of war. It was a peculiar sensation, to switch off my umbilical cord to the rest of the world and listen to the heartbeat of an evening in Kuito. While the days were warm and sunny it cooled off quickly at night. The cloudless skies were a wondrous sight as I had never seen so many stars. City lights usually mask this radiant spectacle, but in tortured Kuito, a city with no lights, the stars would shine for all their worth.

Kuito's tree-lined main street.

Pink stucco terrace houses in downtown Kuito.

Chapter 13
First Breath, Last Gasp

Wei writes....

I felt like I was devolving into a caveman. After only a couple of months my hair was long. I looked tired, almost unkempt, and resolved to write to Karin to request a list of essentials: scissors, thread for mending, and several basic utensils. Strangely, I also wanted a shirt and tie. MSF T-shirts were a monotonous fashion and I felt underdressed when invited to church. My mind needed fertilizing too. I yearned to read and thirsted for a bit of classical music. I also asked Karin to replenish my dwindling supplies of oil paint, as this had rapidly become my main hobby. I had recently completed a painting of the brick oven outside the back door, which wasn't very inspiring subject matter, but the morning light was dramatic. It was covered by a passion fruit vine, bursting with purple and white flowers. I painted a bit each morning at around 7 a.m. to catch the radiance of the new day, before rushing off to work. I also sketched a child whom I had photographed during the immunization campaign. She captured the softer side of Angola: an absolutely beautiful girl, with large innocent eyes and a hopeful look. Augusto, too, volunteered to sit for me. In truth, that sketch was not a good likeness—more like Augusto in middle age—but he was delighted and immediately asked whether I could paint a family portrait. My paints were the best things I took with me; an inspiring way to relax and express what I saw.

Meanwhile the casualties of war continued to roll in. At about this time I received some victims of bomb fragments—civilians injured by aerial bombers. The MPLA claimed it was an accident, but if true, it was a fairly long accident as their injuries occurred over more than a three day period. It all happened around Chitembo, 160 kilometres south of Kuito, where—again, according to what I saw on the casualties themselves—there was some large scale fighting going on, with scant regard to the civilian population.

Two other women among the wounded were victims of landmine explosions that occurred over sixty kilometres apart. Due to the state of the roads, it took them a full week to reach us. Their journeys were agonizing endurance tests and their wounds had become purulent. I still can't find the words to describe that rank and fetid smell. One of these women, called Izabel, was just twenty-five years old. As I used the back of my scalpel to etch the incision line on her leg, I kept thinking back to what we were doing when Karin was the same age. We were already enjoying life together, working, and travelling. That was 1987, the year I proudly showed her my homeland for the first time. It was the year I proposed to her on the West Lake in Hangzhou, so steeped in ancient Chinese history. They were blissful, carefree days. Yet there Izabel was, at twenty-five, losing her leg. She simply lay there, completely accepting as I manoeuvred the Gigli-saw to amputate her dead limb. My heart felt heavy.

I was not sleeping well, disturbed by Lariam (a drug I was taking to prevent malaria) and gunshots that pierced the quiet, to say nothing of the incessant emergency calls. On one of those nights I was awoken at midnight to do a Caesarean. It was a placenta previa: a dangerous obstetric complication where the placenta is attached to the outlet of the uterus, blocking the exit for the baby. I managed to do it quite quickly and returned home to sleep. No sooner did I hit the pillow when our midwife, Emilie, was at the door again. Emilie was an energetic French-Canadian volunteer whose experience extended well beyond her tender age of twenty-three. You learned fast in that environment. She had dark circles under her eyes and was clearly exhausted, but had come to ask me to do another Caesarean. Her patient was bleeding profusely even though the pregnancy was only six months advanced. Twenty-four weeks is close to the world record for the survival of a premature baby, even where neonatal intensive care facilities are available. We did not have any steroids to accelerate maturation of the fetal lung. I rushed to get dressed and on leaving the house, Emilie told me that she suspected that the baby was already dead. I felt pretty depressed by the thought of undertaking such a task, but she rightly reminded me that we were doing it for the mother and her other children. The patient had already lost a lot of blood and it was with a sense of dread that I undertook the operation—another case of placenta previa. The baby girl was tiny and when I lifted the infant out of the womb, she took one small gasp of air and died in my hands. I felt bereft…imbibed in sorrow; the imagery of that moment remains tattooed on my psyche. The mother stared blankly at the ceiling. She had undergone spinal anaesthesia and was awake, so I asked Emilie to translate.

"Emilie, please tell her I am very, very sorry."

Sensitive and gentle, Emilie always treated her patients with great dignity. Before translating my message she wrapped the dead child in a pretty pink cloth, as she had done following the previous Caesarean. She held the newborn gently in her arms and told the mother the sad news.

As I closed the mother's abdominal wound, I couldn't stop the tears streaming down my cheeks. Everyone in the operating theatre was silent. It was about three o'clock in the morning and a serious hush had come over everyone. All you could hear was my sobbing. I was tired, plus I have a real soft spot for children. Maybe I was crying because of what I felt for the mother or was it because we couldn't have our own children? I couldn't stop imagining the mother's reaction to the death of her newborn. I saw so many deaths, yet not many affected me like this. I think I reacted more than the poor mother. She seemed more resigned to the outcome than me, as if it were an inevitable part of the rhythm of life and death.

By now I was looking forward to Karin's arrival and the chance to recuperate a little. I missed her intensely and with no one my age to talk to, it was tough without her. While I had adjusted well to my new environment, I worried about her and wondered whether I was doing the right thing by bringing her there. I was angst-ridden with the dull fear of her coming to any harm. While I knew Karin was incredibly adaptable, I felt so protective of and responsible for her.

(Left) Emilie Chagnon, French-Canadian volunteer midwife.

(Right) The look of innocence, captured during the immunization campaign.

Chapter 14
Domestic Dynamics

Wei continues...

Those weeks before Karin's arrival flew by, although her absence was particularly acute in the evenings when I yearned for company to help me digest the day. Somehow it wasn't the same sharing thoughts with my housemates. I was starting to get to know Erika, although I suspect we quietly acknowledged our differences from the start. It had been years since my student days, when sharing a house with strangers was the norm. Erika was Norwegian and at first she charmed me with her flawless English. Like me, she enjoyed reading, but I soon discovered that she smoked like a chimney. One evening she told me that she thought that none of us really needed to go to university, as it turned us into what we study, rather than what suited us best. She was a dedicated volunteer, even though her attitude was worlds apart from Hong Kong's work ethic, where most endured mind-numbing marathons at work, devoid of real passion. While she had a point, for the most part, we did our own thing.

Team members came and went. It is part of the ebb and flow of life for aid workers anywhere, so I was glad when a Belgian doctor-nurse couple also moved into *Casa Quatro*. It became immediately apparent that Bertrand and Bérengère were a pleasant duo—warm and genial—and I enjoyed getting to know them. More than that, I was grateful for the stock of medical textbooks, novels, and magazines they brought with them. Then a few weeks later, an anaesthetic nurse by the name of Inger arrived. She had been sent by our head office at my request to train the team of anaesthetic nurses. Inger was also Norwegian and was head and shoulders taller than me. We must have looked like the most unlikely pair in the operating theatre, but I appreciated her expertise and I felt infinitely more confident with her around. She too was very easy-going and enjoyed a good laugh, something I valued enormously in the high tensile environment of the operating theatre. I even trusted her to cut my hair. Inger had never done it before, but she said she would give it a go and I was buoyed by her enthusiasm. We must have looked quite comical, as the novice set about her task in high spirits. I sat low in a chair in the back garden while she towered overhead with her scissors, not sure where to start. She peppered her discourse with witticisms as she transformed my black mop with a quick snip, snip. I didn't have a mirror, but the result felt remarkable and I was everlastingly grateful.

While these team members kept me company, I still longed to talk to my wife. For starters I was eager to draw on her management experience. The hospital was chaotic, but I had been trying hard to create a more cohesive environment. At the very least, I sought to establish a greater feeling of mutual respect, increase morale and team effectiveness. It wasn't easy and at times I felt a little demoralized. I guess I demanded a lot, pushing them to plan ahead and be more organized. Up to that point, I had seen little method in the way they scheduled operations—they just randomly took whoever came crashing through the door. While it is hard to plan when almost everything is an emergency, there was still a spectrum and I taught them to classify and prioritize. I gave the trainees a diary and assigned them the task of planning the less urgent operations in advance. Initially, many outpatients didn't turn up at the allotted time, but gradually things ran more smoothly. It was a minor achievement, and I soon learned to take satisfaction from small wins. I also worked hard to upgrade the medical records, as they had not been kept in sufficient detail. For major operations they merely recorded words like "amputation," not naming which of the limbs had been cut. I kept reminding my staff that writing was training itself, as it helped crystallize thinking, to say nothing of the potential value of the records.

Working across the cultural divide with limited linguistic skills required me to be more astute and I had to be careful how I pushed it. One day I noticed that Jesus had been coming late to work. I decided to look into the issue first before taking it up with him, as he struck me as a sensitive fellow. I asked the rest of the team if they knew of any personal problems. No one mentioned anything unusual and just shrugged it off. So with Augusto's help, I broached the subject directly and asked Jesus if there was any particular reason for his persistent tardiness. I was mortified by his reply. To my horror, two of his young children had recently died. I tried to control my reaction. "Two?" I queried gently, thinking I must have misunderstood. As he confirmed the news, my mind was racing. How must he and his wife feel? For a parent to deal with the death of one child would be all too painful a burden, but two? He mentioned that he was organizing a party the following week. "Party" was the word Augusto used, but I assumed he meant a wake as he described it as an event where all the relatives and friends were invited to eat together. They would be remembering the deaths of those who had hardly had a chance at life. I reassured Jesus that his problem was ours and we reorganized things so he could be with his wife in their time of grief.

Had I pushed Jesus too hard? How could I have not known what he was struggling with? Perhaps I had been too preoccupied with little Rita, the girl from Chitembo? Rita and her mother had trekked over one hundred fifty kilometres, taking more than a week to reach us. During an attack on her village, Rita had been shot in the face and half of her jaw had been blown away, along with much of her cheek. She was just six years old. I did the best I could to patch together what remained of her face, but quite frankly she deserved more. Her ability to chew and swallow had been cruelly diminished and she was already in a malnourished state. She needed reconstructive surgery and the services of a talented plastic surgeon, but in Angola all I could do was remove the dead tissue and stitch up her cheek in the hope that we would be able to get some food into her. The team was thrilled that we were able to do that much, but I worried about how she would survive in the longer term. If she could be given soft food, perhaps she had a chance, but life would be tough for a child with half a jaw. Rita and her mother stayed in hospital for several weeks but she continued to lose weight. They had no money, no family to depend on in Kuito—essentially no means of support. Her mother camped in the shelter for relatives, next to the hospital. It was a squalid accommodation: a corrugated open-air shed with two walls, a roof, and dirt floor. There, relatives bedded down in the dust, curled up next to strangers. They cooked on campfires amongst bundles of belongings, tending to their loved ones by day. The facilities were grim but, like everything, they were better than nothing. We all helped Rita and her mother as best we could and closely monitored the child's weight gain. Her recovery was fickle. She needed constant care and, just as she was showing signs of improvement, they disappeared. I was upset, but the nurses explained that there were other children to care for back in

Chitembo. One morning, they simply packed up, left the hospital, and trekked south on foot. Despite the insecurity, they were determined to go home. We never heard from them again.

Absorbed in thoughts of Rita, Jesus, and his wife, I was glad of the distraction of some mail that was waiting for me when I arrived home. I sat quietly in the courtyard and started to read. The message from my father was brief: "I am very glad to hear your health is still in good condition, my international, bare-footed doctor." I was puzzled and read it several times in a vain effort to grasp the full intent. While it was always a pleasure to receive messages from home, I wondered whether the "bare-footed doctor" reference was a joke, or whether it reflected his reservations about what I was doing. In China in the 1960s and 1970s, when the level of medical training and technology was low, Mao sent doctors to the countryside to look after the peasants. As a surgeon, Dad had to spend nearly two years in an underdeveloped part of the country. Mum too was sent away at another time and I remember it well, because, as a child, I missed them enormously. I guess his description of me was not entirely inappropriate, except that my choice to go to Angola was voluntary, while what he was doing in Mao's era was not. I sipped a warm beer…pensively…until the mosquitoes drove me indoors.

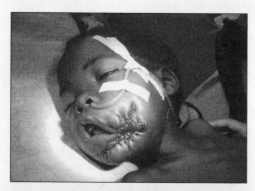

Rita from Chitembo.

Wei teaching the surgical nurse trainees on the hospital steps.

Chapter 15
A Growing Aversion

Wei writes...

I was tired. It had been a long and awful day. UNITA soldiers reportedly attacked a village called Kunhinga, about thirty kilometres north of Kuito. Nine casualties arrived. The youngest, a two-month-old baby, had two bullets through his right upper arm. A second victim had been shot through the hand. It had been completely obliterated and only two fingers were left dangling, while a third victim had been shot through the right humerus, completely severing his arm. Three patients required major emergency operations that night. Judging from the entry and exit wounds on one of the patients, I concluded somewhat erroneously that her bullet wounds were superficial. Moreover, the patient soon developed signs of peritonitis (inflammation of the membrane lining the abdominal cavity) which required an immediate intervention. During the operation I discovered this "simple" bullet had perforated her bowel, causing major damage. It took me ages to repair.

A bullet entering the body at high speed rips a cone-shaped cavity through anything in its path. The entrance wound is generally very small (not much larger than the bullet itself), while the exit hole is large, often the size of a fist. All the structure within its path is shattered to pieces, ripped raw and smattered with bone fragments. You never see that on television as it would no doubt be classified as unsuitable for viewers, while the weaponry that perpetrates it is not. Only since treating the deadly effects of these weapons do I realize just how unbelievably destructive they can be.

It wasn't until days later that I learned why these civilians were attacked. Apparently the government forces had been engaged in another *limpeza* campaign in the surrounding area. They moved the villagers out, searched the area for UNITA supporters, and then tried to resettle the displaced back to their villages. UNITA was thought to have retaliated in order to send the government a warning. Once again the civilians were caught hopelessly in the middle. They said the attack was "small-scale," as it appeared that only rifles or submachine guns were used. Small-scale maybe, but we did three amputations as a result of that attack. Most disturbingly, the baby died as he had simply lost too much blood.

A few days later I was awoken again at midnight to see four emergency patients: all victims of a drunken soldier who shot at random in one of the camps. A three-year-old girl sustained the worst injuries. She had been shot in the foot, but as a child's foot is so tiny the bullet shattered the bone, rendering it unsalvageable. Before performing the amputation, I discussed it with her father, but he just sat there expressionless and concurred. "Sim, sim..." (Yes, yes) he muttered. His weary face betrayed little emotion as he accepted the fate for his beautiful child. She is now incapacitated for life, but I could offer little choice.

And if it wasn't the guns of war, it was the guns of domestic violence. At about this time I also operated on a young woman who had been shot in the forearm by her husband. She had simply arrived home late from a *festa*. Scared by the ramifications of what the husband had done, the family waited one crucial week before seeking our help. When I cut open the rotting bandage I couldn't help but recoil. Maggots wriggled in the puss-filled wound. I wanted to retch as I tried to cleanse the festering injury. All the while, her father-in-law pleaded with me, begging me to save her arm. Believe me, I would have done anything to avoid another amputation and briefly thought about leaving her with a lifeless limb. If only they had come earlier! I tried to explain the dangers of her furious infection. Gangrene was starting to set in, but still he refused. I struggled urgently to make them understand the perils of their decision. Gangrene is lethal, occurring when the tissue is denied blood supply and dies. Infection rapidly invades and left untreated, it inevitably leads to death from blood poisoning.

As the infection spread towards her shoulder, the father-in-law finally relented, but by then her entire arm had to be removed. My patient was just sixteen years old. Augusto then explained more about their village rules and I understood something of the father's hesitation. The perpetrator's punishment was an equal injury. Yet even the village law was not enough to stop that tragedy. They told me the girl's so-called loving husband soon deserted and was on the run.

Incidences like these were commonplace and it didn't take long to develop a passionate aversion to guns. That is not to suggest I ever liked them. In fact, I have never been enamoured by television drama heavy with gun-toting machos. Testosterone-charged, they portray firepower as a symbol of manhood and power. Movies sanitize the malevolent effects of weaponry—the raw unadulterated wounds, the suffering. They package it into benign entertainment. Now I will never be able to watch such nonsense again. Whenever I see guns or armed soldiers, I cannot help but conjure up bloody images of the mutilation they cause. I still hate them with a passion. Guns, so-called small arms! What is small about the suffering they inflict?

Collection of bullets removed from patients.

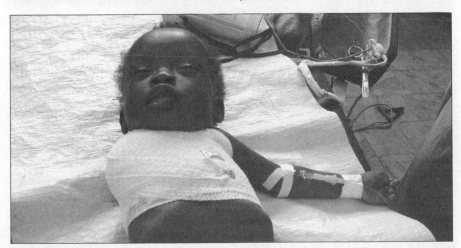

The third victim of the "small-scale" attack.

Chapter 16
Egg and Tomato Sandwiches

Wei writes...

Sabrina left Kuito in mid-September and before her departure we were engaged in a string of parties. With no disrespect to Sabrina, I rapidly tired of these *festas*. Without Karin, parties heightened my sense of isolation even though I did my best to socialize. This was not helped by the fact that my Portuguese left me feeling inadequate.

The hospital staff organized the first farewell party and by the effort they put in, it was obvious that Sabrina was respected for her commitment and courage. During her three-year tenure, the MSF team had been evacuated twice, yet Sabrina stayed behind, risking her life. She had a remarkable reputation among the locals, evidenced by their display of affection at her farewell. The senior nursing staff spent a whole day preparing dishes, including traditional Angolan *funge*. This was the first time I had eaten *funge*, a dry cornmeal paste with the consistency of mashed potatoes that reminded me somewhat of Italian polenta. Monica, our resident Italian, begged to differ. It wasn't that bad, although few of the foreigners seemed to like it. The same women also put on a show to express their appreciation. They danced in swinging steps, singing harmoniously and personalizing the lyrics in praise of Sabrina. After the show, there was more dancing and singing. Angolan pop is very rhythmical and the word "choreo-genic" sprung to mind, although I guess I just made that up. For all my love of classical music, I enjoyed this ethnic pop, finding it infinitely more lyrical than the Western alternative. Even though she didn't know where she was going next, Sabrina spoke calmly about having no fear of the future. She also told me more of what she had lived through during her three years in Kuito: death and suffering juxtaposed against exuberant displays like this and I started to understand something of what she meant.

Sabrina then threw her own surprise party, but this one was a little different and I admit I really enjoyed the outing. It was a hot

Wednesday afternoon and, by chance, my workload was light and I finished operating before lunchtime. We gathered at the office before bundling into the backs of the Land Cruisers and it wasn't long before our motorcade was snaking its way to the riverside. I hadn't been there before, but *Rio Kuito* was on the fringes of the city. Even at that time of the year, the riverside was lush and the grassy knoll where we picnicked was tranquil. Nearby, several women washed their clothes on the banks of the stream as children frittered away time, splashing in the shallow areas. A haphazard array of clothes was laid out to dry. They adorned the nearby shrubs with dashes of colour that enlivened the muddy embankment. It was easy to forget the treachery of the landmines that lurked along parts of that river.

We had egg and tomato sandwiches—not something I would normally choose for lunch—but eggs were a real treat. I can still remember the taste. Then, out of nowhere, hundreds of flies decided to enjoy them too. They descended on the food within an instant, but I could ill-afford to throw it away. The sandwich was just so mouth-watering and I wondered what had happened to reduce my standards of hygiene to that level. I quickly rationalized that anyone would have done the same, as this was no place for etiquette or snobbery. I continued to savour the soggy combination as flies competed with my every bite. As they continued to buzz, a milling crowd of curious onlookers approached us. The children watched us like hawks, eyeing the remains of our sandwiches and soft drinks with a longing that rapidly made me lose my appetite. As the picnic came to a close, the children swarmed the garbage, fighting to snatch the empty cans. Necessity is the mother of invention and nothing was truly garbage. From the moment I arrived in Kuito, I had been intrigued by the ingenuity of the children who made their toys from rubbish. Metal cans were highly prized by these enterprising youth and the oil cans from USAID were the containers of choice. If it wasn't needed as a household utensil, inventive boys fashioned them into trucks. Using twigs for axles and can-stoppers for wheels, a vehicle, complete with suspension, evolved. They copied the only vehicles they had seen with intimate attention to detail: aid-agency Land Cruisers and old trucks used to haul food aid. I was beguiled by their skill and wondered what splendid creations would emerge from these soft drink cans. Just then, the children swooped down on the garbage again when someone attempted to throw the cake crumbs away. The cake was dry: no more than a simple mixture of flour and sugar with a hint of egg, but that was enough for a fight. I felt sad and struggled to swallow a mouthful before handing over what I had left.

But the picnic was a warm social occasion and these moments of respite punctuated the frenetic pace of the operating theatre and I was always glad of a break, however brief. By now I was perennially pooped. I looked forward to the weekends in the hope that I would be able to snatch a moment to relax and recover. So that same week, on Saturday afternoon, I decided to take eight of my staff out for lunch to a small café, called a *lanchonete*. We sat out on the terrace under the shade of thatched grass umbrellas. It had a certain charm, so I settled back to order several rounds of drinks and treated them all to steak and rice. It had been a tough few weeks. The meal eventually arrived and we tucked in ravenously. Chewing the leathery meat was a good exercise for the masetter muscle (jaw). I chewed and chewed and was probably still chewing when the bill arrived. By contrast to Wednesday's prosaic picnic, the meal cost KZR 900, about US$70, an amount equivalent to a nurse's monthly salary. The cost of living in Angola was so out of proportion and nowhere more so than in Kuito, where everything—even the beer—had to be flown into the enclave. Normally a bill of $70 in a restaurant wouldn't bother me, but there it felt wrong, especially as I counted out the money, creating a huge stack of Kwanzas on the table, observed by dozens of penetrating eyes.

The next day Augusto asked me to attend church with him and I obliged. As guest of honour I was forced to say a few words to the congregation, which Augusto translated into Umbundu for me. The service finished before lunchtime so on the way home I bought some warm bread rolls from a street hawker. I invited Augusto for lunch and together we harvested a cabbage from our vegetable garden. I made a salad while the guard climbed a tree for limes to make lime water. Erika set a pretty table in the garden courtyard and as I sat down I quietly reflected on the week's gourmet treats: egg and tomato sandwiches, steak and rice, and now this. That afternoon we savoured rarefied indulgences: a ripe Camembert, a bottle of 1998 Bordeaux, and some Italian salami that we had received by plane from Luanda. For a short moment, my imagination drifted off and I did my best to let nothing mitigate the perfection of the moment. Yet in reality it felt farcical, but such were the contrasts of life in Kuito.

Toy truck made from an WFP oil can.

MSF team picnic, with the children and their treasured cans.

Chapter 17
Absurdity

Wei continues....

I landed in Luanda for my first break and eagerly awaited Karin's arrival. To kill time I wrote to friends and family, telling them about the past two weeks. National Hero Day had come and gone like any other on September 17. The day commemorated both the birth date and funeral date of the country's first president, Antonio Agostinho Neto. He was a doctor and revolutionary who apparently coined that oft-quoted phrase: "Victory is certain." He died just four years after Angola's independence from unsuccessful surgery in the USSR, but is still revered for his contributions to the country's independence struggle. We were expecting more wounded around this anniversary and, while my workload continued to increase, it was hard to determine whether National Hero Day was the contributing factor. We had been receiving a growing number of war casualties, but I was also opting to do some near-emergency elective surgery when I could. Above all, the numbers of new IDPs arriving in Kuito continued to swell. In the twelve months prior to my arrival, the total number of operations was just 1,143. This was already an impressive number, greater than the number undertaken by an average surgical unit with a whole team of surgeons. But by the end of September we were operating at a rate of 200 operations per month. Extrapolated, the annual patient projections were 2,400—a daunting load, which didn't bear thinking.

Patrick, an associate from another aid agency had also accompanied me on my ward rounds just days before. He wanted to meet some of my patients, as he had received a donation from a benefactor, designated solely for women amputees. "Why just the women?" I asked. Feeling uneasy, Patrick tried to avoid the issue, explaining that this was the wish of the donor. Perhaps it was more about modern day political correctness or maybe the donors thought all men were willing soldiers? When I looked at my patients I saw young men and women, equally affected by that rapine war. If they were soldiers they were likely to be reluctant ones, as much a victim as any other. Some had hardly passed puberty. Following the tour of the wards, Patrick obviously saw my point and pledged to secure sixty new blankets for our patients—men and women.

Apart from work I had managed to do little else, except a little painting and writing, yet I was surprised at the speed with which I had acclimatized to the new environment. At the same time, the fascination with my new surroundings had faded. I was scared that I could no longer see the contrast that was so evident on day one, even though writing had become good therapy. I sent much of my writing to family and friends in the form of e-mail letters. That they could be sent in the first place was thanks to the remarkable technology called Wavemail that had been installed in Kuito just months prior to my arrival. With no access to the Internet and only intermittent telephone connections, radio communication was the way of life out there. Through Wavemail our electronic messages were transmitted over a UHF radio to a receiving station at head office in Luanda. From there, they were converted once more and sent via the Internet to my sister-in-law, Ingrid in Istanbul, who disseminated them to a larger audience across the world. To and fro, this process became our psychological lifeline.

As I waited for Karin in Luanda, I befriended colleagues from the office and we exchanged the latest stories. One spoke of the absurdity of a discussion they had had recently with some French businessmen in the oil business. They were in the immigration queue together at Luanda airport. The businessmen had already been working in Angola for two years. When my colleague told them that she was going to the war zone in central Angola, they were surprised. "What war? Is there still a war going on in the interior?" they asked in ignorance. It was a classic example of how forgotten the conflict had become, especially for foreign companies that focused on offshore oil. These men no doubt led a secluded life in the security of a comfortable expat compound, out of harm's way. Two mutually exclusive yet, ironically, intricately linked worlds. While the country generated most of its wealth from oil, the people of Kuito saw none of it. I asked a few of my patients about it and they didn't even know of its existence.

"Oil?" they asked, as if I was having them on. "What oil?" The only oil they knew of was cooking oil from the World Food Programme.

While in prison in Luanda in 1960, Antonio Agostinho Neto

wrote:

> Here in prison
> Rage continued in my breast
> I patiently wait
> For the clouds to gather
> Blown by the wind of History
> No one can stop the rain.[7]

They say the rain finally fell on independence in 1975. However, working amongst the victims of a savage war that had raged ever since, I felt that Angolans were still waiting for the clouds to dissipate—patiently awaiting the end of this never-ending war.

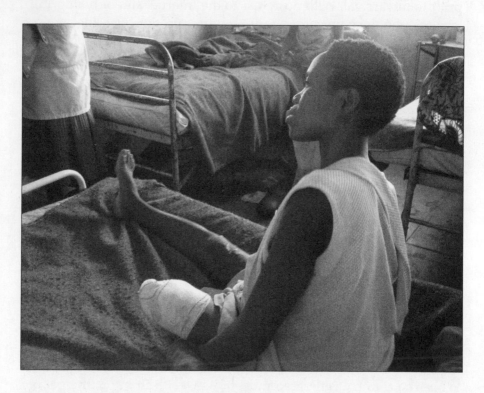

Woman amputee in the orthopedic ward.

Chapter 18
Atlantic Romance

Karin takes up the story...

After months of anticipation, I finally arrived in Luanda. I was pleased to be so close to my new home—just six hundred kilometres from Kuito. The flight from Brussels took eight hours, but we sat on the tarmac for two additional hours while Belgian immigration officials tried to extract a recalcitrant passenger from the plane. Apparently she didn't have appropriate visa documentation, so how she managed to board the aircraft in the first instance was beyond me. The protracted delay at two o'clock in the morning was not widely appreciated.

It was a strange bunch that boarded the plane. As it was the last flight out for the evening, I had time in the deserted lounge to observe the milling passengers: weary businessmen in crumpled suits, aid workers, ubiquitous bag-traders, and priests. Large ladies in bright national dress added a dash of colour to contrast the brown, hooded robes of two elderly monks. They hovered nearby in their own time warp. A quintessential expatriate wife completed the scene. She carried a precious pussycat in a plastic carrier—essential luggage for Angola, no doubt.

I was still miles from Angola when Wei dragged himself from bed in the early hours for the first of two trips to the airport to greet me. I was not the only new team member to disembark. There was another member of our Luanda support team, his Angolan wife, and their baby. We finally arrived, starved of sleep, along with the dishevelled planeload of passengers, minus a few bags that failed to appear. As I waited at the carousel, I caught my first glimpse of Wei waiting behind the barrier outside the terminal. I was instantly struck by his long drawn face, which made him look as though he was in need of a little pampering. We hugged before being whisked off towards the city centre.

It was the red earth that had first struck me from the air and there on the ground, I was struck by it once more. The car was blanketed with dust, inside and out. Red dirt contrasted the tropical lushness and commotion of the city. Luanda, once called "The Paris of Africa,"[8] had all the trappings of a poor, chaotic city, yet I felt strangely positive from the moment I arrived. Quite apart from being with Wei at last, having travelled a bit over the years, the conditions were not daunting, nor was I intimidated by the roughness.

I marvelled at Wei's pidgin Portuguese. He amazed me with his capacity to make himself understood—not bad given that most of this communication was done over a squawky two-way radio. He fearlessly practiced everything he knew and bluffed the rest. On the other hand, I had a mild panic attack on arrival that blanked out every scrap of Portuguese I had learned, so was relieved to discover that French was the lingua franca in our Luanda office.

I spent much of the day in orientation sessions and by sunset we were ready to enjoy a drink in one of Luanda's attractions: a converted railway carriage-cum-bar plonked down on a hillside, overlooking the bay. From this vantage point we looked out beyond the shabby edges of the city to a fiery red sunset over the sea. If we were not abstracted from the surroundings, the panorama could have been one of incomparable splendour. For dinner we ventured to the Ilha, an isthmus embracing the bay that gives Luanda a certain charm. Palm trees swayed in the breeze, while languid waters lapped the shores of the protected inner harbour. The sandy beaches of the Ilha's western shore faced the blue expanses of the Atlantic. During that divine evening—pleasantly mild, with a fresh sea breeze—we gobbled succulent seafood on the beach in a grass hut while listening to the caressing waves. A particularly average bottle of Portuguese rosé tasted sweet between our lips. A post-dinner stroll on the warm sands, past nodding palms, was positively romantic. It was far from what I imagined for my first night in Angola, but I have to admit it was wonderful to be back together after a two-month separation.

The montage of digital photos that Wei showed me on his laptop over breakfast the next morning soon brought me down to earth. It was infinitely more descriptive than any verbal briefing I had received so far. I quickly gleaned what to expect from the arrestingly basic conditions: our new home in *Casa Quatro*, the crushed city of Kuito, the camps, the hospital, and the team members. I also saw graphic photos of Wei's patients for the first time: legs blown away by landmines, a child's arm shredded by a bullet, festering wounds, shattered bones, gunshots, distorted limbs. I gritted my teeth and saw them all through—not out of any ghoulish fascination, but from a real desire to understand what lay ahead. Sparing me nothing, Wei flipped from photo to photo as my stale bread became even harder to digest. I had often helped Wei prepare academic presentations, but those images were taken for the purposes of medical research and had been sanitized. These were just plain in the raw!

We toured Luanda for the rest of the day, not that there was a great deal to see. For a city colonized by the Portuguese for nearly five centuries, there was little of the old town left. Painted in shades of old Macao, the remains of the city's heritage were in a state of disrepair. From a distance, Antonio Agostinho Neto's mausoleum looked imposing, but this huge, crumbling edifice had never been completed. It was rusting and apparently overrun with rats and cockroaches, so we avoided it. Instead, we scrambled up a bluff to the modest fort, which was built in 1576 and completed by the Dutch when they ruled for just seven years in the mid-1600s. Fortaleza de São Miguel is now the Armed Forces Museum, boasting symbols of hollow victories (rusting relics and other outmoded accoutrements) that made the fort seem all the more doleful.

We trudged on through the dust in the sort of heat and humidity that Hong Kong gets in summer before retreating to the cool air of our basic digs—one of several MSF houses around the city. There, between the cool concrete walls, we leafed covetously through a pile of reading matter. I had bought a copy of everything available in English at the airport newsstand in Brussels: a collection of newspapers, current affair magazines, books, and women's glossies, all of which Wei declared to be the best things he had read in months.

Wei returned to Kuito on Monday morning while I stayed on in Luanda for further briefings. That night, in the empty house, I suddenly felt alone and somewhat insecure in that strange city. It was a peculiar mix of excitement and apprehension. The warm evening air was moist and thick with the buzz of mosquitoes. I soon suffered my first bite despite having lathered my body with repellent. With all the talk of malaria, I had been alarmed to find Wei covered from head to toe in bites and had visions of him breaking into fever and delirium. "Mosquitoes?" I'd asked in panic. "No, just bed bugs," he'd replied calmly. I'd felt relieved…for a few moments anyway.

Fortaleza de São Miguel, Luanda.

The Ilha, Luanda, looking out to the Atlantic.

Chapter 19
Kuito Calm

Karin continues…

By Wednesday, I had completed my induction at head office and was eager to join Wei in Kuito. Several colleagues boarded the plane with me in Luanda. After takeoff the plane climbed above the coastal plain, then high up over the escarpment, before traversing a plateau. From Luanda we headed further east than Kuito, to another MSF project in the city of Luena, the provincial capital of Moxico province. There we took on more MSF passengers before heading west, back to Kuito. On the final leg I could see little until the plane burst out of the fluffy cumulus clouds. The nebulous geography of the plateau hid Kuito in its dry expanses until the township and tiny airstrip finally inched into view.

As the plane taxied, I could see Wei standing on the edge of the tarmac among the Land Cruisers. He was surrounded by a small crowd of colleagues who were busy with farewells for Berit, a departing volunteer. For an awkward moment, I didn't know how to feel being greeted by my own husband, speaking a new language, in a strange town, surrounded by people I didn't know and yet with whom he was so obviously at ease. However, with the warmth of their greeting, these feelings quickly dissipated and I was adopted by the group. We threw ourselves in the back of a pickup truck and Wei hugged me tight as we set off for the bumpy ride into town. The ravages of war—the devastation—were the first things to hit me. No house or building remained untouched. It took days to absorb the improbable strangeness of it all: to fathom this melancholy town, full of gutted buildings and homes ripped apart. Yet somewhat perversely, it wasn't long before I felt happily ensconced in my new surroundings. If I closed my eyes to the war damage and shed the image of the grinding poverty, the dusty dry air evoked warm feelings for outback Australia—far western New South Wales, perhaps. Kuito had all the hallmarks of a sleepy country town where life ambled along peacefully. It was easy to be lulled into a false sense of security. Even strangers in the streets greeted me by calling "Amiga" (friend) or "Bom Dia" (good day). In the camps the kids cried "Wa-la-li" (hello) and "Chindella," the Umbundu equivalent of "Gweilo," Cantonese slang for foreigner. I quickly sensed a warmth of friendship lacking in Luanda. At its heart, Kuito had a good feel to it, which made its misfortunes all the more tragic.

On the first day of my new life as the financial administrator, I joined Julio Domingos Mbumba, our local administrator, on his rounds. A warm and, judging by his conversation, learned chap, Julio had an infectious smile. He exuded a gentleness that was immediately obvious as we worked on our first task together. We paid the workers who were rebuilding Kuito hospital. Payday is exciting anywhere, but the scraggly characters that lined up to receive their earnings outside the hospital compound made this one exceptional. Julio unfolded his dog-eared list and began to call out the names when I noticed a spry old man guarding the door. A gnarled nose crowned his leathery face. His name was Nando and was the supervisor who had appointed himself co-organizer of the payday event. He hovered by the door and tried hard to control the lineup as the workers jostled outside to receive their pay.

"Justino Chicapa," Julio called with the airs of a Mandarin.

"Justino Chicapa," echoed Nando to the crowd outside. A wiry man came forth and apologetically approached the desk. Julio passed him the monthly pay. With his tremulous hands he scrawled a signature next to the "X." Justino then scuttled out before Julio called the next.

"Gabriel Vihemba."

"Gabriel Vihemba," relayed the echo before another man came forth.

"Netuno Chikukulo."

"Netuno Chikukulo...Netuno, Netuno." The voice reverberated outside among the assembled. Netuno soon burst forth. Alfredo Ulungui was next to be called.

And so the parade continued. Simply but effectively, we soon completed my first task as financial administrator and paid more than thirty temporary labourers, dollar by dollar.

Julio then took me on a tour of our projects, squashed together in the cabin of the Land Cruiser. We chatted in a mixture of French and English as the juddering vehicle lurched over potholes. He spoke with candour and had an effortless ability to make me feel at home. I was surprised to learn that, although a long-time Kuito res-

ident, his first family now lived in the safety of Luanda. He saw
them at Christmas, just once a year. I was commiserating with him
when, chuckling warmly, he reassured me that it wasn't so bad. He
lived for the rest of the time with his third wife, Domingas Josefa,
and their family in a house close to the office. Julio also told me that
he had trained as a nurse, but didn't feel ideally suited. More inter-
estingly still, he also revealed that he had once joined a seminary
and, totally fascinated, I struggled to reconcile these divergent
lifestyles. His training with a scholarly order of priests in Huambo
(several hours west of Kuito) had taken him into the world of classical Latin and Greek. And now here he was jostling in this four-
wheel drive in the bush and talking of his wives and various families. But Julio's inherent qualities were unique and I instinctively
liked him.

Our conversation moved to the camps for the IDPs, vast areas
that housed the tens of thousands who had fled the fighting. He
explained how each town or village had effectively re-established
itself in a designated area on the outskirts of Kuito. The tiny
dwellings, made from mud and grass, were packed in rows, one
after another. It was here that MSF ran two health posts on opposite
sides of the town. We also visited the feeding centres for the malnourished. It was my first-hand glimpse of the dire situation and I
felt overwhelmed by the enormity of it all.

But the hospital was where the ugly face of this conflict was
most apparent. Days later, I joined Wei on his ward rounds. It was
Saturday and a Spanish camera crew was filming. We were quite an
entourage for a hospital where even the floors were choked with
patients. By far the most confronting ward was orthopedics, where
men, women, and children were crowded together in a basement.
Ventilation was poor and the walls were a depressing shade of concrete grey. Each bed revealed an empty expression. Many were
recent amputees: despondent and gradually resigning themselves to
their lot.

Wei calmly explained each case as the camera rolled: "This child
lost her arm when she picked up a grenade. We had to amputate at
the shoulder"; "This lady was shot by a stray bullet"; "This gentleman put his farming hoe through a landmine while tending his
field." Everyone remained hushed. There was not a whimper from
the patients, nor a word from the journalists. Wei continued his nar-
ration in a matter-of-fact dialogue and, quiet as we were, shock per-

vaded the air. My throat felt tight. A kaleidoscope of emotions overwhelmed me as Wei introduced me to the patients I had already encountered through his letters and photos. Their faces were familiar and I felt as though I already knew them, for I knew their stories and had followed just a little of their plight. It was very sobering. We all filed out in silence.

Camp life.

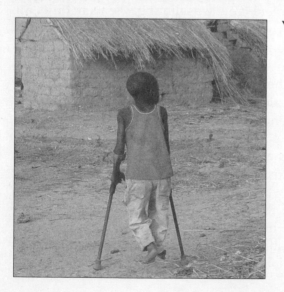

Young polio victim.

Chapter 20
Child's Play

Wei writes...

Karin arrived in Kuito with a complete arsenal of kitchen supplies: spices, aluminum foil, kitchen knives, and groceries—even her own pressure cooker, which was her solution to the tough meat. I didn't want to discourage her, but she would discover soon enough that it would take more than a pressure cooker to make the meat palatable. In any event, she was right that it would help us conserve energy and everything she brought was greatly welcomed by the team.

By then, the rainy season was off to a faltering start, bringing a surge in small-scale guerrilla attacks. I was always one of the first to know of the latest military strategy, as I tended the victims. UNITA's focus shifted towards smaller villages. In the boggy conditions, assaults were made using "lighter" weaponry as they no longer had the muscle to recapture big towns like Kuito. They would kill seven or eight villagers one day and burn a few houses the next.

The victims kept trickling in, but one night's arrival was more uplifting. At first it didn't appear that way when a young woman called Costança arrived with a bullet wound in the middle of her forehead. She didn't even know who fired the shot. Costança looked up at the hospital ceiling as she described how the bullet simply fell from the heavens. It ripped through her forehead and continued its downward path, drilling a tunnel perilously close to both her eyes and through her nose. Amazingly, the bullet exited into her mouth and she lost no more than a tooth. I tested her extensively, but to my surprise and relief there was no damage to her optic nerve. Costança complained persistently of her missing tooth and the hole in the roof of her mouth, and no doubt was confounded by my wry smile. I struggled to convey the miraculous nature of her lucky escape. Costly denture work was beyond the realms of our facilities.

One Monday morning, an ominous tap on the bedroom window cut into my sleep. It was Emilie with news of another Caesarean. The patient had been in labour for two days and Emilie feared the worst. She could not detect the baby's heartbeat. I didn't like the sound of the news that the expectant mother was bleeding internally. Stumbling around in the early morning light, I clutched at anything in the dresser to wear and rushed off.

To our spontaneous delight, less than thirty minutes later we delivered a huge, 4.5 kilogram baby that had been stuck. Frustrated by his efforts to join the world, his bellicose complaint was the nicest start to the day. But this delightful early morning arrival heralded the start of a hectic day. More war-wounded had arrived overnight and we operated constantly until 3 p.m. I snatched a quick break and was foggily swallowing cold leftovers for lunch when I was called in again. A young girl had been seriously wounded. But before starting this operation, another two patients arrived and both were in shock. One sixteen-year-old girl, with her first pregnancy, had been in labour for four days before seeking help. She had multiple complications and had been bleeding profusely. The other, a young man, had a perforated peptic ulcer. As I scrambled to determine the order of these emergencies, the decision was made for me. The young mother died. She was just a teenager.

In the end, it was an injured child whose condition wracked me to the core. To my mind, there is nothing more charming than the unfettered curiosity of young children. And nothing crueller than innocence shattered by the toys of war. Spent weaponry littered the Angolan countryside. That morning a young boy called Nuno and his three-year-old sister, Verônica, were playing in a nearby field. Proud of his find, Nuno picked up a metallic object that was nestled in the grass. Within a fraction of a second his life was terminated and that of his sister hung in the balance. In official-speak it was an UXO, a benign acronym for an unexploded ordnance. The accident was sheer child's play: nothing more, nothing less. Their newfound toy exploded, showering Verônica's body with obliterated pieces of Nuno's. Shrapnel peppered her belly and she sustained multiple internal injuries. Her limbs were fractured like that of a broken doll. Tiny bits of metal perforated her colon, her small bowel, and her left eye.

For this delicate operation I was pleased to have the assistance of David, a British trauma surgeon who by sheer chance was visiting the HALO Trust that day. He had visited the hospital earlier that morning and said he was keen to help out if he could. I had promised to call him if I needed an extra pair of hands, but hardly expected I would be radioing him so soon. Verônica's wounds were extensive. I am not an ophthalmologist nor did we have specialized equipment to perform such tricky surgery. Nonetheless, we had to extract the shrapnel from what remained of Verônica's tiny eyeball. And despite the anaesthetic, in a moment of intense concentration, her right eye twitched. As we completed the delicate procedure, David retched and ran from the operating theatre, unable to face the penetrating gaze of our little patient. In all, her multiple wounds took a full seven hours to repair.

United Nations Children's Fund (UNICEF) claimed Angola to be the second worst place on earth to be a child and with little patients like this, it wasn't hard to understand why. Verônica made a remarkable recovery, but the sight in her right eye was irreparably damaged. But her partial loss of sight was nothing compared to the loss of her innocence and her beloved brother.

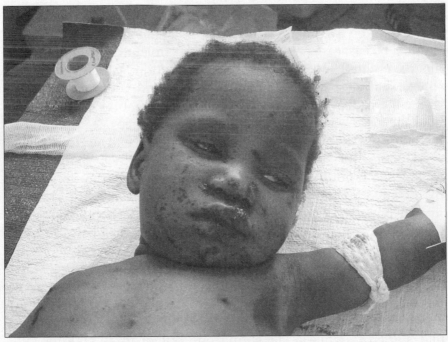

Verônica.

Chapter 21
Something Rotten

Karin writes...

It didn't take me long to realize that something was rotten at the heart of Angola. It hit me the moment I landed in Luanda. From the air, I could see offshore oil rigs and thought immediately that there must be prosperity down there. After all, Angola pumps a lot of oil and is expected to become Africa's leading producer, overtaking Nigeria. The US imports more oil from Angola than it did from Kuwait: a full eight percent of its imports. Moreover, I landed in a country wrecked by war and stricken by poverty, where almost everyone was left to eke out a living.

They called it "The Angola Paradox"—the country that has the potential to be one of Africa's richest is rated among its poorest. The country boasts vast natural reserves of petroleum, natural gas, diamonds, uranium, and gold. It was once a world-leading producer of coffee, sisal, and timber. It has fertile soil and could easily be the region's breadbasket. So where did all this bountiful wealth go? To fund the futile war that ravaged the nation for three decades: almost a lifetime, since the average life expectancy had fallen to just forty years.[9]

The statistics were mind-numbing. As of 1999, Angola was ranked 146th out of 162 nations in terms of human development.[10] By the government's own admission, sixty-five percent of Angolans live in poverty, of which eleven percent face absolute poverty.[11] Corruption was endemic, as Angola was rated the sixth most corrupt nation in the world[12] and this statistic continues to worsen.[13] More than a million people had died as a result of the civil war.[14] Seventy thousand people had been maimed by landmines,[15] resulting in the highest concentration of amputees in the world.[16] Almost a third of the population had been internally displaced since the war had started,[17] while a staggering one out of three children died before the age of five.[18] To make matters worse, there was just one doctor for every 50,000 people in the capital, Luanda. In the rest of the country this statistic worsened to just one doctor for every 400,000 people. That is equivalent to the entire Canadian population queuing for the services of seventy-five doctors.[19] Only twenty-four percent of the population had access to health care and just under half had access to clean and safe water.[20] At nineteen percent,[21] infant mortality was one of the highest in Africa, while a full twelve percent was malnourished. In some areas it was higher than thirty percent. And on it went...

As Wei wrote earlier, we lived in an enclave surrounded by minefields. It was a town where some say one-third of the population died during the heavy fighting. Everyone had lost family members. The majority of Angolans had never known anything but war and could not imagine what real peace meant. More depressingly, no one believed that the war would end. The most common reason for staff members to be absent from work was to attend an *óbito* (funeral). Funerary processions were a daily phenomenon. They passed by our house at all times of the day and night. We heard the implacable cries. Loved ones ululated and sung haunting laments as they carried their dead away to the city's necropolis. The pattern of life and premature death continued, and families suffered perpetual tragedy. Yet, I soon learned to draw enormous strength from their ability to endure.

The children, for example, made my heart melt, constantly amazing me with their ingenuity. They would have been lucky if they had so much as shoes on their feet, but amused themselves in the streets like children elsewhere. They walked and played all over the roads so devoid of vehicles that even I took to ambling in the middle. It was easier than negotiating what remained of the pavements. And when I walked, I loved to observe life around me. It was an easy stroll from one end of town to the other. I particularly enjoyed my stroll to work and back, as everyone was more than friendly. As a matter of politeness strangers always greeted me as they passed. We started to recognize each other and I so wanted to be able to reply with more than a standard greeting, but my Portuguese left me feeling inadequate. How many strangers exchange these pleasantries in our cities today? We never seem to have time. I suspect that over the years I too had become accustomed to Hong Kong's elevator culture where we never acknowledged our fellow passengers. We would stand silently in crowded isolation, clutching our belongings. With eyes fixed firmly upward, we focused intently on the spinning numbers, as if our collective power of concentration willed the elevator to move faster:

34...35...36...37... And when the doors burst open we shot out in our separate directions, oblivious of another day's encounter with fellow man. While there in Kuito, in the middle of a civil war, the stress of modern city life peeled away like onion rings. How absurd it was to find such a relaxed sense of normality among the chaos.

In those first weeks, however, I admit to feeling ill at ease when Wei was called out in the middle of the night. At home alone without electricity, the moonlight cast strange shadows around the house. I would hunker down in bed and stare up at the ceiling through the veil of mosquito netting. Unfamiliar with the nocturnal noises, I lay awake, all eyes and ears, watching the curtains billow in the cool breeze, contemplating what I would do if a stranger entered the house. I knew there were guards out front, but they didn't even have so much as a flashlight. In the pitch of the night, I knew there was little they could do. At times, startled by a crack of gunshots, I would turn to fretting about Wei. Hours would drag on in this way. In due course, he would reappear from the shadows, startling me before crawling comfortingly back to bed. But like most things, I gradually became inured to my new surroundings.

It was in stark contrast to our life in Hong Kong where our first neighbourhood was a frenetic mix of high-rise textile mills and decaying housing estates. I often found myself drawn into thinking about those days, no doubt because of the heightened sense of awareness one has on arrival in a new place. I remember my first years in Hong Kong more vividly than the subsequent ones: the sharp contrasts of Hong Kong to Sydney—a city of superlative beauty. Kuito brought back memories of Sham Shui Po—the decaying suburb where we lived when we were first married. Sticky fibrous soot fell daily on my freshly laundered clothes, as they hung on the line from our thirteenth floor window. Markets spilled onto the streets and squalid shacks lined the canal down Hing Wah Street. In the heat of the summer, all manner of odours pervaded the air. It was oppressively hot and humid. Suffering our first summer without air conditioning, we would lay awake each night, windows ajar, listening to the thrum of the city. Container trucks crunched their gears as they hauled heavy loads up Lung Cheung Road. I spent my spare time shopping in the chaotic street markets and wandering the tenebrous alleyways of industrial flatettes. In the decrepit Stage One housing estates I would listen to that familiar clack, clack, clack of mah-jong tiles echo down murky corridors.

Hong Kong throbbed with vitality whereas Kuito was hobbled and struggled from one day to the next. But the apparent calm of war was bewildering. During the day, life in Kuito still went on in its own resolute way. Dark evenings soon became that bewitching contrast between the danger of darkness and the dreamy calm of night. I eventually learned to sleep soundly until the breaking dawn when the drone of the first WFP Hercules planes would herald the start of a new day.

Grinding maize.

Angola's cruellest statistic: one in three children die before their fifth birthday.

Chapter 22
To Market

Karin continues...

It didn't take long to establish that the market was the only place where commerce seemed to function. Even though a few shops remained, it was hard to identify what was left of the commercial hub. There were certainly no shop fascias, no advertising billboards or neon signs. Two battered roadside bowsers sufficed as the Sonangol gas station, but there was rarely any fuel and few trucks or cars to serve. The only vehicles that roamed the streets were the decaled four-wheel drives of aid agencies: UNICEF, ICRC, Concern, CARE, Save the Children, World Food Programme, Oxfam, and HALO Trust. It was a revealing lineup. One convivial restaurant called The Esplanade graced the main street. The Esplanade was an open-air establishment with a tin roof and concrete floor. It was usually near-empty—hardly surprising given the price they charged for near-inedible pub-style food. There were also a few *lanchonetes* and a disco, but the commercial hub was essentially the market. It was an extraordinarily lively place: crowded, colourful, and noisy in the context of what was available. It was difficult to cut your way through the crowd, the flies, and the children who tried to sell plastic bags at every turn. Wei joked that I was an easy target for the bag-sellers. Instantly judged incapable of carrying things home on my head like any proper woman, I attracted them like bees to a honey pot...to the point of distraction.

The market stocked what could be found in Kuito—nothing much. Vendors organized themselves into aisles by random association. Most of the oddments on sale originally came from China or India: the cheapest of the cheap brands. Some items in the clothing aisles had doubtless been through Western wardrobes. It was like a wilted rummage sale. These garments and shoes were well-worn seasonal rejects: second-hand castoffs from a more affluent society. In fact, this flourishing trade made second-hand clothing one of the top ten exports from the US to sub-Saharan Africa. For as long as I can remember, I have always made a point of donating used clothing to charity. I never could bring myself to throw anything away. Donating seemed to expunge the guilt that comes from tossing away outmoded fashion. I glanced at the range of old shoes with worn soles and broken buckles. I remembered the ones I had thrown away the season before when I spotted something similar for just a few Kwanzas a pair. No doubt the cash that charities earn from the sale of these donations to brokers is an important source of income. But somewhere in my naïve subconscious, I never imagined that the poor didn't get them for free. Used clothing is big business.

On my first visit to the market, I stood there beguiled by the array of fashion when I spied a guy strolling around in an Australian classic: a faded Billabong surf T-shirt. If sightings in the streets were any indication, someone was also doing a great trade in old uniforms. I regularly saw men dressed in uniforms once worn by cleaners and bellboys from swank hotels or attendants at Shell gas stations. I even saw a boy dressed in the uniform of the Oregon State Boy Scouts, replete with achievement badges that he flaunted on his sleeves. But my favourite was worn by one of the guards at *Casa Dois*. The house where we ate lunch each day was a far cry from any hotel, but Domingos sat proudly at the gate, sporting a Marriott Hotel service uniform, and it was nicely ironed to boot.

Elsewhere in the market, flamboyant in their wraparound skirts, ladies squatted in the hubbub with babies strapped to their backs. Small mounds of prematurely harvested tomatoes or onions were on offer for KZR 1 per mound. Cooking oil was sold in tiny quantities—poured into little plastic bags and knotted. Salt was sold by the spoonful, likewise flour. Chorizo sausages were sold one-by-one from tins and it was the same for a precious packet of biscuits. Despite the banter of enthusiastic vendors, I balked at the meat market—enough to turn any meat lover into an instant vegetarian. Flies swarmed around clumps of dark red tissue, dried by the heat of the day. I looked over to the bug-eaten vegetables with relish.

The day of my first visit to the market, we had invited David, the visiting British surgeon for dinner. I attempted our first Chinese meal: fried rice and some steamed leafy greens I'd purchased from an old lady at the market. I say old, but her face was aged by a hard life and she was probably only fifty. The vegetable she sold was called *lombi* by the locals (I later discovered it to be pumpkin leaves) and I was convinced David thought I had raided a hibiscus bush in the garden. With a polite British gesture he gently pushed it aside citing that his mother "never could get him to eat his greens." After mastication and a few gulps of beer, it wasn't really that bad: gritty, if not a bit prickly. That the meal happened at all was quite a triumph because after an aperitif in our mossy courtyard, the heavens opened. I christened our umbrella advertising the 2000 Sydney Olympic Games when the torrential downpour followed me into the kitchen. It was the only protection I could afford the dinner, as a torrent of water streamed through the roof and directly onto the stove. It was not my most elegant of dinner parties, but in the end I was quite proud of my accomplishment.

The commercial hub; oil on sale by the cup.

Chapter 23
The Bush Telegraph

Wei writes...

Mid-October was packed with obstetric emergencies: Caesarean sections, ectopic pregnancies, and the rupture of a uterus during labour. Three of these patients had been in hypovolemic shock, having lost nearly three litres of blood intraperitoneally (into the abdominal cavity), more than twenty-four hours after the onset of labour. They could so easily have lost their lives. I also seemed to be seeing a lot of girls with haematocolpos, an accumulation of menstrual blood in the vagina, usually due to an imperforate hymen. I once thought this to be a rare condition, but there it appeared to be relatively common. Perhaps it was a natural phenomenon, but I began to suspect some of these strictures might have resulted from the insertion of a poultice of potent herbs into the vagina. Traditional medicine could easily burn the delicate tissue, resulting in scarring and the narrowing of the birth passage. In the end, Caesareans were essential for both the mothers and babies to survive.

But not all women were admitted in order to give birth. I remember one young woman who arrived the same week. She lay on a stretcher clutching at a pain high in her leg. On examination, I became suspicious about the position of the penetrating bullet wound and coaxed her to tell me more. Gabriela spoke in a faltering voice about having resisted the sexual advance of a policeman. "Sexual advance" is how my staff explained it to me, but I quickly surmised from her traumatized state that she meant attempted rape. The policeman had blown a hole through her upper thigh, just centimetres off his target. Gabriela had been shot for resisting him. Visibly frightened, she cowered from further discussion and clung to my arm as I arranged for her immediate transfer to the operating theatre.

I guess I never expected to be confronted with so many indirect victims of war. With health care pushed back to rudimentary levels, women became the most vulnerable. In Angola, one mother died during childbirth for every fifty-four children born.[22] This was one of the highest rates in the world. Perhaps not surprisingly, only seventeen percent of mothers[23] were attended by someone skilled in childbirth and most of these beneficiaries were in the larger cities. Anywhere in the world, fifteen percent of pregnancies meet with complications. One in twenty requires surgery, usually a Caesarean, but with so few surgeons out there, many women and unborn babies meet with certain death. In fact, an Angolan woman had an astonishing one in eight chance of dying as the result of childbirth. This was already twice the African average.

I am prompted to tell you this because, in addition to several Caesareans that month, we also treated a patient who had endured a difficult birth. Prolonged pressure, exerted by the baby's head on her pelvic bone, led to extensive damage to her bladder, rectum, and vagina, rendering her incontinent. Known as an utero-vesical fistula, this debilitating condition is believed to affect more than two million women worldwide.[24] This statistic understates the reality, as little data is collected to determine the real magnitude of the problem. Fistulas typically occur when a teenage mother cannot deliver her child because it is too large for her pelvis. Malnutrition compounds the problem, retarding growth of the pelvis. After a prolonged and agonizing labour without medical care, the baby often dies and the mother is left with a hole between her bladder and vagina and sometimes even her rectum. While the operation to repair the torn tissue is notoriously difficult, I felt particular sympathy towards our patient, as left untreated and incontinent, she risked being ostracized. The acrid smell of uncontrolled urine and feces streaming down their legs often leads to abandonment by their husbands and even expulsion from their community. Stigmatized and ashamed, these social outcasts are amongst the most pitiable and the least acknowledged group of sufferers in the developing world.

In a forlorn state, our patient had travelled huge distances, through inhospitable terrain, to seek our help. The smell of her wound on arrival was overwhelming. With other operations complete, we started at 11 a.m. in the hope that we would be spared further emergencies. I am no gynecologist and the procedure was new to us all, so the surgery progressed slowly. It sapped the powers of concentration of the entire team and it was well after ten o'clock that night before we finished.

Once again, I was grateful for the steaming hot meal that greeted the team when we finally made it back home. By morning, news of this marathon operation had already spread around town. Some spoke of a renewed sense of pride in our standards of surgical care. While I remained worried about our patient's progress, she was happy and recuperated well. Within days the entire team was basking in a sense of accomplishment. This alone was worth the effort, to say nothing of the quality of life our patient could now enjoy.

Although it didn't occur to me at the time, the unofficial bush telegraph is a powerful communication channel. From that point on, our outpatient consultations began to grow at a relentless pace, faster than emergency operations. We doubled the number of sessions and, like a sponge, the demand quickly expanded. Some travelled enormous distances on foot. The arrival of large numbers of displaced people in Kuito and the opening of some roads into the province were undeniably the main causes. But that did not account for the number of townsfolk who came forth with long suffering afflictions. They arrived with a vast array of advanced conditions, many of which I had never before encountered. In they marched with classic textbook pathologies: tuberculosis, elephantiasis, ascaris (worms), old war wounds, and gross tumours, to name but a few.

"But doctor, you fixed my friend, so I thought you could do something about this," said a gnarled old man. Like many patients, he didn't know his age. We tried to guess by asking how old he was at independence or when Kuito was first attacked. Still he wasn't sure but proceeded to drop his pants to reveal a massive hernia the size of a watermelon. He had endured it for over a decade!

A young lady came to me one day with her face completely shrouded in a scarf. I instinctively knew that she was trying to camouflage something embarrassing. In a private room she plucked up the courage to reveal her face to me. It took my breath away! Like an encrusted parasite, a large blackened tumour grew on her translucent face. She could no longer see through her left eye. For a young woman, robbed of her beauty in this way, I felt an overwhelming sense of compassion. Adriana suffered from albinism, a genetic condition resulting in the lack of pigmentation in the eyes, skin, and hair. This condition is not uncommon in Africa, but the consequences are severe in the unrelenting sun. The hot rays had ravaged Adriana's delicate white skin. For years she cowed from public gaze as the condition worsened. At a glance it appeared to be a particularly gross melanoma, a very serious form of skin cancer, but I had no facilities to complete the diagnosis. I explained the situation and difficult procedure with due protocol, but she yearned to savour a quality of life we all take for granted. The surgery was a difficult, perhaps cavalier, undertaking out there in the bush. After excising the tumour, I undertook reconstructive plastic surgery using the rotational flap technique, which uses the surrounding facial skin to cover the defect. Adriana stayed in hospital for months, as she didn't want to face the outside world until her wound had completely healed, but I soon suspected she liked being there. She became a willing helper in the wards. As her wounds healed, she gradually she began to uncover her face and her extrovert nature started to shine through. With renewed self-confidence, the joy she exuded with each passing day was worth more than I could have ever imagined.

However, for many there was little we could do. In reality, we could only accept patients whose conditions were life threatening or whose livelihoods were seriously compromised. Many required complex reconstructive surgery, a luxury beyond the medical care available in Angola. There was enough work to keep an entire team of general surgeons, oncologists, plastic surgeons, gynecologists, ophthalmologists, and physicians busy for a lifetime. We treated as many as we could and my heart sank each time less serious conditions were turned away—something unthinkable to me before this.

And as for the hidden issue of utero-vesical fistulas, in 2002, the US government cut $34 million in funding to the United Nations Population Fund (UNFPA) over the Bush administration's concerns about abortion in China. Sadly, it is this very same fund that sponsors programs in prenatal care to help prevent vaginal fistulas.

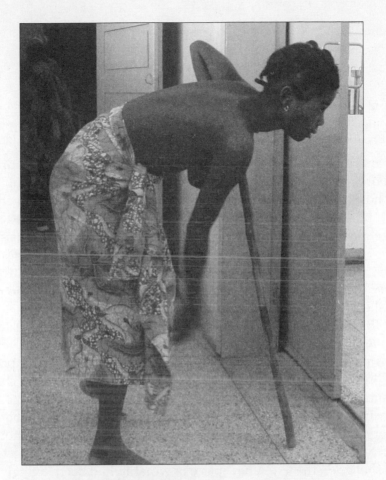

Patients walked for miles.

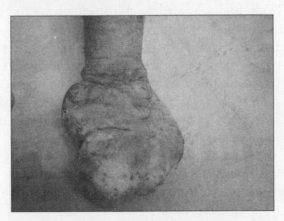

Left foot disfigured by elephantiasis.

Chapter 24
Sunday Best

Karin writes...

Sporting an ill-fitting suit, white shirt, and loud tie, Eduardo stood in our doorway, clutching his Bible. He had the day off from the hospital and had been badgering us for weeks to attend church with him. The bright morning light illuminated his silhouette. His huge platform shoes were as prominent as his ever-infectious smile. Like a life-sized caricature of the classic door-to-door salesman, Eduardo's Bible could well have been the latest edition of *Encyclopaedia Britannica*. In this dandified getup, Eduardo had come to take us to church on that sunny October morning.

A clash of flamboyant colours greeted our eyes. As he led us through the streets, I understood instinctively where the expression "to dress up in Sunday best" came from. Sunday, the most important day in the weekly calendar, was here. Upon arrival at the church, Eduardo guided us proudly through the milling crowd to meet the preacher, whose obeisance bestowed far more honour than we deserved. His church was a shell and, as I stood wondering how the service was going to be held amongst the rubble, Eduardo directed us to a shelter on the left. A new place of worship had been lovingly constructed adjacent to the basilica-that-was. But this new church had no walls, half a roof, and was clearly still under construction. Roughly hewn tree trunks, placed vertically at metre intervals, defined the building frame and supported smaller sapling branches that formed the roof beams. Piece by piece, sheets of plastic or warped sheet-iron were gradually forming what would one day become a complete roof covering. The floor was just a patchwork of dirt and thinning grass. As we were led up the grassy aisle, guarded whispers from the congregation made it feel no less of a holy place.

We were directed to the side rows of the imaginary apse, where we sat among the senior church wardens. We tried to balance our chairs on the uneven ground as I observed the curious podium: an old concrete slab from which a rusted reinforcing rod protruded. I eventually worked out that it was the foundation of an outhouse that, like the adjacent church, had been obliterated in a mortar attack. A symbol of resilience, the outhouse floor was now the preacher's lectern—a stage from which he would launch renewed hope for the future.

The congregation began to swell, spilling through gaps in the makeshift walls. I was counting the people around me, which had reached over five hundred, when I was interrupted by a long chain of singers snaking their way down the aisle. Dancing rhythmically and singing harmoniously, they heralded the start of the service. Their rousing voices gradually worked to a crescendo. It was mesmerizing music sung with such passion that I was immediately swept away by its energy. As the service progressed, various groups took turns to sing their praise of the Lord: a young women's choir, a men's choir, a children's choir, the modern, and the traditional, in Portuguese, in Umbundu. The drummer hopped nimbly from the ground to a seat nearby. His limbs, ravaged by polio at an early age, hung lamely from the bench, but he clutched a drum between his knees and played with a joie de vivre that inspired with each beat. An elderly fellow gently nudged me, offering his treasured hymnbook. We felt obliged to accept his kind gesture. Frayed at the edges, it was printed in both Portuguese and Umbundu. I used it to sing my first hymn in Portuguese and to utter my first words of Umbundu. I stumbled along, mouthing as best I could. I still don't know exactly what I was singing, but as it was a hymn, I got the general gist.

As the service progressed I became increasingly aware of the man on my right: a fit handsome fellow of about my age...younger perhaps. He began his lament during the first hymn. Keening, wallowing in raw pain, he propped up his face with anguished hands. In a feckless attempt to comfort him, I tried to hold his left forearm as we sang the next hymn together. But I sensed that he felt disquiet at my strangeness. His palpable agony distressed me more with his every sob. With his spirit harpooned and fustigated, loss oozed from every pore. At that moment, the preacher began to read the list of parishioners who had died in the past week. There were close to ten names on the list in a congregation of five hundred. When the name Maria was read out, the man lurched forward and let out a mournful howl. He had lost his wife.

My mind filled with images of my own family as we sang the next hymn together; images of happy, comfy times together, contrasting this poignant scene around me. A mixture of homesickness and pathos overcame me. I pressed my tongue hard against the roof of my mouth and sang harder, straining to stave off my tears. I looked up above, straight through the half-finished roof into the azure sky and the heavens above. I had been in Kuito almost one month and suddenly felt the emotional impact of it all. I yearned to run from the church and cry out loud in privacy, but I couldn't abandon the moment.

At the invitation of local friends, we joined congregations of varying denominations several times after that, but none touched me quite the same way as that first service. Later in December, Wei painted a portrait from a photo taken at another marathon service we attended. It was Augusto's church, arguably one of the most impressive buildings in the city. It looked better than the hospital. It is somewhat ironic that the churches were the first buildings to be rehabilitated. That day the pews were crammed with parishioners, but Wei was captivated by one particular face in the congregation. It was that of a woman, electrified by the words of a fire-and-brimstone preacher. For an amateur I think he captured her well—her sense of hope. This huge painting now hangs in a prominent position at home and serves as a daily reminder of the people of Kuito.

Since our return, a surprising number of people have asked us whether we are Christians or whether God lead us to work in Angola. While we respect all religions and cultural beliefs, we have no particular religious beliefs or affiliations. Although many have been surprised to hear our reply, it was MSF's non-religious credentials that appealed to us. And if forced to define our beliefs in the form of an "ism" it would be the non-theistic and inherently secular ethics of humanism.

A face of hope in the congregation.

…captured in Wei's painting.

Chapter 25
Day Care

Karin continues…

War makes no distinction between a Saturday and a Sunday, therefore, like all those years in Hong Kong, Saturdays were workdays. After all, the malnourished needed feeding and the sick were still ill. Given my responsibilities for human resources, I chose Saturdays as the day to visit the various programs, to get to know both our national and expatriate staff and the great work they did. On one of my first such visits, I toured the nutrition program, which was managed by Christelle, a nurse from Belgium. She was the longest serving volunteer on the project and spoke English with a delightful, lilting accent, but with her fluent Portuguese, she outshone us all. When I first met her, she appeared frazzled and I was a concerned about her overworked state. After that visit I understood why, as there were simply hundreds under the care of her team. They were completely overloaded and there had been little time for holidays in the twelve months since the nutritional emergency had started.

While the WFP provided food for the displaced people, MSF was involved in the medical treatment and care of the more seriously malnourished. The facilities ranged from supplementary feeding (for the moderately malnourished) to therapeutic feeding (for the severely malnourished). These critically ill patients also often had complications resulting from other medical conditions.

We started the day with a visit to Day Care, a monitored feeding program for children, where over one hundred fifty children were admitted. Each day, mothers brought their children to receive medical care and fortified food supplements. I followed Christelle on her rounds, one of several she and her team conducted throughout the day. She took the time to explain the signs of malnutrition as she skilfully checked their eyes and feet. Oedema, an accumulation of fluid, frequently in the feet, was a classic symptom. She also explained the complexity of malnutrition and how children in particular can deteriorate very quickly. The recovery progress is slow and fickle and demands vigilance. Children could seem happy and well in the morning and be seriously ill by the afternoon: alive one minute, gone the next, even if they consumed the supplements. I trailed behind Christelle as she attentively checked child after child. The patients' carers, sometimes just young siblings, settled around the walls of the tents. It was an unhurried process. Perched on grain sacks to keep them out of the dirt, they spooned food from a plastic mug into malnourished mouths. Some recipients looked despondent and lifeless.

Finding the tents airless and stuffy, I wandered outside into a milling crowd. The onlookers stood hauntingly before me on spindly legs, but had bigger smiles than you could elicit from children with infinitely more reason to be happy. They were enigmatic. At first I was embarrassed to use our camera but soon realized that it provided great entertainment. In the absence of toys, a foreigner with a camera was a real crowd-pleaser and the digital images were magic before their curious eyes.

We then checked on proceedings at the centre's kitchen, which was of the same basic standard as the one at the hospital. It too had a dirt floor. Several hearth fires smouldered in the open-air structure of corrugated iron. Workers laboured to stir the maize slop in blackened cauldrons. The kitchen seemed to work well enough, but made my mice-infested one in *Casa Quatro* look positively futuristic.

When Christelle was finished we strolled, dog-tired, across to the therapeutic centre where the more serious cases were referred. Patients were housed in traditional thatch buildings emblazoned with MSF logos. We wandered in to meet Bertrand, the Belgian doctor. Typically, the prevalence of tuberculosis and malaria complicated the recovery for the severely malnourished. On entering the hut, I instinctively wanted to apologize and throw myself in reverse. I gasped as I observed the gaunt patients: they were little more than lifeless apparitions. There is no dignity in starvation.

Despite my unease, Bertrand took time to explain his issues. It was there that I learned more about pellagra, a rare vitamin B (niacin) deficiency, which, until then, Wei said he had only ever read about in medical school. The condition presents as a dermatosis (skin disease) affecting sun-exposed skin. It is more common in populations whose staple carbohydrate is maize, which is low in niacin. People who depend entirely on food aid (usually maize) are obviously more vulnerable. Bertrand described the clinical features known as the 3-Ds: dermatitis, diarrhea, and dementia. The most common sign was called Casal's necklace, a ring of dermatitis around the neck where the skin was more readily exposed to sunlight. Fortunately, we only had a few cases of pellagra at that time, but in the period before the summer harvest, known as the hunger gap, Kuito had previously reported up to fifty cases a month.

I remember hosting the fleeting visit of a pompous European diplomat around this time. He clearly had no time for aid workers and laughingly suggested that we had confabulated our statistics on pellagra. He quizzed us on why they were out of line with incidence rates in the rest of the country, then strode through the hospital bombastically pronouncing it to be one of the best in Africa. Despite our startled looks, he implied we didn't warrant further funding from his nation. Then off he went, leaving us to ponder the art of modern-day diplomacy. Yet, nearly one thousand cases of pellagra had been reported in Kuito that year and it was widely believed that the entire displaced population suffered from some degree of niacin deficiency. Fish is a good source of vitamin B, but Kuito was hundreds of kilometres from the sea and stocks in the rivers were limited. Nuts should have been easy to grow but, like most things, they were no longer farmed in any great quantity. Farming had collapsed and ongoing insecurity was the root cause of the nutritional emergency.

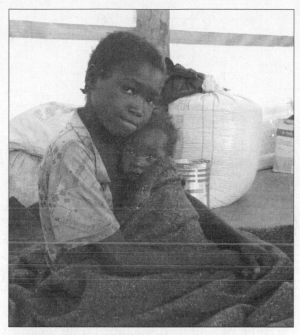

Sibling responsibility.

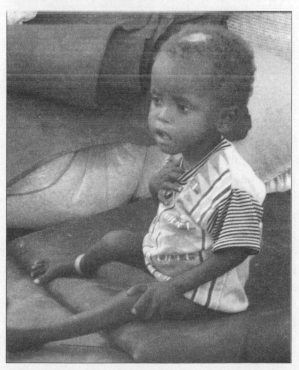

Just one of hundreds of malnourished children
at the Day Care centre.

Chapter 26
Gémeo

Wei writes…

"How can this patient possibly have a pulse of seventy beats per minute?" I asked urgently, during my round in Intensive Care. The critically ill patient was pale and sweating—clearly in shock. Yet the nurse reassuringly pointed to the readings on the patient's chart that been diligently recorded throughout the night: 70, 70, 70. A pulse rate of seventy beats per minute is consistent with that of a healthy adult.

"But you simply can't have that pulse rate and be in shock," I explained, exasperated.

I seized upon a nurse with a wristwatch and asked her whether she had checked the patient's pulse. "But I only wear my watch for adornment. It doesn't work," she replied, with no hint of embarrassment. I then checked the patient's pulse rate myself and it was a disconcerting 120 beats per minute.

I tried hard to suppress my antipathy towards the government for allowing hospital care to rot in this way. For weeks, I had been frustrated by my failure to foster a culture of systematic checks. I had tried hard to instill a little basic discipline in patient care. Yet it took me until that day to get to the heart of the issue. It was not for the want of trying, but my instruction to methodically record pulse rates was debased by my own oversight. I peered around the walls. Until then, it had never crossed my mind. There were no clocks, and I had never noticed. With no wristwatches, the methodology had metamorphosed into a best guess. I immediately ordered wall clocks for each ward.

Intensive care units are normally characterized by bleeping monitors that assist with patient care. In Kuito we had no more than a single nurse serving seven very sick patients, with no equipment—a superhuman expectation for even the most experienced nurse. Most of the hospital staff was inadequately trained, although MSF nurse trainers were trying really hard to improve things. As for the medical equipment, there was no oxygen, ventilator, or cardiac monitors—essential standards for most surgical units. In fact, there was less equipment than a basic ambulance would have in many countries today. Apart from intravenous drips and urinary catheters, there was little else. In the operating theatre there was one diathermy (a surgical heating instrument commonly used on the tissue to limit bleeding during surgery) and it didn't work. We had also been known to run out of medication. What was more, years of endless neglect had induced a particular attitude. For instance, we regularly found MSF hospital supplies for sale at the market.

Shocked by the perilous state of our patients that morning, I went as far as reprimanding a nurse who had abandoned her post before her replacement had reported for duty. I was ready to explode, but, again, there was a simple explanation. A shortage of trained nurses meant that many of the women whom I had assumed to be qualified were not fully trained. Many still attended nursing school. The nurses working nights attended school during the day. That morning they all had an examination. No one reported for duty and there was simply no one to replace them. Without my knowledge, intensive care patients were left to fend for themselves. Morale at the hospital had been further eroded by the Ministry of Health's failure to pay staff for eight months. I felt I was merely providing symptomatic relief to a system rotting at the core. The entire hospital was creaking, but to wallow in frustration was a futile pastime.

With these depressing problems still fresh in my mind, I moved on to another day. We stabilized the patient in shock and I proceeded with my usual operating list. After the third operation, we ran out of sterile theatre drapes. The rainy season had started and the drying of drapes and gowns became more unpredictable. With no electricity and no dryers, we relied on washerwomen and the sunshine. The green drapes were laid out on the grass to dry before being sterilized in the autoclave. When it rained, the chain broke down. I suspended the list and called in additional emergency supplies to be sterilized.

The respite was short-lived as Monica referred two more patients that afternoon. Monica had a feisty personality and an acute sense of humour. In her lively Mediterranean way, she rolled with the punches and knew when to bring laughter to an overwhelming situation. Above all, she cared. As a pediatric surgeon, I was particularly keen to receive her first patient: a three-day-old baby born without an anus (imperforate anus). He had a distended abdomen. Alarmed by the late diagnosis, I asked why it took the parents a full three days to discover the baby had no anus, but never did understand the answer. I classified it as a "low-type," meaning I was able to attempt the operation with just local anaesthesia. This was something no one would dream of doing under better circumstances, for an infant may cry or move at a critical moment. We were ill-equipped to put a newborn under general anaesthetic, and fortunately the baby was a model patient allowing the mother to resume breast-feeding immediately.

Another Caesarean followed before Monica called me again, referring a nine-year-old boy with appendicitis. Monica, ever interested in surgery, decided to scrub. While up to our elbows in the appendectomy, Emilie rushed in to announce an urgent case of eclampsia (pregnancy-related hypertension that leads to convulsions and coma). Eclampsia is rare in countries where prenatal care is developed but has a high mortality rate of up to twenty percent. In fact, I had to admit I had never seen a case. However this patient had already suffered three fits and was unconscious. There is no other treatment in a place like Kuito than to get the baby out quickly by Caesarean section, so I asked Emilie to bring her over. Inger started the spinal anaesthesia while I finished the appendectomy.

There is nothing like the birth of a child to brighten the spirits. "Whaaaa…" the baby bellowed energetically. Everyone was so elated that we momentarily failed to notice something unusual as I pulled out the placenta. Hooked on assisting, Monica was first to spot it.

"Hey, what's that?" she quizzed.

"It's another baby!" I announced with excitement.

Three seconds later another "Whaaa…" and the mood was infectious. "Gémeo! Gémeo!" (Twins! Twins!) we all cheered.

And to my relief, the mother awoke from her coma three days later. I still reflect on their birth: a moment suffused with joy, doubled happiness that bloomed from tortured surroundings. The entire surgical team felt like proud parents.

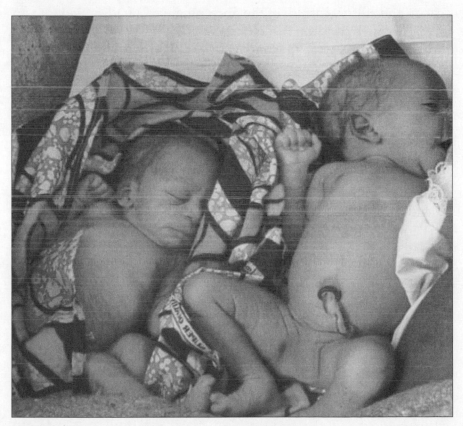

Gémeo.

Chapter 27
Three Dollars a Day

Karin writes...

By November, days oscillated between the crisp cool of the dry season and sultry warmth of the oncoming wet. I had settled into an enthusiastic rhythm at the office. At the end of the day I often recorded my thoughts, long after the last of our employees had left. Our staff included about ninety full-time and two hundred part-time employees whose work covered a wide range of tasks across the project. Among other things, Julio and I were responsible for making sure they were paid. The administrative office was often hopping with casual workers who had helped dig latrines or unload cargo. Endless queues were a feature of the daily hubbub outside our window. At the allotted hour they would come to collect their recompense: three dollars a day. It might not sound like much but consider that nearly half of Africa's 570 million people live on as little as one dollar a day.[25]

This particular day started with a trip to the airport to welcome a new volunteer. The plane was late which probably explained why a team of women was still sweeping the tarmac. With small straw brooms in hand, they were strung out across the entire runway. Bent double from the waist down, the task was arduous. As the unrelenting sun beamed hotly on the tarmac, they swept up excess grain that had spilled from the WFP plane that morning. It was a captivating sight. Just then another vehicle arrived, and I wandered up to chat. Two middle-aged men climbed out and introduced themselves as photographers from *National Geographic*. I motioned them in the direction of the cleaning detail and suggested the women would make a vivid portrait, but their interest lay elsewhere. I was fascinated to learn of their assignment on diamonds—the so-called dirty diamonds that were being trafficked beyond UN sanctions. They were winding up an extensive adventure that had taken them to the heart of places like Angola, Sierra Leone, and Congo. We chatted for a while, and before the plane landed I asked them when I could expect to see their photos in print. "Not for a while," one joked.

"The *National Geographic* moves at a glacial pace," laughed the other, as they threw their camera gear on board.

I welcomed the new arrival with a strange reassurance, for by now I already felt like an old hand. Eventually I made it back to the office to be confronted by Dona Teresa, the office janitor. In lively gestures that transcended language, she showed me that thousands of ants had invaded the sugar. She was not amused, and unaccustomed as I was to dealing with problems of that magnitude in corporate life, I listened intently. The tin cupped in her palms was teeming with them. Teresa's leathery face captured years of toil in every wrinkle, while her convivial smile revealed a sweet soul underneath all of that. Even so, she seemed out of place in an office environment, not that it was fancy by any stretch of the imagination. Despite our relatively modern facilities, Teresa still chose to boil water outside on charcoal and squealed each time the phone rang, as if for the first time. She loved to answer it and bellowed down the receiver as if everyone was hard of hearing. Her voice resonated through the whole house with grating regularity. Teresa was hardly shy, having already taken a distinct liking to my cheap raincoat. It was no more than a plastic bag with press-studs down the front, emblazoned with the slogan of my last sales conference, but she made it obvious enough that she liked it. I was quick to promise that she could have it on my departure, and from that day forth I was convinced she was counting the days.

"Ai, ai, ai." I shrugged in an "oh well" kind of way when she presented me with the infested sugar crystals. I had assumed that she would just ask me for another hundred Kwanzas to replace it. Dona Teresa was always asking me for money to purchase sugar. The office workers consumed this luxury as if it were life-giving nectar. But she just wandered away, preoccupied with the container cradled in her hands. Hours later she returned and proudly presented me with a bowl of white crystals. "As formigas?" (The ants?) I queried. Forming pincers with her fingers, Teresa nimbly demonstrated how she had eradicated the problem. She had diligently removed each ant—thousands of them—one by one. But at US$4.50 a kilo, sugar was expensive, equivalent to one-and-a-half-day's salary for a labourer.

By that afternoon casual labourers were waiting outside for their pay. One by one each worker came forth responding to the roll call that Julio delivered in his amusingly official tone. He doled out the cash. Towards the end of the procedure, he called a second time for someone who had failed to show at the allotted hour. A waif burst forth—his face aglow with an impish smile. He had no shoes and his pants were filthy and frayed. He threw me a furtive glance before announcing confidently that he was the missing worker. He had helped to unload the plane, he proclaimed. Julio looked unconvinced, his skepticism obvious as he turned to talk to me. In a voice mingling pity with contempt, Julio switched to English to fill me in. He asked for my opinion. The waif cocked his head on the side and turned towards me with downcast hush-puppy eyes. He instinctively knew that payment now hung in the balance. Was it misery or superb acting? The urchin looked as though he lacked the stamina to lift more than his dusty feet, let alone lug heavy cargo, but I was taken by his plucky attitude. We quizzed him some more about the time, location, and contents of the cargo and he stood his ground during cross-examination.

He was no more than a child, but reaffirmed he was the legally mandated age of eighteen. It was hard to tell in a place where malnutrition leaves some teenagers looking like they have hardly reached puberty. I was wondering how much he had learned from others waiting in the queue about the payload, when pity won out. We eventually gave him the benefit of the doubt and his three dollars. The urchin beamed widely as he attempted to scribble a signature on the payroll sheet. His eyes squinted as he focused on the seriousness of the task: spelling his assumed name. He then threw me an impudent smile and quickly absconded with his loot.

Supplies arrive as another volunteer departs.

Chapter 28
Headcount

Karin contines...

After a depressing week spent analyzing statistics on child mortality, I volunteered to help with a population survey in the camps—anything to get out of the office for a bit. While I had commissioned plenty of consumer research in my marketing years, this was a survey from an entirely new perspective. As my Portuguese was still elementary, I stuck with Paulo, one of our supervisors who spoke English.

Marooned within the tiny enclave that the so-called security zone afforded the displaced, over one hundred thousand people had set up camp. The sanctuary that Kuito offered was little more than ten kilometres across and conditions were dire. Yet in these camps, MSF managed a team of home monitors: local residents who were employed to collect data from among their own people. With residents checking in this way, the sick were discovered earlier and sent more promptly to the nearest health post for attention. Statistics on births, deaths, population movements (arrivals and departures), health problems, and general living conditions were systematically tabulated to provide a fast barometer in an ever-changing situation. We shared this data with other NGOs to help plan the relief efforts. As the homeless moved continuously, the data collection process was fraught with difficulties. Accuracy also suffered when large numbers of dispossessed scrambled to register twice so they could increase their chances of receiving double the meagre food rations. This might well outrage the self-righteous, but I could easily imagine myself attempting the same, if faced with a similar plight. While this distorted our data, the statistics still provided us with an essential overview and enabled quick identification of problems, such as outbreaks of infectious diseases.

On that overcast day in early November we headed out of town to Trumba camp, one of more than twenty-five camps nestled on the hilly expanses surrounding the city. However, on arrival, the *Soba* (village chief) greeted us anxiously with the news that counting was not appropriate since a child had died overnight. The villagers were tending the deceased child before the burial began. As a sign of respect we pushed on to neighbouring Andulo camp.

Like any market survey we moved from door to door, street by street, interviewing the residents and assessing their general living conditions. We counted dwellings, the number of latrines, access to communal water pumps or wells, adequacy of shelter, plastic sheeting, blankets, cooking pots, and immunization cover. Some residents proudly produced their immunization cards while others stared blankly at us. Progress was slow.

The poorest of Kuito's poor lived in these camps, in conditions the likes of which I had never before witnessed. Dry thatch was lashed to twig frames with anything they could lay their hands on. The shelters were cobbled together using shredded sack as string, but more often just strips of tree bark. Living on a shoestring took on a whole new meaning when I came upon a thatched hut that was literally lashed together with an old shoelace. Hearth fires spluttered in the middle of the huts. A sooty smell hung heavy in the air. In these drier months, the search for wood and thatch took villagers further afield and deforestation became yet another economic tragedy. Neglected by their government and in desperate need of shelter and fuel, people tore at trees and grass that they needed to survive. In the dry season it became hard to find, meaning villagers were forced to walk up to thirty kilometres across precarious terrain to obtain supplies. I was beguiled by their tenacity.

With every step, an entourage of curious children swelled our ranks. They posed in fascination for my digital camera. With infectious smiles they peered down the lens as if determined to see the miniature people inside—those who appeared on the liquid crystal screen. I was charmed.

At *Rua 4, Casa 22* we came upon a tiny hut of Lilliputian proportions. Few of these dwellings were tall enough to allow you to stand inside, but this one was particularly diminutive: the roof stood a bare metre from the ground. With its thatch scrappy and loose, it could have been a dream cubby house for an imaginative child, but there it was a home. A young girl, aged twelve, and her ten-year-old sister came running over to us. Elsa, the elder of the two, took up the story. Her tattered skirt wafted around her spindly frame. She explained how she and her sister, Rosalina, had been orphaned after an attack on their village in September. They had fled with their neighbours and proudly explained how they had built their little cubby house themselves. It leaned precariously to one side and was unlikely to keep out the first drop of rain. I peered inside and eyed an oily rag thrust in the corner. The embers of a spent fire sent curls of thin smoke up through the gaping roof. I could see no blankets, clothes, or cooking pots. Smoke permeated my lungs and a stale whiff of poverty invaded my nostrils. Elsa answered our questions with disarming maturity. We marked them for special attention but had to push on to the next hut.

An already leaden sky had been growing darker all morning. The thunderclouds moved in and with them the first real rain of the season. The heavens suddenly opened, pelting warm raindrops against the thirsty earth. It soon turned the dust into a quagmire and we were forced to abandon our survey. We retreated to the Land Cruiser and headed for the nearby health post, pursued by the entourage of children who ran precariously behind. Despite our protestations, raffish young boys played tag with our rear bumper and the wheels soon sprayed them with muck. They were fearless of vehicles and cared for nothing more than the fun of the moment.

Out of the rain, in the tents at the Belo Horizonte health post, I found Anne-Sophie, the Belgian nurse, in charge of camp health. She was directing a team of nurse's aides, as they struggled with burgeoning patient numbers. Despite the frenzy of activity, she exuded style and I marvelled at her refusal to let the dire surroundings disturb her air of femininity. The health posts treated more patients than the hospital in any given month and that day diarrhea was an overwhelming problem. Anne-Sophie and her team were finding it hard to keep up with the demand in the dispensary, so I plonked myself on a metal trunk and quickly became engaged in the tedious task of counting tablets that were dispensed to the afflicted. The rain teemed against the tent walls. As dust turned to slush and slush to rivulets, I couldn't stop thinking about Elsa and Rosalina in their tiny cubby house.

Elsa and Rosaline and their Lilliputian house.

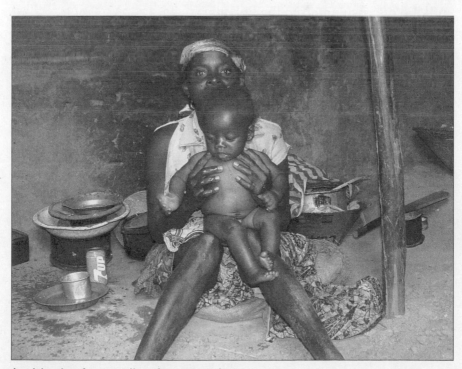

Inside the four walls of a camp hut.

Chapter 29
Baby with a Broken Arm

Karin writes…

I sat down to write my story about the camp visit when Wei asked me if I wanted to go to the *Banco de Urgência* with him. It was turning into our regular Saturday afternoon outing. He had just treated a five-month-old boy whose mother had been run over by a military vehicle. Miraculously the baby had been thrown clear of the vehicle, sustaining little more than a broken arm and a nasty bump over his eye. His mother was still missing, believed to be dead, and no one knew anything about the rest of his family. The infant had not been weaned and with no special formula milk available Wei was concerned that he was at risk of dehydrating. Wei showed me how to make the next best substitute. We grabbed some Nido milk powder from our pantry shelves and hastily made some diluted milk before rushing off to the hospital.

The *Banco de Urgência* was housed in a partially rehabilitated building that had sustained considerable damage. A corrugated iron roof had been tacked back on, exposing the rafters. It was a dim, depressing place. On busy days, patients filled its beds and spilled onto the floor. Stretchers came and went with monotonous regularity. Everyone seemed to talk in uneasy whispers, while hoards of nervous relatives hovered outside.

Gingerly, I stepped over a man with a bloody gunshot wound to his knee. His glassy eyes glared through me into space. Tucked out of harm's way, I found the little boy crying alone on a bed at the back of the room. We didn't know his name, but as soon as I set eyes upon him I nicknamed him *Fei Tsai*, Cantonese for Little Fatso, as he was cute and pudgy. As babysitting has never come naturally, I dithered over the next problem. How was I to transfer the milk from the screw-top bottle to the baby's mouth? Stumped, I radioed Monica to ask where to find a baby bottle. She simply laughed and said: "Just use a large syringe." Of course. How silly of me!

As Wei busied himself with the wounded, I lifted Fei Tsai's bruised body off the bed. I was terrified I would cause further injury and gently carried him out into the warm sunshine. I settled myself on a balcony bench, where I attempted to inject milk into his tiny mouth. Fei Tsai's miniature lips puckered around the syringe as if it were his mother's nipple. He sucked with vigour, for he was thirsty. Neither of us was an expert at this. Milk trickled haphazardly between the creases of his chubby neck and seeped between my legs. I felt warm and soggy, but nevertheless we spent blissful hours together this way. With one eye swollen shut, he stared quizzically through the other before drifting off to sleep. He stirred only when I tried to put him back on the bed at the end of the day. Fei Tsai whimpered until he felt the reassurance of my touch once more and I was loath to leave him. I begged Wei to take him home for the night. But Wei was right. It wasn't correct protocol to just waltz off with a nameless orphan from a hospital. I could have adopted him on the spot.

Reluctantly, I returned to *Casa Quatro*, but several hours later Wei was called again to *Banco de Urgência*. Fei Tsai's mother had arrived. The soldiers had finally managed to lift their vehicle off of her and villagers rushed her in when they realized she was still ticking. She was not dead after all, just unconscious and had sustained only minor injuries. Wei treated her for little more than a concussion and Fei Tsai was never happier to see that his next feed wasn't from that big plastic syringe.

But every small victory seemed tempered by another loss. The following evening we had planned a dinner party with a selection of friends from the other houses. I persisted with my attempts to improvise and cooked another Chinese meal. I set the table before the house was suddenly plunged into darkness when the solar cell failed, leaving us stumbling around in dark shadows. With little more than the moonlight to guide us, we could barely negotiate the corridors but had the battery back in action to greet our guests. Then like a circling vulture, the hospital ambulance glided quietly to the front gate. They needed half the party-goers. Emilie, Olivier, and Wei dashed off, putting a damper on the evening. Tall, young, and erudite, Olivier loved his work as a physician and was ever eager to learn some basic surgical techniques from Wei. It was only a Caesarean and I had expected them back within the hour, but as the evening dragged on I knew that something was amiss. The remaining guests stayed on, but eventually their ranks dwindled and the evening fizzled out. Still, there was no sign of Wei.

When finally I heard voices at the door I rushed to greet them, but I could tell from Wei's ashen face that something had gone wrong. The sixteen-year-old mother had suffered a cardiac arrest on the table as a result of the spinal anaesthetic and died. Wei and Olivier both tried to revive her for almost an hour. They had brought a child into the world without a mother. It was a solemn way to end an evening. A hollow feeling ruminated from within.

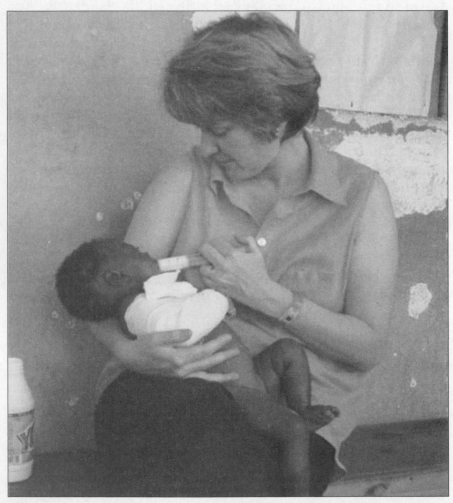

Karin and Fei Tsai on the balcony of Banco de Urgência.

Chapter 30
Development & Decay

Karin continues...

"Pela paz, democracia e desenvolvimento, reconstruamos a pátria."
— Government slogan for the twenty-fifth anniversary of
independence, November 11, 2000

"For peace, democracy and development, let's reconstruct the homeland," screamed a T-shirt that Wei had exchanged with a colleague for the one on his back. He came bounding home after the National Day celebrations at the hospital, flaunting the souvenir that proudly declared Angola's twenty-fifth anniversary of independence. Quite apart from the wishful thinking it declared, I felt a heightened sense of anguish by the political statement Wei was making in those times of insecurity. After all, I could see no peace, democracy, or development and very little reconstruction. I also wondered how Angolans reconciled these concepts of progress while witnessing the general disintegration of their nation.

With due protocol, the hospital administration took its official *festa* quite seriously. There were the usual speeches and cake-cutting ceremonies, singing, and dancing, but a conversation Wei had with a member of the staff was more interesting still. A fellow colleague chose that day to reminisce wistfully about a bygone era. He talked candidly of his time as a soldier in the Portuguese colonial army, recounting stories of the years prior to independence. Such was the mix of feelings about the past, present, and doubtful future on what should have been a proud occasion for the nation.

Celebrations took place around town, but the security situation had deteriorated. That week, the hospital received several landmine patients, all victims of new mines; some placed just seven kilometres away. There were also more gunshot victims. Claims of police brutality towards civilians were on the rise, and as a result the whole team was under tight security constraints throughout the weekend. For that reason, we didn't get to see the parade through the main street—small as it apparently was. My frustration was heightened by my failure to get to the heart of how locals felt about it all. It was exasperating to be so linguistically challenged because I yearned to understand how people were managing inside themselves. Yet, whenever I probed, I only induced a confused mixture of nationalistic pride peppered with that tired refrain: "Angola tem muitos problemas!" Said with a weary air of resignation, this comment rarely invited further discussion. It was always a bit of a conversation stopper: "Angola has many problems!" An iconic understatement clouded by an unspoken past and lingering uncertainty about the future.

The anti-colonial war for independence started in the 1960s in a move against the Portuguese colonial administration. Independence finally came to Angola, but its faltering start was a mere foretaste of the crises to follow and things went wrong right from the beginning. The country lurched from one disaster to the next. The South African government invaded on the eve of independence in August 1975, claiming the need to quell rising dissent from SWAPO, an organization calling for independence in neighbouring Namibia. South Africa ruled Namibia back then and SWAPO operated bases from southern Angola. In its race to Angola's capital, the South African army came within two hundred kilometres of Luanda before being pushed back. This predatory move prompted Zaïre (now the inaptly named Democratic Republic of Congo) to send troops from the north in support of a third group called the National Liberation Front of Angola (FNLA). Despite Chinese backing, this move was short-lived and the group collapsed soon after. More significantly, all of these shenanigans provoked Cuba, with covert support from the USSR, to send thousands of troops to bolster the government's control of the capital. If this sounds truly absurd, it was. The real interests lay far away. Moscow had become paranoid about China's growing influence in Africa, which, at the time of Angola's independence, was overshadowing the Soviets.

Things also took a leap backwards on independence, when Portuguese settlers left en masse, meaning much of the country's educated and technically qualified personnel evaporated overnight. To make matters worse, the MPLA pursued an unsustainable development model that precipitated economic ruin. The newly independent nation stumbled into an economic crisis and even more war.

Moscow and Havana provided the government with all of its

military needs. Billions of dollars of equipment and assistance poured into the country. Castro lent combat troops, pilots, military advisers, technicians, and engineers. As the insurgency expanded, so did Cuba's military presence. By 1982 there were 35,000 Cubans in Angola, a number that grew to more than fifty thousand by 1988. Over three hundred thousand Cuban soldiers served in Angola over a sixteen-year period.

Ever suspicious of the USSR's intentions and control of massive oil reserves, the US, through the CIA, was soon running covert operations to support the opposition. Together with South Africa, they armed Jonas Savimbi's UNITA. Even though he had been trained in China, Savimbi was a master chameleon and soon became a willing recipient of Washington's largesse. This complex chessboard-like game brought Angola into international focus. It remained there until the end of the Cold War when, like the setting sun, it sank from view. Once the Cubans were out of the way, the US was free to switch sides and support the government, leaving their old ally Savimbi to re-establish arms suppliers among numerous nation-pieces of the former Soviet Union.

During our months in Angola some said: "The war is over, but there is no peace." I had difficulty digesting the paradox. Angola was a country of graveyards and the disenfranchised population could draw no comfort from this play on words. Kuito's own necropolis was overflowing. There were makeshift graveyards in the camps and the main city cemetery was just at the end of our street. It wasn't safe to go there until soon after we arrived, after the UXOs and mines had been cleared. The wall surrounding the necropolis was scarred with shrapnel and the chapel was completely gutted. It was a mournful place to stroll—nothing of the restfulness one anticipates for those who have met their end. Row upon row of freshly dug graves anticipated the arrival of new occupants. Simple wooden crosses demarcated resting places for the latest victims along with poignant symbols of the lives they had lived: a WFP oil can, a prosthetic leg, a shoe. Mounds of fresh dirt were garnished with wilting wildflowers. Angola *tem muitos problemas* indeed.

Official cake-cutting ceremony at the hospital for the twenty-fifth anniversary of independence.

Kuito Cemetery. Graves adorned with USAID oil cans.

Chapter 31
Electrified

Karin continues...

Our logisticians were indispensable: undeniably the backbone of the projects. During the first few months, most notably on Sunday evenings, we had rationed town-supply electricity on several nights per week. It came on at 6 p.m. for a few hours. On alternate nights, another part of town enjoyed the benefit. I looked forward to the moment that the light bulbs would glow from pale to bright, heralding the start of our privileges, and I rapidly learned to make the most of this luxury. In truth we preferred solar power, but this system did not generate enough for more than two very dim globes and the battery tripped with monotonous regularity. There were times when we simply went without power for weeks and, while I was loath to bother him, we finally called on our logistician, Arnaud, for help.

Arnaud was an easy-going Frenchman whose permanently tousled hair made him look as though he had just climbed out of bed, no matter what time of day. But when it came to the technical demands of the project, he was a wizard and provided competent leadership to the team of logisticians. That day, Arnaud arrived with a small generator in his pickup truck that soon put all of Wei's electrical gadgets back into service. Until then we had to walk two kilometres to the office to charge his computer battery. Arnaud also explained the mystery behind our lack of power, as it had happened before. Apparently the main cable had been hauled away by the electricity authority to be given to someone else. Our guards had been too afraid to say anything when workmen scaled the power pole to carry it off. With a chronic shortage of cabling, this sort of thing went on all the time. Arnaud had been advised that we had two options: pay to have it reinstalled or supply our own cable. We scoffed at the proposal. Where to find an electrical mains cable? In the end we caved in and resorted to a noisy generator. It was a gas version, which made a racket and detracted from the splendour of light.

Arnaud went out of his way to make sure the team was well looked after in addition to a heavy workload on the projects, but it wasn't long before he moved on to another assignment, in Afghanistan. While we were sad to see him go, an irrepressible Italian called Roberto soon replaced him. Roberto proved himself to be a tireless worker and an outstanding pasta chef. Despite his culinary skills, he was conspicuously thin. His belt wrapped twice around his waist and clothes hung loosely from his lean frame. A hand-rolled cigarette drooped from his lips. He lived on a simple diet consisting of pasta, sugar, and nicotine, and each meal was rounded off with anything resembling chocolate. His sweet tooth was so insatiable that we were constantly trading our tins of Mont Blanc crème dessert for something we found more palatable. Once we coerced him into savouring a cup of Chinese tea and watched in wonder as the cup overflowed with multiple scoops of sugar. We suggested politely that adding sugar to Chinese tea was akin to adding Fanta (another of his favourites) to Chianti Classico, but our protestations failed to perturb.

Roberto could turn his hand at anything and did so with gusto. Our chairs were as hard as boards, but he did his best to repair the odd assortment we had cobbled together in the dining room. He was also determined to eradicate our bedbug problem, which filled me with hope. Smarting weals were driving me wild. I itched incessantly and when I overcame embarrassment to share my exasperation, Roberto commiserated and his team sprung into action. I came home one lunchtime and thought for a moment that we were having a yard sale. A team of workers was hauling the mattresses into the sunshine. The entire contents of *Casa Quatro* were spread around the garden. Roberto directed proceedings as they fumigated everything in sight and pummelled our bedclothes on the concrete washboard. The bugs stayed at bay for several weeks and I didn't have the heart to tell Roberto when they returned. We never did rid the house of those maddening little mites.

We had been without a field coordinator for weeks, but at about that time Katelijn arrived to fill the spot. An MSF veteran, she was well versed in the operations of nutritional programs and was not new to Kuito, returning for her second mission. Katelijn was a Flemish nurse who had studied music and the viola before nursing. We invited her over for dinner soon after her arrival. In our own little epicentre of culture, she and Wei quickly became engrossed in a conversation about Shoshtokovich and Brahms. Wei was delighted to announce that we had a CD of both in our small collection and put them on for us all to enjoy. We thought it sounded divine, but in truth it was barely audible over the drone of the generator we were yet to become accustomed to. Anyway, Katelijn struck me as having a no-nonsense style and intuitively knew we would work well together.

Arnaud with the local logistics team.

Chapter 32
Chook Capers

Karin writes...

We had covered the window with a blanket. It was Saturday and we didn't want to mar the delectable prospect of a good sleep-in with the idea of sunlight knifing through our window. But all in vain! Even before sunrise, a rooster heralded the new day. We had become used to hearing roosters each morning but this one was especially close and it was still depressingly early. Cursing the *chook* (a delightful colloquial Australian term for chicken), we arose bleary-eyed and after breakfast decided to read in the warmth of the bright morning light. As we settled in around the study window, we watched one of the guards as he tended a rooster in our backyard. The rooster's foot was tethered to the papaya tree in the shade of the garden.

"Oh, the guards are going to raise chickens," I surmised out loud.

"Bom dia, João. Este é o almoço?" ("Morning João. Is that lunch?") Wei joked half-heartedly, calling to João through the open window.

"Sim, sim," João confirmed, in his immensely good-natured way. We chuckled quietly to ourselves, imagining he had not understood Wei's accented Portuguese that early in the morning.

Some time later I went to the fridge in search of the things that I had asked the cook, Dona Madonna, to buy. With the conditions in the meat market as they were, I still hadn't plucked up the courage to do my shopping in person. We had invited the team for dinner and I had asked her to buy some chicken. On opening the fridge I discovered there was nothing there. "That's strange," I thought. "Dona Mado is always so reliable." I stood there, door ajar, pondering for a while until the penny dropped. Oh no! João wasn't joking. That rooster tethered to the papaya tree was indeed our *almoço*!

At the risk of sounding sexist, there are some household tasks that fall clearly into the male domain: barbequing, unblocking drains, emptying the garbage, catching mice, ridding the house of creepy crawlies. The slaughtering, plucking, and gutting of chickens is clearly another chore linked to the Y-chromosome. To my surprise, Wei relished the idea—a throwback, no doubt, to his youth in China, when he fought with his brother over the visceral duty. He claimed great technical expertise with the hatchet and as he is a qualified surgeon, who was I to doubt his capacity to dispatch our feathered friend with panache?

For a moment, I took pity on the bird and toyed with the idea of buying our rooster a girlfriend. "We could raise chickens," I proclaimed. But thoughts of the cacophony at dawn soon put a stop to that frivolous idea. In fact, Roberto had been eyeing our generous backyard for weeks with this in mind and had already tried to convince us of the merits of a daily supply of fresh eggs.

As we weren't ready to launch into plucking a chook, we went vegetarian for dinner and it was another twenty-four hours before we found the courage to bring the project forward. Wei and I sat in our study discussing epicurean options for our basic broiler: chook with tomatoes, chook with avocado, chook and onion soup. I cast a sympathetic eye across the lawn at the handsome bird. His grey-speckled plumage was striking as he basked in the warmth of the afternoon sun.

I guess until then I hadn't thought about it much, but somewhere between our feathered friend and the chillers of a modern supermarket, a clinical and dehumanizing (or should that be de-animalizing?) process takes place, allowing us to divorce our emotions from the stuff going down our gullets. I longed for the sanitized sanctity of a supermarket: to see a plastic-wrapped pack of marinated chicken wings or boneless chicken thighs. I yearned for a pack of tender chicken breasts, although Wei often laughed at this idiosyncrasy of the English language: the curious concept of a chicken with mammary glands.

Finally, we could prevaricate no longer and Wei launched an all-out assault. But on observing the great surgeon bearing down with a shiny knife, our attentive chook escaped his tether. He took off at high speed with Wei in hot pursuit. And don't ask me where in his Australian university education he ever learned such nonsense, but as he belted along behind, Wei sung the schoolyard ditty: "Captain Cook chased a chook, all around Australia." I was laughing as I watched from a safe vantage point. With the chook firmly in the lead, they darted in and out of the bushes, and lapped the mango tree. They raced through the vegetable patch, round and round the pomegranate tree, and under the wire fence. When our chook finally darted in the direction of the street, Wei called on João for backup and our chook was skilfully recaptured. Perhaps to get the last laugh, Wei plonked the chook head first in the freezer. Rigor mortis feet, complete with toenails, leaped out at me every time I opened the door. Until then my favourite Cantonese Dim Sum had been *Fung Tsao* (steamed chicken feet), but my penchant waned by the hour.

I don't remember ever eating that chook, but I am sure we did. However, I do remember spending days picking up speckled grey feathers from around the house, gentle reminders of who really ruled the roost.

Our chook (the dinner).

Chapter 33
Deng's Visit

Karin continues…

Wei operated at a cracking pace throughout November. Although he did his best to stay positive, he was showing signs of fatigue and was in need of a holiday. By the end of that month we managed to organize a short break. At first it was a holiday to nowhere as colleagues in Luanda advised us there were no available seats on flights to any neighbouring countries. Even flights to the coastal cities of Benguela and Lobito were full. In any event, I needed to leave Angola, as securing a work permit was a protracted procedure and my visa was due to expire. So we packed our bags for lovely Luanda in the hope that we could sort something out from there.

A replacement surgeon was to arrive from Brussels, so Wei busied himself preparing a thorough report. I took over as editor and in the process learned about changes to the surgery department. Wei had devised a new way to plan operating lists, revised gown regulations, implemented new handwashing and swab-counting procedures, and also introduced a clean zone. They had improved interdepartmental meetings, morbidity and mortality records, ward round procedures, and patient records. Rosters were reorganized to improve care and much-needed training had been secured for the anaesthetic nurses. Wei had also increased ward-round frequency and at the same time his outpatient consultations were up 300 percent. While these measures may seem rather basic, changing entrenched habits in any environment is not easy. All the while, the number of operations performed had increased by over eighty percent.

In spare time, Inger and Wei had also worked hard to computerize the operating data. This gave us the first accurate analysis of the workload. Some interesting figures surfaced too. Not surprisingly, ninety percent of operations were emergencies. The rest were still gross conditions like large hernias and tumours. Twenty-one percent of operations had to be done in the first hour of arrival (Caesareans, ruptured uteruses, and so on) and a further sixty percent within twenty-four hours (landmine amputations, bullet wounds, fractures, and abscesses). Just nineteen percent of operations could be delayed by a day. By the end of November, Wei and his team had amputated fifty-eight limbs due to bullets and landmines, drained 108 abscesses—performing 614 operations...but such was life there in our own mini *M*A*S*H*.

Around this time, Dr. Francis Deng visited Kuito. He was Kofi Annan's representative for the IDPs. In reality, the United Nations High Commission for Refugees (UNHCR) had no real jurisdiction over Angola's internally displaced until they crossed an international border. However, I helped Katelijn write a document to detail the critical health situation of Kuito's displaced and we presented this to his delegation. Up to thirty percent of Angola's population had been displaced by the armed conflict, yet only a small minority had crossed into neighbouring countries and become refugees. This massive movement of people occurred in two waves. The first, in the early 1990s, saw almost two million Angolans flee their homes because of the renewed conflict. They went mostly to provincial centres and the capital, Luanda. While some were able to return in the intervening period, the resumption of war in late 1998 resulted in the further displacement of 2.6 million people. All of the country's eighteen provinces were affected. There were 120 locations for IDPs scattered across Angola, with one of the largest rural-based concentrations settling in Kuito.

When Deng's visit report was published, we were pleased to see that our comments on the health and nutrition situation had made their way into print. Deng said that the humanitarian action was constrained by the prevailing climate of insecurity, characterized by banditry and armed attacks. Humanitarian access was severely hampered by logistical problems. Much of the infrastructure was destroyed. Many roads, even in the town of Kuito, were like creek beds, and road access throughout the country was limited. Bridges had been destroyed and landmines were still being placed on main routes. The state of Kuito's airstrip and its importance to the relief effort made international news again following the report. Deng commented on the appalling living conditions of the IDPs and was struck by their overriding sense of despair. He went on to say that he was "seriously concerned at the lack of effective protection accorded to the physical security and human rights [of the IDPs], ongoing harassment, systematic theft of food and non-food items by

UNITA, government armed forces, and the national police." His report referred to incidents of rape and violence, forced conscription, and forced relocation. He also spoke of an "alarming landmine situation...extreme levels of deprivation...and inhumane shelter conditions."[26]

When I read this I was initially struck by the almost banal nature of the words, the predictability of it. Yet, perhaps, I underestimated its effect, as from then on we started to see a little more interest from the outside world. Just before we left for our break we were busy hosting visitors at *Casa Quatro*—mainly photographers, journalists, and cameramen. A Japanese photographer arrived along with a freelance photographer from Switzerland. They were soon followed by Diego and Caco, a documentary team from a popular current affairs program of *Rede Globo*, the largest television station in Brazil. We often had a full house and enjoyed chatting until all hours about life in the enclave. It was as if these strangers had parachuted in from the outside world, like old friends dropping in for a chat. Soon enough they were gone again, but we always enjoyed the distraction and the chance to meet new friends and to catch up on the news of other places.

Andulo Camp.

Chapter 34
Ambush

Karin continues…

Even when we arrived safely to Luanda at the start of our vacation, we were still reeling from the shock of the events of Saturday night. We had been home sharing a meal with the Brazilian TV crew, and we were chatting almost apologetically about how quiet things were, when Bento suddenly appeared at the door. He knocked politely, but I quickly sensed the gravity of the situation through his urgent whisper. The ambulance was idling outside. A baby had been shot in the gut.

As if acting on instinct, Diego switched on his spotlight and started to film. Wei searched frantically for his two-way radio, as Bento urged him to come quickly. I scrambled to find a charged radio battery but, before I could, they headed for the door. In the maelstrom, Caco shoved a microphone—somewhat disconcertingly, I thought—under Wei's mouth in an attempt to conduct an interview. They stumbled down the path and out the gate. From the door I watched as the ambulance pulled away and sunk into the night. The evening was dead still.

I cleared the dishes and whiled away the hours, waiting anxiously for more news. By midnight, I knew something was seriously wrong but crawled into bed to get some rest. I slept fitfully. At about 3 a.m. I awoke with a start as Wei crashed heavily onto the pillow, letting out an exhausted sigh. He was clearly disturbed and mumbled something about having done everything he could. I sat bolt upright to listen to him tell me that he didn't think the infant would survive the night. In a defeated tone, he described how the baby had been shot through the liver and had lost too much blood before arrival. But, worse still, others from the same shooting didn't even reach the hospital. Slowly and deliberately, the whole gruesome story came out and then we both drifted off into our own troubled thoughts.

The phone rang early on Sunday morning. Wei listened intently and put down the phone with a sense of passive resignation. The baby had died overnight. The details of the whole story were hap-hazard. Confusion prevailed and it wasn't until Monday that we learned that commandos stationed in Kuito were at the centre of the story. They were part of the government's elite force being used for a major offensive against UNITA to the east of the city. The story around town was that some of these commandos went in search of women during their night off. From there things went hideously awry. Drunken and aggressive, they accosted a pregnant woman in the street. She tried to escape by running to the nearest house. They pursued her and somehow a couple, their seven-year-old son, and baby were shot at in the house where the lady had taken refuge. The husband escaped unharmed. Abandoning his dead wife, he ran to the hospital with their dying infant in his arms. In doing so, he raised the alarm.

By this stage the man knew his wife had sustained fatal injuries but was insistent that his boy was still alive back at the hut. The ambulance set off, first to our house to collect Wei and the camera crew. After dropping them off at the operating theatre to treat the infant, the driver left in search of the wounded boy. The male nurse on duty at *Banco de Urgência* accompanied the vehicle. It lurched over rutted roads on a starless night with the driver peering into the gloomy shadows searching for the hut. As they approached, a hail of bullets rang out. They had driven into an ambush.

The driver was first to be hit. The nurse in the seat next to him was shot twice in the head. He slumped forward onto the dash-board. The driver struggled deftly to turn the lumbering vehicle around in the dark, narrow lane. In a forlorn hope, the driver could do nothing more than hurtle full-speed back to the hospital. Tragically, the nurse was dead on arrival in his own pool of blood.

Manuel Vitangui, a respected head nurse in charge of Wei's orthopedic ward, was one of the few truly experienced staff left in Kuito. He had given years of dedicated service. Manuel was a hus-band, a father, a respected member of the community, and our neighbour's brother. He was shot and killed while trying to do no more than his job: trying to help others. Manuel had simply been the one rostered on duty that evening. And, as if to add to the injustice of it all, Manuel supervised the ward that cared for the ugliest face of Angola's conflict: the landmine victims.

It was all so sinister, but the stories changed quickly. The first culprits were said to be *tropas*, the common name for government troops, drunk and in search of fun. These claims were quickly repudiated and rumours circulated that it was UNITA or *banditos*, a well-understood euphemism for the army or police. But when you need to live in the so-called safety of a military-protected area, there is wisdom in mendacity. No one wanted to openly accuse the government of such brutality.

The entire team was in a sombre mood: collectively despondent…grieving…fearful. With death all around us, we struggled to understand the meaning of this irrational killing, as if it were somehow the first. Wei was devastated. I felt physically sick. Manuel had been in my personnel meeting at the hospital just two days before. Although employed by the government, MSF so valued his contributions that we supplemented his salary. We attended Manuel's funeral with hundreds of his family members, friends, and staff from the hospital. They had lost another experienced colleague from their dwindling ranks. We all ruminated for weeks.

Senseless killings like that happened all the time in Kuito and many other towns throughout Angola. But out there we seemed to develop whatever built-in mechanisms we possessed to allow us to live with this terror. But, when the horrors were personalized, the pain came through, closer to the nerve. It wasn't until Monday afternoon when we were in Luanda and officially on vacation that I suddenly felt that I needed a break. Just before closing time, we rushed into a travel agency, secured seats and put down cash for two tickets to South Africa. We left first thing the next day, yearning for space to reconcile what had happened and to put these first months into perspective. It's funny how impressions change. On that trip, Luanda almost looked exciting, even prosperous. What a contrast to my first impressions when I found the city poor and desperate. As the plane lumbered into the blue skies and veered south I wondered how we would find Johannesburg on arrival.

The rehabilitated buildings of the Provincial Hospital of Bié with an MSF flag flying.

Wei in the operating theatre.

Chapter 35
Wild Game

Karin continues...

After a therapeutic week in South Africa we were back in Kuito. A full moon shone brightly through the window as I wrote about our first break. We had spent the first few days of our wondrous holiday acutely aware of the luxuries around us: the comforts of electricity, running water, hot showers, and mobile phones. We hyperventilated with excitement on entering a bookshop and felt a thrill while sipping divine wines in a swank restaurant. We were like two kids in a toy shop.

We scooped up a travel guide upon arrival in Johannesburg and flipped through its pages, while soaking up the comforts at the Holiday Inn. A nature holiday was a spontaneous but calculated choice. From Johannesburg we took to the roads with glee and headed first to a private game reserve at Kruger National Park, near the border with Mozambique. The park ranger advised us of the security regulations. "Do not walk unaccompanied back to your room at night...as lions and other wild animals roam freely through the compound," he said. We must have laughed, as he seemed a bit perplexed by our reaction. "Don't worry, we're used to security warnings," Wei reassured.

With the beauty of the bush as our backdrop, we had time to mull over life in Angola. Satiated with sightings of exotic wildlife we headed south, skirted Swaziland, and stumbled upon the Saint Lucia Wetlands. There we went in search of elusive hippos and crocodiles. It was a magical ride, kayaking through the still reeds as the water lapped around us. This caressing beauty helped us lick our mental wounds, while the domestic comforts and hospitality of our friends in Durban nurtured a sense of normality. In many respects it was crazy to have driven more than 2,000 kilometres in six days, but it was enormously liberating. It was as if moons separated us from Angola's conflict, yet in reality we were little more than 2,000 kilometres from that cauldron of carnage.

Back then, just six short years after South Africa's freedom from

apartheid, the country had deep-seated problems: incredible dispar-
ity in living conditions, the government's blundering approach to
the AIDS pandemic notwithstanding. Despite that, we left South
Africa feeling optimistic, but the gloom soon descended as we
returned to Angola.

For starters, pandemonium prevailed in Johannesburg when we
tried to check in. The flight had been overbooked and, like excess
luggage, we were shunted unceremoniously. Waitlisted for a TAAG
flight (Angola Airlines) the following afternoon, we trudged back to
the Holiday Inn with thoughts of one last hot shower as the best
consolation. It wasn't until some twenty-four hours later that we
knew we had arrived safely in Luanda — two hundred passengers
broke into spontaneous applause. After a few bone-jarring thuds,
we bounced down the runway and were home.

It was a scrum inside the terminal. A power failure had thrown
baggage retrieval into chaos. As the carousel ground to a halt, the
crowd clawed in the dark to locate their bags. We laid claim to ours
and scuttled outside to gasp some fresh air and escape the general
mob. The still, warm air enveloped us. It was getting dark and
Duarte, our driver, was late and we had no way to contact the office
We spent an irritating half hour fending off touts who buzzed
around, trying to sell all manner of services. Duarte finally arrived
and with an apologetic shrug, blamed traffic congestion en route.
We negotiated our way through a sea of prying hands before throwing our bags in the back.

Our vehicle had made little progress in the car park when a
policeman flagged us down. He declared that our driver had committed an offence and the hefty fine was payable immediately in
cash. Duarte was annoyed but climbed out of the car whereon
barter-style negotiations ensued. Before long, the steely-eyed policeman approached and bossed Wei into the back seat. Our apprehension kicked up a notch when his oafish mate arrived and proceeded
to wedge himself in too. It was the smallest of cars, but Wei gallant-
ly sat in the centre as we desperately exchanged glances in an
attempt to assess what was going on. No one uttered a word. The
head policeman climbed in the front with his rifle, seemingly oblivious to the fact his wide shoulders rubbed an MSF sticker banning
weapons from the vehicle. Our anxieties reached a crescendo as we
sped off into darkness, squashed together in the tiny car. The steamy
night was dank and listless and the streets became narrower and

more menacing. Any hope of following landmarks disappeared. Duarte did not utter a word, but I could see from behind that he too was a bundle of nerves. Pearls of perspiration formed on his neck and my own heartbeat was audible.

In the crushing darkness the policemen motioned our driver to stop. It was a baleful precinct, but Duarte pulled to the side of the road. He switched off the engine and after an endless pause turned off the headlights. Through the murky shadows I could see a high barbed-wire fence—a police or military installation perhaps? Both policemen climbed out and beckoned Duarte, who let out a worrisome sigh. He followed them with obvious hesitation. We watched as they marched our driver stealthily into the shadows well beyond our view, leaving us perched uselessly in the back. Wei and I reassured each other with empty words—it is what one instinctively does at ambiguous moments. My blouse was sticking to my back and it wasn't just the oily warmth of the evening. By then my fears had reached their zenith.

After an apparent eternity, our panicked driver reappeared looking agitated. "Gasosa, gasosa!" (Soft drink, soft drink!) he muttered urgently. In an aggrieved tone, he divulged the amount he had negotiated. At US$8 it was an expensive soft drink, but by now we were familiar with inflation inherent in the *gasosa* euphemism. In a fleeting moment of indignation, I contemplated resisting, but, in reality, we were not about to argue. We quickly figured it was a cheap escape from certain volatility. Our nerves rattled, we dipped into our wallet and paid up. Duarte then sped off at high speed. On our way back to the main road we observed that we had indeed been parked outside a police station. Our two friends had simply hitched a ride home and pocketed a handsome salary.

It was hardly surprising that we rapidly readjusted to life back in our familiar surroundings. We were welcomed by another power cut at *Casa Quatro*. The shower dispensed a burst of icy-cold water and even my wimpish aversion to this embracing start to the day paled in significance. The house was leaking, the phone was on the blink, and the bed bugs were biting. The strange thing was, I had to admit, I was glad to be home.

The next day, Roberto read us the riot act on propane gas: there was no more and none foreseen—not one more bottle. The arrival of the wet season had cut the recently reopened road. Wei and I made a pact to stop boiling so much as a pot of water to reserve the rest of the gas for cooking. I admit to seriously debating the merits of using our last reserves to heat water for a bucket-bath compared to the trials of cooking dinner over a charcoal stove outside. But it was the absurdity of it that riled me more. In a country flush with oil and gas, charcoal was the only accessible fuel to meet more than eighty percent of household needs.

Preparing breakfast at Casa Quatro over charcoal.

Chapter 36
Against Odds

Karin continues...

Emergency surgery increased a further thirty percent while we were away, and by mid-December we feared that it was a sign of worse to come. UNITA was traditionally more active during the rainy season as it suited their guerrilla tactics. Landmines, too, came to the surface with heavy rain and it wasn't hard to understand why: by then the rutted streets around Kuito already look like creek beds with all the topsoil eroded.

One night soon after our return, for want of something better to do, I decided to accompany Wei to the operating theatre. There was only one ambulance in Kuito, so the same one that had been ambushed two weeks before came to collect us. The word "ambulance" is a bit of a misnomer for an old white van, stripped bare and not even equipped with a first-aid kit. Perhaps that's why the hospital director saw fit to second it for his personal use with frustrating regularity. Although it was back on the road, the damage was clear. I eyed the small hole where a bullet had shattered the windscreen and injured the driver and turned to look at the puncture hole in the cabin door. It was level with Wei's ear. Visions of Manuel being mortally wounded flashed before my eyes. The bullet had cut like butter through the metal. We sat motionless where his life had ended—our skin clammy and crawling. Wei reached out and reassuringly held my hand but neither of us uttered a word. It was a chastening moment—an intensely private memorial.

I never had the opportunity to see Wei operate in Hong Kong, so the two emergencies I witnessed that evening were a tough initiation. I donned the appropriate green garb and tried to make myself useful in the theatre. As there was no running water, I poured jugs to help the team scrub. I idly swatted insects that buzzed around the lights while the team readied themselves for the first patient. Wei was incensed because the *instrumentista* (scout nurse) was too drunk to report for duty, leaving Malaquias and him to cope single-handedly. I felt superfluous and was of little help. I hardly knew the difference between a clamp and catheter although I was enthralled by the array of stainless steel instruments from which to choose. I thought forceps would have come in one or two configurations, but the tangled mess of metal that spilled out of the autoclave onto the side table fascinated me. Wei's lack of humour about the situation that evening was palpable, so I refrained from asking a series of burning questions about it all.

The first patient was a small girl who needed an explorative laparotomy (an opening of the abdomen). I can say now that a laparotomy is not the most elegant of procedures, but I managed to watch it without retching. I had assumed that it would be a classic "blood and guts" procedure, if there is such a thing. In my ignorance, I had imagined that our intestines somehow swam around on the inside in a pool of blood, but not so. A silly presumption when you think about it, as I knew all about veins. I guess I gleaned my ideas from television dramas, so it was quite a surprise to see so very little blood. Wei sliced through the skin drawing but a few drops. He pulled the incision wide open, slid the clamps deftly into place and set down to work in a matter-of-fact kind of way. The power of concentration was mesmerizing. Although my description may not be quite as succinct as a surgical textbook, the procedure went something like this: pull out the guts, search around in the metres of intestines, find what you want, repair it, and stuff it all back in, in seemingly no particular order. This last part is rather difficult as the intestine has a rather ignoble way of popping out again. Finally, stitch it up and that's that. I was captivated.

Throughout the first operation, a twenty-one-year-old woman, with far more serious wounds, waited calmly on a trolley in the corridor. She gave no hint of discomfort despite her hideous wounds: a stab wound to the abdomen and a gunshot wound to the leg. The bullet had shattered the bone and blown a huge hole in her knee. The small entry hole looked innocent enough until the larger, tatty exit hole was revealed. My stomach churned. Arlete had come from Camacupa, some eighty kilometres away, having endured six days in the town's hospital with no doctor or medical supplies. In that week, her injury had festered and the acrid stench of rotting flesh was infinitely more overwhelming than the sight of her wounds. As Malaquias wheeled her into the theatre this smell filled the air. I fiddled with my facemask, using one hand as an additional barrier to the odour. I had always assumed that they were worn to protect the patient, but without a mask's filtering effect breathing in such close proximity was enough to make one gag. I watched the team's nimble work and listened as Wei reassured them that they would be able to save her leg. I looked on with skepticism. When he inserted his finger in the puss-filled stab wound to further investigate, I surmised he was undertaking some sort of primitive laparoscopic (keyhole) surgery. His exploration revealed a perforated intestine. With multiple wounds to fix up, the operation dragged on for some time, and it was late before she was wheeled into the recovery area.

What amazed me, as a complete novice to the medical business, was that people didn't die instantly from such horrid afflictions. Wei often spoke encouragingly of the body's amazing ability to heal itself, and we certainly saw the power of nature in that environment. Unless an artery is severed, the blood clots and eventually the bleeding stops. Through nature's strange process of selection, most who made it onto the operating table endured and survived. Obviously an unknown number did not, but those who made it to the hospital had often already survived long periods without care. Weak as they were, many survivors clung onto life. Their open wounds may have been rank and fetid, but they hung in there. However, Arlete's appearance worried me. It was as if her femininity had been drained. On the way home, I asked Wei about her breasts: the way they were prematurely atrophied and fell lamely from her chest. How shrivelled they appeared for one so young. Wei sighed as he revealed his deeper concerns. "Arlete's biggest problem," he said, "was not her grievous wounds, but malnutrition." He was obviously more worried about his emaciated patient than he had previously let on.

Arlete clung to life, but only for six more weeks. She endured but did not survive. We still talk about her often, how she stayed in intensive care for weeks: malnourished, wasting, responding to nothing. We all wanted her to keep death at bay, and, for a hopeful while, she became an enigmatic symbol in the raw struggle against the odds. We tried everything and no one more than Wei. He constantly gave money to the nurses to buy her sugar drinks. We pandered to her fancies, although she had few. In the early days, she wanted fresh mangoes, but she soon became too ill to eat them. Nasal-feeds of liquid milk supplement failed to lift her, nor did any of the drugs he tried. A recurring infection wracked her emaciated frame.

Despite an aura of imminent death, she hung on to life and we held on to the irresistible belief that she would turn a corner and recover. To find her still alive in intensive care became a minor victory in itself, although I am still haunted by her cadaverously frail body and that harrowing look in her eyes, as if she knew death lurked in the shadows. As she continued to waste, Wei continued to obsess. Had she been treated elsewhere, a course of total parenteral nutrition (nutrition via intravenous drip) would have surely saved her. But there we had none and with her skin stretched like parchment paper between her ribs, she teetered on the precipice. In her weak and sallow state, infection raised its angry head and ravaged her body even further. Death finally descended and we felt totally defeated. Arlete was gone and with her a little more of our hope.

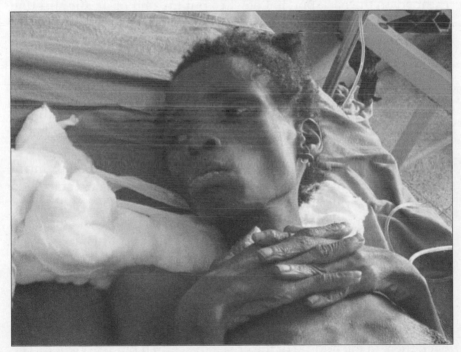

Arlete.

Chapter 37
Nuninhibited

Karin continues…

Sister Imaculada stood coyly in the office corridor, her back pressed against the wall. A baggy white tunic hung loosely over her willowy frame, a sensible hand-knitted cardigan covered her shoulders. She had come as an envoy for the Reverend Mother. Our office, I should add, was a converted house. Julio and I sat in what was probably once the maid's quarter. The office for the health post was camped on the back porch. Logistics put up a bit of plastic sheeting to partition the lounge/dining room and there were three offices in the bedrooms along the corridor. The reception area was restricted to the hallway and somewhat amusingly our meeting was to take place in what was once the master bedroom. Katelijn insisted that I join, ostensibly to add weight to the occasion. I wasn't sure I liked the inference, but perhaps my grey hair was showing. With her assistant Frederico, a part-time Pentecostal lay-preacher, we had a quorum and the meeting began.

In as authoritative a tone as she could muster, Katelijn introduced me as the *administradora de finanças*. After all, Sister Imaculada was there to discuss the weighty financial matter about MSF camping on church property, but we were not exactly illegal squatters. Twelve months prior, the arrival of large numbers of displaced with severe malnutrition led to an emergency that stretched the feeding centre beyond capacity. To cope with demands, we asked the church whether we could set up a second centre in the corner of their disused garden. The convent was gutted and abandoned by the nuns, who had moved opposite to a row of freshly renovated bungalows. Back then, in the middle of the crisis, the church kindly obliged. The garden was obviously once a pretty location, full of conifer trees. Our tents were pitched in the needle-sweet shade and CNS-2 (Supplementary Nutrition Centre No. 2) soon sprang into action, screening and feeding malnourished children.

Mothers were asked to report to this centre with their children for a weekly medical checkup and received fortified supplements. A further two hundred thirty or so severely malnourished were under more constant care at the therapeutic feeding centre, attached to the hospital. More than three hundred new children were still being admitted each week, and nearly three thousand children were cared for at the two centres. Each day, streams of weary mothers lingered patiently in endless queues with their sleeping or crying babies strapped to their backs. They waited for hours to be processed. It was a thoroughly dehumanizing process, but options were limited.

Sister Imaculada sat, hands clasped in her lap, eyelashes cast downwards to avoid eye contact. She lifted her head and said all she had to say in staccato fashion. I smiled politely, listening intently. I frowned and raised my eyebrows intermittently at what I hoped were appropriate moments, pretending to understand everything she said in her rapid-fire address. After all, Sister Imaculada couldn't have known that my Portuguese was elementary at best. Although my role was just to add weight, I was secretly worried that she might address me in Portuguese on a financial matter. She was tough going and I could only snatch the general gist of what was being said, so was relieved to learn that Katelijn had also struggled to follow her nervous oratory. That said, Sister Imaculada's point was clear enough and Frederico filled us in later on the finer nuances. The church, bless it, had decided that enough was enough! MSF had been parked on their land for too long. They now wanted US$500 per month in rent.

"Five hundred!" we protested. Sister Imaculada just nodded.

"But this is outrageous," Katelijn queried, as if she was not hearing correctly. "Here in Kuito? To pitch a few tents on that land, that corner of disused garden, that twelve months ago no one wanted because it was full of unexploded ordnances?" Katelijn continued, lividly. But Sister Imaculada quietly advised that she was just passing on the message.

"But we don't even pay that for larger pieces of land with a building—a warehouse, office, or a house," we explained incredulously. Perhaps she would pass on the message about how out of touch they were with the dynamics of the Kuito property market. Quite frankly, we strongly objected to paying anything at all on principle. After all, we were there to help the people of Bié and the emergency nutritional situation was not of MSF's making. It was our ultimate goal to close the centre as soon as it was practical to do so.

Toying with the large silver cross that hung from her neck, she maintained an angelic smile. "All those people," she added, some-what more querulously, "lining up there every day opposite our bungalows. Well you know...the latrines smell...and they don't even know how to use them properly!"

"Well the poor need to go to the toilet too, Sister!" Katelijn retort-ed frostily, her neck now blotchy-red with rage. Frederico jumped diplomatically to rescue the moment, giving Katelijn a moment to cool down. "But surely the church and MSF—humanitarian organi-zations at heart—have the same objective of helping the poor?" said Frederico, in a humble plea.

Exasperated, we finally offered US$100 per month, not as rent, but as a gratuity to acknowledge the church's kind contribution to the relief effort. But Sister Imaculada repeated that since she was only the messenger, she could not agree to our offer. But if her bash-ful demeanour were the only guide, no one would have surmised the meeting was not going well. When we asked for an audience with the bishop, she responded glibly that he didn't bother himself with such matters. We would have to put our counter-proposal in a letter to Mother Superior who resided in the safety of Luanda. With an imperious tone in her voice, she asked if we could fax it over.

"What?" we gasped. "A fax machine? In Kuito? Do you have one?"

"No, the Sisters don't have a fax machine here," she replied prissily, but added that Mother Superior in Luanda was blessed with one. It was on the tip of my tongue to ask whether she had an e-mail address, but I held back. We would have to wait for the next plane to send our letter.

Weeks later, the reply arrived. Written in convoluted Portuguese, we struggled to comprehend the nuances. Embellished with a florid signature, Mother Superior had spoken. The church had sanctimoniously decided that the land was needed for other reasons: it was to become a playground for the needy. Play on an empty tummy, we wondered? In short, it was an eviction letter, with a gracious three months notice. But we were more than ready to move. In Angola we saw charity from all perspectives and mar-velled that Africa had become the world's last successful recruit-ment ground for the nunneries.

The Kuito property market.

Church property.

Chapter 38
Another Truckload

Karin continues...

As Christmas approached the days became blisteringly hot. Dazzling, undiffused light poured out of the sky and I longed for the inviting afternoon rain. And when it rained, the morning's swelter was extinguished. As the first pellets fell, the searing pavement responded, making steam rise like the morning mist and infusing the air with muggy warmth.

In mid-December we were also privileged to receive three visitors from Hong Kong: Chung, a photographer, Elaine from MSF, and Eric, a cameraman-journalist from the popular station, Radio Television Hong Kong (RTHK). The plane they hired to reach us looked no bigger than a mosquito when it popped out of monsoonal clouds and bounced down the runway. I was there on the tarmac to greet them and felt an instant affinity with these strangers. Wei was soon delighted to be speaking Cantonese and news of home filled *Casa Quatro* with a special warmth. They arrived to the usual caper: no electricity, no gas for our generator, no clean water (despite the pouring rain), and several household leaks. But they brought the most divine treats imaginable, including an entire pantry of Chinese ingredients: dried mushrooms, soya sauce, oyster sauce, noodles, dried shrimps, Chinese tea, and even Vegemite to spread on my breakfast bread (no self-respecting Aussie should ever be without it). We felt so spoiled. There was no doubting that our support team in the Hong Kong office was the greatest.

I was embarrassed when Elaine innocently asked who cut Wei's hair. It wasn't the most becoming style, so I tried to evade the subject and avoid telling them about my little slip-up with the trimmer. Thankfully Wei couldn't see the other side of his head and up until then, everyone had been more than polite about it. I had always cut Wei's hair when we were first married, but I had obviously lost the skill. In the days before our guests arrived, Wei suggested I use the trimmer on his battery-operated razor to tidy up his hair. He sat in the courtyard with a towel around his shoulders as I set to it with overt confidence. Within seconds I had razed a hole in the middle of his dark hair. In a quiet but frantic effort to correct the error, I razed another. Still convinced I could improve the situation, I fearlessly kept going until it was apparent that I was working towards a hopeless cause. It looked like I had plonked a bowl on his head and made a skinhead of the rest.

Hairdos aside, we had a fun-filled time, entertaining the entire team with Chinese food. It was a short but joyful week, although their stay wasn't devoid of drama. It was Emmanuelle's birthday party that Friday evening. We were celebrating in *Casa Três*, joshing each other lightheartedly, when Eduardo arrived to collect Wei. A truckload of injured had arrived at the hospital, dampening the party spirit. We all moved off in convoy to the hospital. The victims had come from Andulo, an important diamond-mining town 120 kilometres to the north. Roughly hewn branches had been lashed together with grass to make primitive stretchers. They covered the floor bearing motionless people with broken bodies. Eight patients were crowded into the small room at *Banco de Urgência* with the full complement of wounds: from gunshots to landmines, beatings and stabbings. Katelijn radioed Inácio, the Brazilian-born representative from the United Nations Office for the Coordination of Humanitarian Affairs (OCHA), who arrived soon after to record the patients' stories—we had been hearing so many unsubstantiated reports of atrocious guerrilla attacks. As UNITA had been particularly active across the province, we needed to learn as much as possible about the security situation beyond Kuito.

Most had been wounded during the previous week and even the freshest wounds were already three days old. One man sat in the corner with a criss-cross of machete chops to his face. He told us that UNITA had held him down and delivered slash wounds to one side of his head as a warning to others not to support the government. He had been turned into a veritable walking billboard for life. Another man with a badly dislocated hip was also present. "But it looks as though you have been suffering this condition for some time?" Wei queried. "Yes, several months," he concurred almost apologetically. On learning a truck was going to Kuito, he seized the opportunity to seek long overdue treatment. As his case was not urgent, he was asked to wait. A shredded thigh stump was all that remained of a young girl's leg as she lay there quietly. It was amazing how composed everyone was in emergencies like this. The entire team worked in silence. Perhaps it was a reaction to the atrocity, but the victims endured their pain, without so much as a whimper or a moan.

The lighting in the *Banco de Urgência* was grey and shadowy. The brightest light that night was from Eric's video camera and he used it to Wei's advantage on the more serious wounds. Meanwhile, the camera rolled. I used a flashlight to illuminate the parched skin of a man on the floor, while Inger struggled to insert a drip. The man was clearly in shock, but she fumbled in her attempt to find a vein. She could barely detect a pulse. Feeling more desperate with every moment, she passed the job to Eduardo, who also had no luck. The patient hardly winced as they repeatedly punctured his skin in the shadow of my flashlight. More used to inserting drips into the veins of tiny newborns, Wei came over to assist and succeeded just as the torch faded. After what must have been more than an hour, we all parted in a sombre mood. Wei stayed on to stabilize the patients and returned home late for a few hours sleep before operating non-stop the next day.

All these patients recovered in the weeks ahead, but in the run-up to the Christmas festivities, we were left to wonder whether their arrival heralded more hostilities. At the same time, we received news that Wei had graduated in absentia for his Master of Surgery, and that his convocation for a Fellowship of American College of Surgeons had been held in October. Set against that backdrop, these things, once all-important to our lives, seemed singularly remote, almost irrelevant. We barely stopped to acknowledge the moment.

When Chung and Elaine departed we both felt a little depressed but were pleased that Eric was staying on. Sharing bizarre circumstances with strangers make for special friendships. Elaine, Chung, and Eric have remained friends. Elaine went on to a further mission in Afghanistan and a photographic journal by Chung called *Crying Angola*[27] was published in 2002. Eric stayed behind until early January to work on a documentary for the popular current affairs program *Hong Kong Connection*. His documentary, *I'm Crying Alone*, went to air just prior to our return and was well received. It was both compelling and compassionate. The patients from Andulo feature in the film. By year end, Eric went on to win the humanitarian award from the Journalist Association of Hong Kong and the Foreign Correspondent's Club and we were proud of his attempt to bring attention to the plight of average Angolans.

His documentary moved people in ways that often came to light most poignantly. On our return to Hong Kong, a middle-aged lady approached us at the end of one of our talks. Eager enthusiasts, keen to hear more first-hand experiences, swamped Wei. She hovered shyly in the middle of the auditorium until it emptied. As I was starting to pack up, the lady approached me to ask if she could have her photo taken with us. I felt slightly embarrassed by her request, but it was obvious she wanted to talk. She described how she had been deeply moved, and how Eric's documentary had compelled her to attend our talk. Her voice quavered as she described how recent hardships made her contemplate suicide. Her sadness was palpable. She had chosen to end her life, but marked one of her last nights by watching television. By chance, she had tuned into Eric's documentary and was quickly absorbed. I tried to catch Eric's attention, beckoning him to join us. "This must be the lady you just told me about," I whispered as he wandered across to join us. "...the one who sent an e-mail to the television station to say she had changed her mind about suicide after seeing your program," I said, marvelling at the coincidence. But she was not. She hadn't sent an e-mail. She was yet another soul who had been inspired by his work. I was moved by the way in which she laid her emotions before us. She wept as she described how the powerful message of *I'm Crying Alone* changed her; how she compared her own predicament to the residents of Kuito and now counted herself as lucky. She came to thank us, and I was touched. We had our photo taken together and within minutes she slipped away quietly. Even today I often think about that sensitive lady and wonder what has become of her.

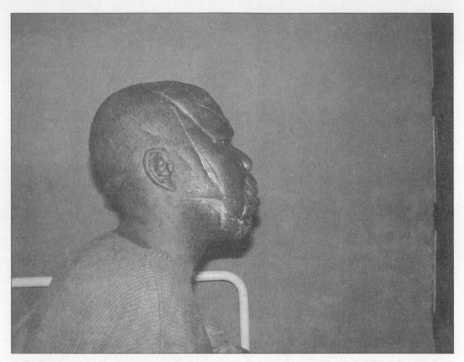

UNITA's walking billboard.

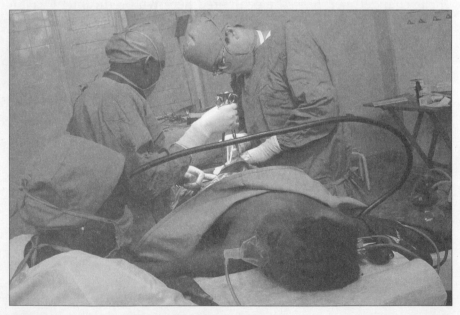

Operating on another patient from Andulo.

Chapter 39
Feliz Natal

Karin writes…

With Christmas only three days away we were taken by the near lack of suggestion that the festival was approaching. Some coloured lights adorned a Christmas tree high on the roof of the tallest building. This slum tenement was akin to a gutted and scaled-down version of Kowloon Walled City, now lost in Hong Kong's history. It was quite a Christmas symbol, with its broken concrete floors and twisted reinforcing rods. Here, families bedded down for the night at a precarious height, with no walls between them and the street below. Yet high up, those coloured lights twinkled. In Kuito we found it especially hard to get into the festive spirit, knowing that for most people Christmas would be just another day of grinding poverty. We knew that the churches would be full of people singing and dancing, no doubt as a way to forget their woeful existence as much as in praise of the Lord.

We were otherwise both in good spirits, uplifted by our visitors. In the weeks after Chung and Elaine left, the Hong Kong-generated entertainment induced me to pepper my desperate Portuguese with bits of Cantonese. I became even more incomprehensible to our ever-patient staff as I bumbled my way through each day. From then on I was convinced that my brain was programed to understand only one notional foreign language—a complete fruit salad of Cantonese, Mandarin, French, and Portuguese, seasoned with a couple of words of Umbundu. Plenty of spice, but all-round *confusão*. I took lessons twice a week to improve the situation, but the words drilled into my reluctant brain lacked sticking power, and I was crippled by my inhibitions. Or was it just old age?

As Christmas Day approached we learned that our food order would not be arriving from Luanda in time, so I set about to find a way to add a little Christmas cheer. Special deliveries like this were real luxuries, so it would have been a huge treat for the team. I knew that plum pudding wasn't everyone's tradition, but with my Grandma's recipe at hand I applied myself to the art of substitution.

For apples I found a type of pear and for brandy I used beer. Brown sugar was a mere memory, but I had bought a packet of cane sugar in South Africa and it was a worthy substitute. Every second egg I cracked looked like it was about to hatch. I couldn't find a suitable pot in which to cook, so instead I used a saucepan and removed the handles. I had no string to tie it, so improvised with our personal supply of Colgate waxed dental floss. I mixed the recipe early one morning and took it to the office to boil over a small electric plate using power from the office generator. But the water was reluctant to simmer, and I rapidly became tired of jumping up from my desk to check on its progress. The demands of the day were taking precedence and when we needed to use an office machine, I had to switch off the hotplate. It took me an entire workday to complete the task and I hoped the real proof would be in the pudding.

That night, with my mission accomplished, I settled back to reconcile my yearnings to be with my family with my new sense of belonging in Kuito. I reflected on the fact that every year, from all over the world, we received Christmas cards adorned with peace-on-Earth-type greetings. Until then it was something I found quite banal, almost corny, so I rarely stopped to consider the real meaning. I would eagerly flip the card open, keen to read what was written on the inside. While I knew that peace on Earth was too much to wish for, I dreamed of peace. It felt idealistic at best, but after more than thirty years, Angola deserved a little respite.

Tallest building in Kuito.

Longing for peace at Christmas.

Chapter 40
Silent Night

Karin continues…

It was amazingly quiet. Christmas came and went largely without incident and it was a unique chance for the entire team to spend some quality time together. On reflection, this was the period when the real soul of our team emerged. We enjoyed each other's company enormously and had developed a unique bond of friendship.

Christmas Day started routinely enough. As Wei headed out the door for his hospital round, Eric and I decided to go along. We wanted to distribute some presents to the children. My family had recently sent hoards of gifts. My little nephew had also contributed presents from his second birthday party. With needy children everywhere, we weren't sure how to make the best use of the câche, but decided on the children in the orthopedic ward. So we loaded a sack full of chocolates and gifts and set off to play Santa Claus.

One day in the orthopedic ward was as dull and grey as any other, and it was with angst that I entered that distressing place. The agonized cries of patients during dressing changes echoed through my mind and I braced myself for the worst. But on Christmas morning all was calm. In the first bed, we greeted two listless girls as they lay side by side, their legs suspended high in traction. We reached out and gave them matching koalas and they squealed with delight. My heavy heart lightened its load. In the adjacent bed we gave a yo-yo to an older boy, who instantly tried to dismantle it until Wei demonstrated how it worked. Wow! Did that get them all excited! These children held their simple gifts with such innocent wonder that an otherwise ordinary moment suddenly went well beyond the magical. We continued from bed to bed. Among all of those presents, I had two pairs of shoes to give away. In a ward full of landmine victims, this needed to be handled carefully. As Wei continued to dole out the gifts, I surreptitiously checked under the blankets in search of a child with two legs. Wei suggested Alberto, a young boy who had lost both of his arms in their entirety after playing with a hand grenade. His limbless upper body swayed from side to side as he struggled with gut-wrenching determination to sit erect on the bed. I held out the gift to his armless torso and panicked momentarily, not knowing what to do. Alberto spontaneously raised his feet to grasp the new shoes between his feet and gurgled as I unwrapped a chocolate and popped it into his mouth. His eyes danced.

I was down to the bottom of the bag and noted anxiously that there was still one child in the far bed. I dug in once again, willing myself to find something. She smiled with anticipation. I laid my hands on one last gift. It wasn't much—just a simple cardboard cutout of a scene from *Winnie the Pooh*. Her eyes sparkled as I reached out and presented her with the image. She stared right into my eyes as she took the picture in her hands and placed it gently in her lap. Winnie the Pooh, Eeyore, Kanga, and a pot of honey. I wondered what could these characters mean to this child? Then a bashful smile inched across her tiny visage. She looked down in wonder at Winnie and his friends and let out a shriek of delight. I will always cherish these Christmas moments.

That evening, we all pitched in to prepare a special dinner at *Casa Dois*. We filled the room with colourful decorations and set a pretty table with candles and some flowers from the garden. Despite our varied backgrounds the team hummed, and we all felt particularly close at that significant time of year. For our Christmas feast, we had long resolved to cull a few of Emilie's pet rabbits while she was not looking, but the surprise arrival of our Christmas food order made this unnecessary. We sat down to a well-timed turkey and a few bottles of wine, surrounded by a cargo of supplies that arrived at the last minute. Despite the obstacle course sustained in the making, my Christmas pudding was delicious. Conversely, my Christmas cake was a disaster. Having never perfected the art of cooking in a traditional brick oven, I burnt the cake to a cinder, much to Roberto's chagrin. Wei delivered two Christmas babies early that evening, before we dined and sang carols together. We reminisced, talked of our families, and crooned along with Charlotte Church, the only festive CD on hand. As if on cue, the stars shone with a gemlike intensity. It was a charming evening and a Christmas we will simply never forget.

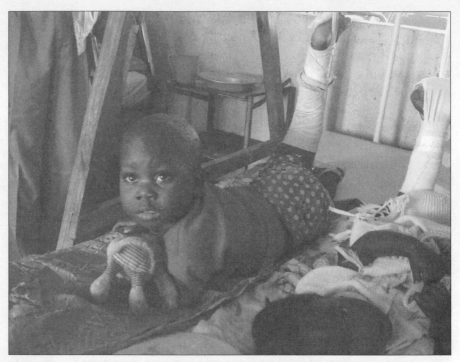

The girls share a bed in the orthopedic ward.

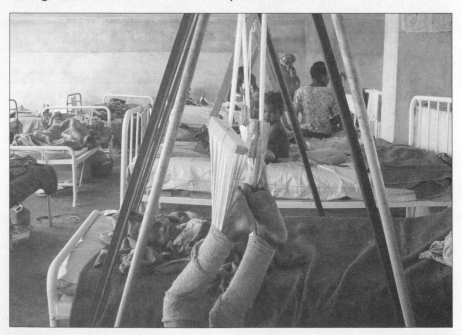

Christmas Day in the ward.

Chapter 41
Retracing Steps

Karin continues…

The days between Christmas and New Year were as disjointed as they are anywhere. We all had that upbeat festive feeling, grounded in the knowledge that there was still work to be done. It was during this time that Eric and I went in search of Elsa and Rosalina, the two orphan girls whom I had encountered back in October. Eric became interested in their plight, so we set off for Andulo camp to find them. The vehicle chortled over yawning potholes, now slushy with the arrival of the wet season. There was a green lushness to everything, made all the more dramatic when set against the orange mud. Green maize shot up at random, like a shock of hair on a balding head. The camps looked surprisingly moist and fresh, in stark contrast to the toast-dry conditions that struck me when I had first arrived.

The vehicle cut slowly through the swamp of humanity and general mêlée that defines camp life. But the wet had changed the place so much that I struggled to get my bearings. We parked and were walking down the narrow path between the adobe huts when the old *Soba* ventured from his, just as he had done before. Our translator engaged him, but in a nonchalant tone the *Soba* mumbled something and shook his head. I didn't need to understand Umbundu to know that the girls were no longer there. He was not sure where they had gone, but said they left soon after they arrived. And that was that. I guess I was not surprised to find no trace of their hut. The ground had already been turned into someone's vegetable plot. The hut would not have withstood the first downpour, but in this sea of people, we had no hope of locating the girls. Elsa and Rosalina were gone and so was their cubby house. Eric inhaled deeply on his cigarette and I suspected by now he was wondering whether I had just dreamed them up.

With nothing to film, we shuttled back to the Land Cruiser whereon the driver explained he had to start his daily rounds, collecting the sick from the camps. It would have been a long walk back to town with all the camera gear, so we decided to tag along for the ride. Several kilometres further eastward the vehicle waded through flooded roads towards Kunge. This settlement was pinned on the side of a gentle elevation at the extremity of the security perimeter. The crumbling railway station sat idly beside, acknowledging the town's past importance. A rusting army tank punctuated the edge of the decrepit structure. The once proud *Estação de Silva Porto* (Kuito Railway Station) was mined, dangerous, and out-of-bounds. Strangely though, I always felt a peculiar affinity with Kunge. Hard to explain really, for there was little of the town left. The flourmill had been razed, as were most signs of prosperity. But I am sure my sentiment had something to do with a primeval love of the Australian bush, as there was a cluster of commanding eucalyptus trees on the fringes of Kunge. Their massive canopy rose above it all. They were tall…imposing…resilient—so tall that you could see them from as far away as Kuito. That day, swaying in the breeze, their silvery leaves flashed monochromatic tones against the grey-bellied clouds that lingered overhead. No one else seemed to take any notice, but these symbols of endurance filled me with hope.

We pushed on through the slurping mud, turning south towards Katala, the most remote camp in the vicinity. The road tracked alongside the *Caminho de Ferro de Benguela* (Benguela Railway), once heralded as key to Angola's economic development. For decades, the Benguela Railway remained one of the few pieces of infrastructure in the entire country but, like everything else, it was idle and rusting. The Portuguese laid three thousand kilometres of track, but only about twenty percent was still operational, and the railway functioned to just three percent of pre-independence levels. The Benguela Railway was the largest of four lines and was about 1,350 kilometres in length. A ninety-nine-year lease for its exploration and construction was awarded to the British in 1902 because of their unrivalled record for steam-engine technology and for laying tracks in remote areas. Construction on the Benguela Railway began in Lobito on the coast and then extended up to the highlands and across central Angola to the border town of Dilolo. The ultimate destination was Lusaka in Zambia. The prize was the riches of the copper mines, which were shipped to Angola's ports. The railway brought action to Angola's rural hinterland and Kuito was strategically situated along the track. Kuito, Huambo, and dozens of other towns like them, started to boom. Both Zambia and Congo (then Zaïre) depended on the Benguela Railway, making it a focus of attention during the height of the Cuban-Soviet aid to Angola. Acutely aware of this, Savimbi regrouped in Bié and pursued hit-and-run guerrilla tactics to damage important infrastructure. The Benguela Railway was a key target. Most of the track is now in ruin and no one seemed to recall when a train had last arrived. Ravaged by years of war, it was another fitting symbol of economic decay.

What was left of the railway line ran past Katala camp. In fact it was one of the first camps I visited when Julio showed me around on my arrival, but I was too disoriented that first day to realize that we had been driving on the very edge of the security perimeter. On this particular day, however, I scanned the nearby minefields from the same spot and searched the grassy horizon with a sense of foreboding. Katala camp was a lonely, isolated place. I eyed the first line of defence: a row of flimsy grass huts, which brought back a flood of terrifying stories that a colleague had told me one evening. She had interviewed numerous victims of an attack that occurred just weeks before our arrival. Drunken soldiers had burst out of the night into this camp. They separated the women, ransacked and looted their homes, then callously raped them before disappearing into the darkness again. Embarrassed and traumatized, these women took days to trickle into the health posts to seek medical help. No one ever caught or punished the perpetrators of that heinous crime. It was simply added to the invisible tally.

Our visit that day was mercifully less eventful. We were there to check the situation with the home monitors, pick up the sick, and transfer the more urgent cases to the hospital. Stripped of their coping mechanisms, these villagers were particularly vulnerable to malnutrition and disease and daily checks were a vital link in their chain of survival. With Eric's help, we loaded the stretchers and before long the Land Cruiser was packed with an amalgam of patients. Crying children and anxious relatives crouched among bundled belongings and we all clung on for the bruising ride to the hospital.

Katala camp.

Sibling responsibility, near Kunge.

Chapter 42
Filming in Katabola Camp

Karin continues…

We turned off the main road and negotiated the rutted path that snaked past the banana trees to Katabola camp, nestled into the southeast slopes, overlooking Kuito. It was Saturday, December 30. Eric wanted to do some more interviews, which is why Wei and I were taking him out early to the camp close to the airport. On our approach, the driver gingerly inched around a sapper unearthing a mine, just metres from the edge of the road.

We didn't have to walk far to find newsworthy material and just a few paces within the compound, Eric set up his camera. He began to film an amputee who was eager to demonstrate his dexterity as he tended a small vegetable patch. The camera rolled while the ex-solider explained how he had lost his leg in the battlefield. Wei and I left Eric to his work. We wandered around the compound, the epicentre of camp life. Wei's life as a surgeon forced him to miss a lot of what happened beyond the hospital even though he had long wanted to see more of life in the camps, especially the distribution of food. Although completely devoid of the usual hubbub that day, I had seen similar compounds when WFP grain was being distributed. So there in the middle of the deserted compound, I tried to explain it to him as best I could…but I have to admit it is one of those things you have to see with your own eyes. About 200,000 of Kuito's inhabitants, including 40,000 malnourished children, depended entirely on food aid, so food distribution was a real feature of daily life. Recipients thronged the compound, jostling for a position in queues that snaked around the perimeter. Each woman or child clutched an empty oil can in one hand and a grain sack in the other. To while away the empty hours the village *Soba* sometimes led a chorus in which they sang, clapped their hands, and swayed to the rhythm—their silvery cans gleaming hotly in the sun. I never ceased to be amazed at the cheer that could be rallied from the dispossessed.

Weeks earlier I had witnessed food distribution in Andulo camp.

I had wandered into the logistics shelter: a simple wooden hangar that, by night, was packed tightly with new arrivals— woebegone peasants sheltered from the wet. By day, CARE used it as their main locale for distributing grain for the WFP. I was awed by the level of organization and stared at it for minutes on end. An old man stood in a pond of maize and mechanically scooped buckets of kernels into the recipients' bags. A litre of oil, a scoop of beans, a bag of maize, and a small quantity of salt were monthly rations for an entire family.

Wei and I wandered on and engaged the *Soba's* wife, who wanted to sell us some small wicker baskets. The baskets were intricately woven from grass and shredded WFP grain sack. As I marvelled at her handiwork, a villager suddenly implored us to come quickly. Someone was ill in one of the huts. I told her that we would return momentarily to collect our purchases before we followed the messenger along the narrow paths. Deep in the village we found a lady, crumpled on the dirt floor of her hut. Her shrivelled breasts looked like ruches of leathery fabric. An unweaned child howled by her side. Struggling to focus in the dim light, Wei crouched down to examine her and five minutes later we were carrying her to the Land Cruiser. We motioned to Eric to pack up quickly and were off.

In the vehicle, I offered with a gesture to nurse her baby, as our patient needed all her strength to maintain her posture and hold on for the ride to town. I took the willowy child from her, and, as I planted him on my lap, a sour smell of poverty poured into my nostrils. His hair was a shade of yellow straw and his scalp encrusted with scabs. Patches of hair were tinged with the telltale signs of malnutrition. Thick snot oozed from one nostril and was smeared in dried patches on his upper lip. True to his predicament, he whimpered miserably for the entire journey.

It was still early when we arrived at the hospital so, after depositing the patient at *Banco de Urgência*, I headed to the office, but the pungent smell of poverty clung to my clothes. My T-shirt reeked. I took it off and put it on backwards in a vain effort to suppress the odour. Longer still lingered the image of that baby with his scaly scalp. All of this was depressing and distracting enough in theory, but to have been physically imbued in it gave quite a different impact. That day I couldn't stop obsessing about Angola's cruellest statistic: about one out of three children dies before they reach the age of five.[28]

Delivering food to them wasn't easy. In the weeks before we left Kuito, guerrillas fired at a WFP plane as it approached the Kuito airstrip. The plane was servicing the distribution centres in the camps. Fortunately, no one was injured. Then on June 8, 2001, another cargo plane was fired on and damaged near Luena airport. Finally, on June 15, 2001, the crews of two WFP-chartered planes reported seeing a missile exploding in their flight path from Catumbela to Kuito forcing the UN to temporarily halt both cargo and passenger flights nationwide. The attacks on these aircraft, painted white and clearly marked with the WFP insignia, endangered not only aid workers but also the provision of vital humanitarian assistance to hundreds of thousands of IDPs. Due to poor roads and ongoing insecurity, sixty percent of all inland food aid in Angola was delivered by air. More than seventy percent of WFP's food aid beneficiaries in Angola were women and children.[29]

Eric filming in Katabola camp.

Chapter 43
Ano Novo

Karin continues…

Perhaps even guerrillas go home to celebrate the New Year—the week between Christmas and New Year was surprisingly calm. We had noticed a buildup of military and police on the streets just before Christmas. They assembled a large posse and then raided the suburbs for suspected UNITA infiltrators. Able-bodied men were hauled off for identity checks. Many of our staff was caught up in it all and we regularly sent Armando to secure their release. Afonso, a guard from *Casa Quatro*, was badly beaten because he wasn't carrying his MSF identity card. That news ricocheted through our office and we scrambled to ensure each employee carried appropriate identification. Police also drove around the streets with megaphones threatening to throw drunkards directly into prison; indeed, anyone found shooting or even making too much noise would be arrested. Maybe these heavy-handed tactics had paid dividends. From then on our nights were no longer punctuated by the sound of gunshots and life at the hospital was delightfully uneventful.

For our New Year gala dinner each volunteer brought a national dish to *Casa Dois*. We busied ourselves with the preparations and were all having fun until I broke out in a feverish sweat. Wei was at the hospital as usual, so I quickly asked around about the symptoms for malaria. I was convinced I was in the throes of joining the ranks of team members who had caught it. From its sudden onset, my temperature soared and beads of perspiration streamed down my face. I slunk home to bed and crashed onto the lumpy mattress. I slept fitfully, failing to stir for further celebrations with our local staff at midnight. I thrashed about, dreaming wildly. I awoke disoriented and stared through the shadowy veil above. A kaleidoscope of colours swirled above before the mosquito net and the watermarks on the ceiling came into focus. I was in my bug-ridden bed. *Casa Quatro*. Home.

The next morning I awoke feeling rotten and was soon subjected to Wei's Olympian-style check-up. My fever had subsided and in the end he was convinced that I had no more than a good dose of Angolan flu, infinitely better than malaria. While my start to the new year may have been inauspicious, I considered my escape light compared to Eric. We arose bleary-eyed to find him sitting at the dining table, nervously working his way through a third cigarette. Without any encouragement, his story unravelled.

He had risen early to film the sunrise and symbolically catch the dawning of the new year. We didn't hear him creep out of the house before the first light of day. The weather was dull and light rain was falling. Working for the first time without his translator, Eric set up his tripod in the middle of the town's main boulevard. He faced eastwards to catch the first glimpse of the rising sun. Suddenly, out of nowhere, an angry army commando burst forth and demanded he hand over the camera. Eric realized instantly that the soldier was drunk and with quick thinking tried to buy time. He offered an array of items from his pockets. Nothing seemed to entice. The commando wanted the camera and snatched it, pushing Eric towards a derelict building. At that critical moment a policeman appeared, enabling Eric to break free. The kindly policeman gestured to Eric to run. Dishevelled but unharmed, Eric snatched his tripod and ran, leaving the two adversaries to fight it out in the middle of the street.

Aside from the attack on Eric and my fever it was a beautiful day. By now we were used to the twists and turns of Kuito life. That same afternoon we were enchanted again by the irrepressible Angolan joie de vivre. New Year's Day, normally a dull day spent nursing a champagne hangover, was never so lively. From the balcony, we watched a merry parade of children troop from house to house welcoming the new year with song and dance. They stopped outside our home to charm us with their harmony in exchange for some sweets. It was a delightful, good-natured variation of Halloween and we were more than happy to dole out what sweets we had left.

Wei takes up the story…

The respite didn't last for long. On New Year's Eve, while the world was celebrating, a small village named Belo Horizonte was under attack. It took four days for the victims to arrive. What we had thought to be a quiet holiday was actually a harbinger. Among the wounded, I received a small boy who had been shot in the back while running away. He was just eight years old. I removed a bullet from his abdomen—brassy yellow, about the size of a child's finger. He recuperated well, but many others lost their lives, including the boy's younger brother. Even some of those who made it to Kuito were not so fortunate. One woman with a bullet in her brain died three days later. She was in a coma on arrival and I could do nothing except cover the tiny wound from where her brain spilled.

I was rattled, but the brutality continued. The dreadful wounds that rolled through the doors never ceased to astonish. In that same week I performed the most loathsome surgical undertaking of my entire career. Although not a war wound, I blamed the futile fighting. A newborn baby had died during the birthing process and it took two whole days for the distraught mother to reach the hospital. Despite various attempts, I could not dislodge the swollen baby from the birth passage and had to resort to very intrusive surgery to remove the dead child. I found every second of this odious task almost too much to bear. The mental nausea lingered for days.

Eric returned to Hong Kong that same day. With my mind preoccupied, I can't remember the farewells, but was sad to see him go.

War damage along Kuito's main street. Residents continued to live among the rubble (see bottom right).

Chapter 44
Of Mice and Mangoes

Karin writes…

To peals of laughter, Inger regaled us with a story of how she discovered hairy, grey mice carcasses choking the roadside gutters. Having never seen a mango seed dried by the tropical sun she surmised that Kuito had been suddenly overrun with a plague of oval-shaped rodents. In reality, spent mango seeds littered the streets in January with such abundance that one could have been forgiven for thinking hairy paving stones were in vogue. It was mango season. A large mango tree and a huge avocado tree graced our backyard and were laden with ripening fruit. The plump produce fell with the predictability of the chime of a grandfather clock—perhaps a very old clock with a rather muffled, sloshing sound. They invariably hit the corrugated plastic that covered the entrance to our backyard emergency bunker. We never had to use that grim, dank facility, and I was convinced it was home to bats, mice, spiders, and other insects that didn't bear thinking.

My first encounters with a bat in the house induced spontaneous hysterics and mice provoked a similar reaction, much to Wei's amusement. What is it about these creatures that reduce me to a blathering fool? In fact, mice were a real issue in the wetter months. An indigenous family of rodents nested in the roof of our house and descended on the pantry with persistent regularity. They gnawed at anything in their path and deposited rodent pellets like calling cards in all manner of places. I requested a simple mousetrap in an effort to curtail the plague. Weeks later, when we finally received the traps, we were surprised to discover that each had been fashioned by hand—even the spring. They would have been exactly the same as mass-produced models if they hadn't been the largest mousetraps I had ever seen! While Kuito mice were big, you could have caught cats in these. Temporarily revoking the Hippocratic Oath, Wei trapped five mice in the first night. With each thunderous snap the cull progressed with such precision that I thought we had eradicated the problem. However, when sinking my teeth into a small bread roll at breakfast one morning, a gritty sensation made me blanch. Despite their chewiness, these crusty rolls, called *pão*, had become a favourite. Baked in a brick oven, we bought them fresh each day from one of the roadside vendors. On closer observation my alarming discovery was mice droppings freshly baked into the bun.

In the early evenings, mice would occasionally scurry across the living room floor, reminding me it was already too dark to write. As electricity was a fading memory, we were forced to adjust to nature's clock. We learned to go to bed early and get up when the sun streamed through our bedroom window. But none of this seemed to matter much. Watching life go by like this made us realize just how insignificant our modern-day concerns and preoccupations could be. Confronted with Kuito's privations, we rapidly discovered that we were happy, healthy, and well catered for, and little else mattered.

I learned to be creative with the four basic staples available in the market: funge, tomatoes, onions, and avocados. It didn't matter that none of the teacups had handles, that our glasses were screw-top jam jars, or that the coffee table was held together with masking tape. No one was bothered that the dinner setting was an eclectic array of oddments, where nothing matched and there were never enough to go around. We'd take turns or I'd ask my guests to bring what I didn't have: extra knives, plates, and spoons. No one flinched when you served straight from a saucepan or spooned the dessert into mugs. I washed and reused everything, including my precious stock of plastic wrap and tied knots in broken elastic bands. The toilet no longer flushed, the bathtub was stained yellow beyond repair, and there was no hot water. But from the moment we arrived, we were immersed in a new code of behaviour: utilitarian, practical, without fuss. Everyone simply rolled up their sleeves and got on with it and this appealed enormously to my Australian psyche.

We also took pleasure in things we had never had the time to enjoy and our backyard was central to this. After a period of cooler weather, the heat returned and with the rain our garden burst into beautiful blooms. The backyard was lush with ankle-deep grass. We sat out under the trees as often as we could, languidly adrift in the tropical stillness, broken only by the scch…ump of falling avocadoes. Tanguy, our Belgian logistician, joined us from time to time. Wei and I were enormously fond of him. Tanguy and I did basic training together in Brussels back in August, so we shared a common bond. A self-effacing law graduate, he was an unlikely candidate for the rough and tumble world of logistics in the African bush. I was convinced he didn't know his way around the back end of a generator, to say nothing of a radio, but he seemed to take it all in his stride. His passion was humanitarian law and, like Wei, he was an optimist. One superbly sunny Sunday, while sprawled out on our lawn, we shared a glass of wine and chatted for hours about far-flung subjects like family expectations, careers, dreams, and aspirations. It was always a convivial way to pass the hours until the mosquitoes drove us indoors.

Tanguy and Emilie, the Canadian midwife, were part of the French-speaking contingent that lived in *Casa Três*. For most of our stay, the two weren't great friends and Tanguy even suggested that he didn't like Emilie very much. But something strange happened towards the end of our stay: they fell in love.

In the garden at Casa Quatro.

Chapter 45
A Hand or a Life?

Karin continues…

Rather than sit at home twiddling my thumbs, I preferred to accompany Wei to the hospital, especially on Sundays. This was by now part of our weekend routine. On the first Sunday of 2001, I tagged along, as several patients had arrived overnight and were in need of emergency surgeries.

I clearly remember the first operation on the list that day. It was for a boy who had been shot in the leg and it was a relatively straightforward affair…or at least I was becoming more familiar with the routine. The boy had sustained a broken bone from the impact of the bullet. Wei worked nimbly to clean the wound and set the limb in plaster. Before long the boy was wheeled into the recovery area. But within minutes there was a ruckus in the corridor and Wei bolted from the theatre to investigate. I too was curious and joined the small throng of people crowded around the trolley. The boy was trying to tear the drip from his vein.

"Wo-o-o-o-o! W-o-o-o-o!" he howled pugnaciously, as if surfing successive waves. "Wo-o-o-o-o!"

"What's wrong?" I asked.

"It's the ketamine—the anaesthetic," declared Wei. "He's delirious. It's making him hallucinate," he added, as he helped to pin the combative patient to the trolley.

"Wo-o-o-o-o!" Like a fish trapped in a net, the boy thrashed wildly.

His vociferous cries echoed through the corridors. It sounded like a chamber of horrors, and I fretted about his family waiting outside. I popped my head around the door expecting a sea of upset faces, but no one gave the impression of anything unusual. The boy's strength was superhuman. He was determined to free himself. Wei worried about the undue stress on his broken limb and the fresh plaster cast. It took the strength of four men to secure each limb and contain his struggle before he finally drifted into a fitful sleep.

With the cries of post-operative patients resonating through the corridors, the recovery room often sounded like something from an old ghost movie. But Wei repeatedly assured me that it was little more than the ketamine, which was the safest general anaesthetic to administer under those conditions. Hallucinations were merely a disconcerting side effect, as was the tendency for some patients to start moving about on the operating table before surgery was complete.

Our second patient that day was a soldier who had sustained serious wounds to his right leg and right hand after an anti-tank mine accident. In comparison to the number of civilians we treated, we didn't receive many military casualties in Kuito. The army preferred to treat them in their own facilities, so there was no way of knowing just how many soldiers died or were injured in this way. Wei started the operation thinking that he would try to save his hand, but would have to amputate the soldier's leg. He was therefore pleased to discover some blood supply to the foot. The patient's tibia protruded grotesquely at a 90° angle and, as I observed the procedure, I quickly concluded that orthopedics was far harder to watch than surgery to the abdomen. The brute force needed to align the bones made my stomach heave. Wei literally swung on the spaghetti-like limb, pulling with all his bodily might in an attempt to align the twisted leg and reduce the fracture. He pulled, pushed, and shoved the shattered bone back inside the skin, bandaged it, and applied a plaster cast.

Jesus told me the soldier's name was Vincente. Before the ketamine was administered, Vincente begged Wei to save his cindered hand. It was his right hand and I understood his concern, but even I could see that the tendons and bones were crudely exposed. The skin was charred to the edges of the wound. After repairing the leg, Wei preoccupied himself with cleaning the injury. While he loathes amputations, he became unconvinced that the hand could be salvaged and was sure the artery had been severed. The soldier's fingers were bloated and the skin was already black and necrotic. We wheeled him into recovery and went home, but Wei was worried and hours later he returned to the hospital to check on the patient.

Despite the gravity of the wounds, Vincente steadfastly refused to allow the amputation of his dying hand to proceed. Wei pleaded persistently, but in vain. In a desperate fight against time, he summoned the family, who by chance lived in Kuito. They too failed to persuade. A hand or a life? He bravely braced himself and chose death, which slowly and inevitably enveloped him. Even with antibiotic treatment and debridement the rotting flesh harboured infection. Septicemia soon attacked with a vengeance. Wei had been torn between the need to respect a patient's rights and the anguish of watching another man die. Two days later, Wei came home and told me in a desolate voice that Vicente succumbed. And another family lost a son.

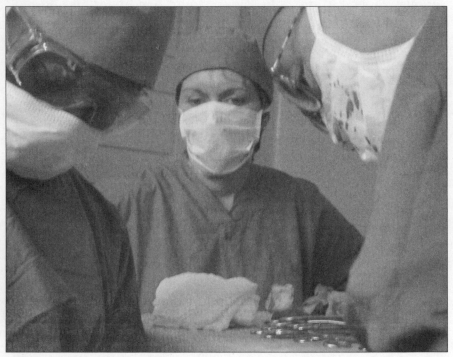

Eduardo, Karin, and Wei.

Chapter 46
Back to School

Karin continues…

It was straight out of *Jungle Book*. I was on my way home from work in light rain when I came upon four schoolchildren parading in a row, squealing with delight as they jumped puddles together. They had each plucked a huge elephant ear-shaped leaf and were frolicking around, gripping the stalks as umbrellas. Cuter than Mowgli, I half expected Baloo the bear to appear.

These snotty-nosed children provided me with immeasurable entertainment on my walks to and from the office. I befriended a raffish few, who loved to taunt me with a few words of English. "What is your n-a-m-e?" they called, enunciating every letter. They dared each other to bully me in their own naïve way. "Amiga, me dê o dinheiro!" (Friend, give me money!), one chanted defiantly. All they wanted was to evoke a silly response. They squealed innocently and soon ran away. They went back to their mud puddles, never concerned about the success of their monetary demands.

The children were crazy about soccer. I walked past a dust bowl that was used as a soccer field on my way to work and watched barefoot boys kick a ball around with great competitiveness. But the balls were not real soccer balls. They had been simply fashioned from rubbish, using strips of plastic bag, rags, and string. The boys wound these cast-offs up tightly, until they took on a spherical shape that more or less responded when bounced. The rest was like soccer anywhere and the crowds were just as enthusiastic.

Schoolchildren were easy to identify as they often walked to school with their own seat on their heads: an empty oil can or a tiny wooden stool. I had no idea whether the children I befriended attended class, but each day I passed several schools. To stop the rain from coming in, the paneless windows were covered with grass matting or bricked up. A thin gap was left at the top so some light could enter. One pockmarked secondary school told its own story. A rocket had ripped away part of the classroom wall, high up on the first floor. Part of the floor had also been vaporized, leaving mangled reinforcing rods, exposed and rusting. But life went on as usual. The desks were neatly arranged to avoid the gaping hole and students attentively faced the blackboard. There were no outraged parents worried for their safety and no one suing the government for negligence. Everyone respected the inherent dangers and carried on regardless. A spent rocket casing hung in the middle of another huge hole at the end of the corridor. It was beaten with a stick to announce the start of class. This was Kuito's best school, as most didn't even have desks. Schools everywhere had scarce resources, including teachers.

Kuito residents proudly told me that the town was once renowned for its standard of education. The Ovimbundu people of the region were considered Angola's most educated, and scholars were still treated with reverence. Education was respectability. However, I noted how people were more inclined to reminisce about education as if it were part of some bygone era. Their wistful remarks were full of hoarded hopes and postponed ambitions.

While MSF's efforts in Kuito helped prop up a collapsed health system, the education system was in an equally dismal state. In some schools there was one teacher for every seventy pupils.[30] Even that statistic was grossly overstated, as it did not take into account the large numbers of teachers who had already dropped out of the system altogether, due to the subsistence wages they received. Only half these teachers had finished any more than seven years of school themselves, and in some provinces most teachers had no professional qualifications at all. Many had not even finished basic schooling, so the quality of education was declining and dropout rates were high. The fact that only two in five children attended school reflected a truer picture. Of those, eighty percent were in grades one to four and only twenty-seven percent ever reached the fourth grade.[31]

Augusto used to teach English some afternoons at one of the church schools and asked us to join a class. We hiked along the narrow paths between the huts of suburban Kuito to find it. Chickens scattered and dogs barked as we jumped puddles to avoid the mud. A hand-painted sign assured us that we had found the right place. It was nestled among the trees, a modest establishment with mud walls, a tin roof, and a dirt playground. A beam of sunlight streamed through the window as Augusto welcomed us inside the dark room. The classroom was crammed with children of all ages and our presence caused a commotion. To the amusement of the students, I found myself a tiny desk at the back of the room after Augusto had introduced us. Looking down at the dirt floor I observed that most children wore shoes, so surmised it was a relatively affluent neighbourhood. Wei was invited to take over the lesson: a simple text about a book and a desk, a window and a room. He was in a lively mood, so it wasn't long before the children echoed his words in an animated chorus. While I am not sure that they really understood the text, they clearly enjoyed chanting the words as Wei pointed to each on the blackboard.

These children were the lucky ones—without proper birth certificates, parents could not register their children for secondary school, making prospects for the displaced even bleaker. Not surprisingly the IDPs in Kuito rarely arrived with appropriate documentation. As a result the literacy rate in Angola was at best a dismal fifty percent and even lower in the rural areas. The main reason that children didn't attend school was economic, but lack of accessibility was also a factor. Years of neglect of this key to progress left the nation with a bleak future. It will take generations of well-directed initiatives to fill the void. Even today more than one million Angolan children remain out of school,[32] with primary school attendance at just fifty-eight percent.[33]

There were also an estimated one hundred twenty thousand child soldiers serving throughout Africa at that time.[34] The reality of this situation was perhaps best illustrated by an amputation Wei did in January on a young soldier called Jaime. Jaime was a skinny runt, just fifteen years old, a boy drafted into a war he didn't understand when he has fourteen years old. Both sides of the conflict had been accused of kidnapping and drafting young boys like him. Jaime still cried like a child in need of his mother each time they changed his dressing. With his adolescence stolen, he faced life without a leg when any other child would normally be running free in a schoolyard.

En route to school.

Outdoor classroom near Katabola camp. Children squat on small stools and empty USAID oil cans.

Chapter 47
Weight Watchers

Karin writes…

There was a nationwide strike of government workers in mid-January, meaning things slowed at the hospital. Wei received fewer patients than expected, so it was a relatively quiet time. It isn't often that I support strikes, but I was encouraged that Angolans still found the energy to send a protest message to the government that neglected them so blatantly. After all, a hospital worker's monthly income ranged from just KZR 220 for a cleaner to just KZR 2,000 for a nurse. At the prevailing exchange rate, that was between US$10 and US$100 a month and inflation was rampant. The majority earned a subsistence wage at the lower end of this scale. To put this in perspective, the price of a small egg was forty cents, a litre of cooking oil or a bag of charcoal was US$2, while a chicken cost US$7.50. Low salaries were one thing, but getting paid was another. In the prior year the hospital staff waited some eight months before being paid their meagre earnings retrospectively. So who could blame them for withdrawing their services that week? But, by the end of the week, the strike had petered out without comment from the government. The staff felt even more slighted than before.

I offered to help in the Therapeutic Feeding Centre weighing malnourished children because of the staff shortage. The task was simple enough, but I quickly realized that handling the malnourished was more confronting than war surgery. In a building styled on a traditional village meeting house, with a thatched roof and dirt floor, we faced a long queue of mothers and their starving children. We asked each mother to remove her child's clothing and then, one-by-one, helped the child into a pair of plastic pants. We attached these pants to a strap that was latched onto a meat hook, connected to the scales. The children dangled there, sometimes scared and screaming and sometimes too weak to react. We then recorded their weight.

When the vicious cycle of malnutrition begins, lack of food soon leads to lack of energy. Immense fatigue sets in. Bit by bit the affected become apathetic. They no longer have the strength to move or to engage in what you think they desire most: food. Through this deprivation, the stomach begins to waste and they lose their ability to consume large quantities of food. Mechanisms regulating hunger wane. Surprisingly, the person is no longer hungry or thirsty and they rapidly become dehydrated, especially children. But lethargy doesn't dull the pain. Atrophied muscles and cracked dehydrated skin compound the intolerable suffering. Malnutrition ruthlessly wracks the entire human body, which then becomes fragile and more vulnerable to disease.

"I'm dying of hunger!" How many times had I said that, I pondered. When ravenous after a hard day at the office? After skipping lunch or while trying to shed a few excess kilos? How apt and inapt was this pedestrian expression? Yet these tiny mites were literally dying of hunger. They were nothing more than clichéd bags of bones. Their rib cages protruded as if they had swallowed a birdcage. Each time I hung another on the hook, I struggled with a primeval desire to turn and look the other way. There were scabby kids, smelly kids, kids with lice, kids in rags—the filthiest rags I have ever seen masquerading as clothes. Consciously I knew they needed nothing but warmth and compassion, but any desire I may have had to cuddle them evaporated spontaneously. I forced myself to treat them with the same instinctively warm behaviour I would otherwise use on cute, clean children of the same age. What is it that makes us want to block the sight of those we sense to be so near death? The shockingness of it all, I guess. I strained myself to override instinct with intellect. As the morning drew on, I reflected ruefully on the scourge of obesity sweeping our own society: the impact on our health services, the money spent on diet food and gym memberships. Then I hung the next child up on the hook. We continued to record their weights: 5.3 kilos, 5.5 kilos, 6.1 kilos—just a few kilos more than the weight of a healthy newborn baby. Yet, they were not babies at all, but children of four, six, seven, or perhaps even nine years? It was so hard to tell. Chronic malnutrition dulls development of the human body. It stunts growth and renders the afflicted less mentally agile, making it harder still for them to break the cycle of poverty.

We scribbled their weights on little pieces of paper and gave them to their mothers. This was their ticket to special rations. We went on measuring and calling out the weights, child after child. But then, as always, something happened to induce a little comic relief.

"4.9 kilos, 6.7 kilos, 5.3…11.3…14.6…12.1 kilos."

"Hey, hang on here, what's going on? You don't look malnourished to me," my local colleague queried. She turned to address the queue. "This queue is only for malnourished children. Please stand aside if your child is not malnourished."

A dozen people moved to the left.

"So why did you bring your children here?" we asked curiously.

"Oh, my kid has a fever and, with the strike, the outpatient clinic is closed," said one.

"We saw this queue: the nurses, white people handing out tickets…and…" replied another.

We sighed, but how could we blame them? We found them a doctor and went back to our work at the Kuito Weight Watchers' Club.

With our task complete, I went to lend a hand in the wards where the severely malnourished were monitored around the clock. I say "ward," but it was just a tent pitched next to the hospital. The beds were tightly arranged and crowded with patients and family members. As it was feeding time, I was asked to help ensure the patients drank their entire allocation of supplemented milk. This gave the two MSF nurses, An and Emmanuelle time to finish the daily medical checks.

Katelijn also came by and as we worked together she explained an interesting phenomenon. She asked me to try to get the child to hold the cup in his own hands and discourage the mother from spoon-feeding. In her experience, when a child interacted with the food they achieved better results. By contrast, a child that is fed passively rarely drinks as much. Moreover, it is a mother's instinct to spoon-feed a frail child, as the very act symbolizes caring. I was fascinated by the psychology of it all, and, from my small sample, I think that she was right. Keeping the children active and stimulated is also important therapy, but with over two hundred seventy children, feeding and medical checks took precedence over play.

At the end of my rounds I saw a child in the last bed at the back of the tent. He was being cared for by his grandmother, also not a picture of health. The metal bed squeaked as I sat down and tried to show the child how to hold the cup. A sour smell invaded my nostrils. Grandma spoke no Portuguese, but managed to tell me his name was Graça—an unusual name for a boy I thought, but it was not uncommon in Kuito. She let me take the lead. Graça's eyeballs sat low and heavy in their sockets. His face was sallow and despondent. As I tried to wrap his bony fingers around the orange mug, I sensed all his energy had been sapped. Graça mechanically lifted the mug to his mouth just as the blanket fell away. I instinctively turned my head away and scrambled to hide the shocking sight with the covers. I felt nauseous, but was angry with myself for having flinched so publicly at the sight of his impending death.

I was so disturbed by the way I had reacted to his cadaverous body that I felt obliged to return the next day to help him some more, as if this somehow absolved me of my behaviour. But Granny wasn't there. Even from the door of the tent, I could see that the bed in the back corner was empty. Bed-by-bed, I scanned the entire ward, looking into vacant eyes. Graça wasn't there and then someone casually told me that he had passed away that same evening. I had helped him eat his last repast. At a low ebb, I left the tent with tears streaming down my face. Graça—graceful. There was little grace in his death.

Malnourished mother spoon-feeds her dying child.

Chapter 48
BBC and a Pomegranate Tree

Wei writes...

Snail-mail via head office in Brussels was particularly slow and by the New Year the news drought seemed particularly dire. Even out-of-date magazines hadn't arrived for weeks. So I scaled our pomegranate tree to put us back in the real world, or at least the *BBC World Service's* version of it. But what has the BBC to do with a pomegranate tree? For months we suffered from such poor short-wave reception that listening to news on the radio was at best an irritation. Hours spent fiddling with the dials and readjusting the aerial induced little more than extra frustration. We eventually gave up. Without television, *The Economist*, daily newspapers, or a radio, we rapidly degenerated into a rather uninformed household. Weekly dispatches arriving via Wavemail from a dear friend in Sussex were the only real news reports that staved off complete ignorance. Each week, he faithfully wrote a newsletter called "Letter from England," modelled on Alistair Cook's prolific dispatches of a similar name. We looked forward to each edition.

However, one day while tinkering with the radio, I discovered that the secret to success for short-wave radio reception was a long piece of wire and a strategically placed pomegranate tree. So we started to fill in the missing pieces of the US election charade and the Filipino-Estrada fiesta among other things. One night we even tuned somewhat nostalgically into a dispatch on the changing face of old Beijing. The hutongs, playground of my childhood, were disappearing and with it thousands of years of history. I felt melancholy, but news of home was still honey-sweet. Little by little, we started to feel like part of the world again, even though it just highlighted for us how the larger world had so little time for what was happening in the country from where we tuned in on the world. Angola didn't even get a passing mention.

The great wet season continued and the downpours of January were torrential. Thunder seemed to seek us out and the lightning dazzled even the darkest night skies. Like frenzied kettle drums, the thunder would build to an explosive crescendo. Lightening would first flicker and then angrily knife across the blackened sky. Even more disturbing were the huge military-type explosions that accompanied some storms. I don't know whether they were controlled explosions of UXOs or whether the thunder set them off, but it was at times difficult to distinguish the two. The wild tempests would eventually peter out into the soothing sound of water cascading off the rooftop. It poured noisily into the concrete courtyard. Shortly after, we would hear that ominous drip, drip...plip-plop, plip-plop—water seeping through every household crevice. The house leaked like a sieve and it was then time for the bucket brigade. Progressively, the house smelled musty, so Roberto helped me place more plastic over the roof, which we secured with rocks.

The advantage of all this rain was most evident in our garden. Karin had brought seeds with her and the vegetable patch soon sprang to life. We harvested spinach for salad and the tomato plants bore fruit, even though the bugs often helped themselves before we did. All manner of herbs shot up like rockets and burst into bloom before we could savour them.

With the rain, the main street turned to a muddy river and the side streets to swollen creeks. There was sticky mud everywhere. But it brought tragedy too. Bento's nephew was killed after being struck by a bolt of lightening in one storm and this was not uncommon. I encountered my first such patient: an elderly lady admitted after the first heavy rains. She had been sitting indoors in her grass house where she had been struck. Amazingly, she survived with little more than a large burn to her forehead and a profusion of singed hair.

In late January, there was also a mine accident, which occurred within the city security limits. An anti-personnel mine placed on top of an anti-tank mine obliterated the victim. Another attack occurred a week later, leaving us to wonder whether things were becoming unstuck again. We fretted about its proximity, as it was less than fifteen kilometres away and four people had been killed. Quite a line waited for me at *Banco de Urgência* that morning. Many were bleeding from bullet wounds, so I asked whether the four dead had been military or civilians. Someone replied that since the local radio station had confirmed the deaths they must have been civilians. The government, they explained, would never broadcast deaths of their own military personnel. I hadn't thought of that.

It was also about this time that we learned that Laurent Kabila,

President of neighbouring Congo, was dead. Although what we heard was at times heavily dependent on rumour, we learned that he had been assassinated. Angolan troops were flying in to Kinshasa by the thousands, ostensibly to help maintain the peace—not something they were renowned for. I remember being puzzled by why Angola was so quick to move, but surmised the government was keen to tighten its grip on UNITA's supply lines through the Congo, both for arms and diamonds. Angola had also joined Kabila in oil exploration and, in a remarkable parallel, resource-rich Congo had also seen non-stop warfare. Six neighbouring countries were drawn into the fray and the resulting humanitarian situation was every bit as desperate, if not worse, than life in and around Kuito. This was hard to imagine.

After the rain; remnants of an adobe house in the suburbs.

Chapter 49
The Snake Baby

Wei continues...

It was Chinese New Year Day. Peter, an anaesthetic consultant from Belgium, had just arrived and I was pleased of his help in theatre. He stayed for two weeks to review anaesthetic procedures for the team. On the auspicious first day of the Year of the Snake I started my operation list as usual. Then...

"Wei, Wei, para Emilie." A call came for me over the radio from our midwife.

"Yes, Emilie," I replied, detecting her plea for urgency.

"Wei, I have a woman with post-partum hemorrhage and she is in shock. I am sending her to the operating theatre now!" On arrival, the patient was bathed in blood and looked weak and pallid. I examined a small vaginal tear that could not account for the amount of bleeding. She had to be bleeding internally, so I immediately performed a laparotomy that confirmed my worst fears. Blood gushed out like water from a tap and it took me a while to control the uterine artery.

"Blood! Get blood!" Peter shouted urgently.

But there was no blood. Since stocks in the hospital blood bank were limited, we routinely had to ask the family to donate on the spot each time a patient was in need. But the patient's husband was not there and she had no other family members around. Peter poured Haemocel solution through the drip to replace the volume of blood being lost. It is usually said that blood is thicker than water, but, in this instance, the blood was as thin as water, so diluted with the infused solution.

Sensing her life ebbing away, Peter shouted again over the radio. "Blood! We need someone to donate blood immediately!"

About a minute later, I caught a glimpse of Tanguy at the door of the operating theatre. He had responded to the call, gripped by the intensity of the moment. I was deeply moved by his gesture. Emilie had also managed to convince several nurses to donate.

After what seemed like an eternity, Peter reassured me in a calm voice. "We have three or four units of blood now. Do whatever you consider to be the safest."

With the bleeding under control, I put my fingers on her aorta but there was no pulse. She had already died. The blood had come too late.

At two o'clock that morning, this thirty-year-old mother had given birth to a little girl—The Snake Baby. She was probably one of the first babies born on Chinese New Year's day, certainly in Kuito. This alone was cause for celebration. The baby was her seventh child, which no doubt contributed to her uterine rupture. When Emilie came to work that morning, she had found the mother lying in a pool of blood. In the dark of the night, without electricity, the maternity staff simply hadn't noticed the bleeding. For more than seven hours, her blood leaked into the baby's swaddling cloth.

Distraught by the loss of life on my operating table, I turned and walked out of the theatre, tearing my gloves from my clammy hands. Visibly shocked by the ordeal, Emilie stood at the door, cuddling the cutest baby girl in her arms. She sobbed when I told her that we had lost the mother. I took the baby and held her gently in my arms. At that quixotic moment, I drowned in her beauty and contentment. The morning sunshine streamed across her tiny face. She frowned and looked up at the world with one eye, the other eye closed. She lifted her little right hand, spread her tiny fingers and pushed her miniature index finger against her forehead, as if pondering the moment. Did she realize that her mother had died, just eight hours after she came to the world? I felt a damp patch on her lemon-coloured blanket, and thought she had wet herself. Looking down I saw that it was blood: her mother's blood that had soaked her blanket. I held her tenderly, lost in sorrow. Learning to cope with a preventable tragedy was always the hardest. I felt totally diminished.

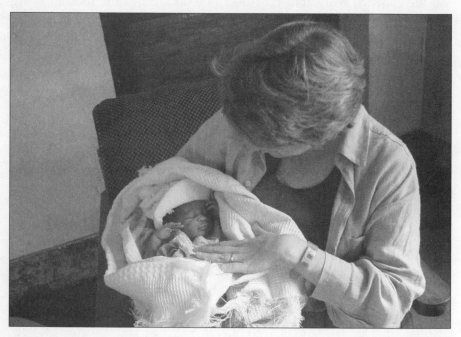

Karin holding the Snake Baby. The team cared for the child for the first day until we could locate a relative to breast-feed the newborn.

Chapter 50
At the Desk

Karin takes up the story...

While life in the operating theatre dominated our lives, my life at the office added a touch of routine to domestic chores, like cooking meals for those who worked late at the hospital.

Teams of doctors and nurses need support wherever they are and, even in a war zone, the administrative requirements are voluminous. Officially, I was responsible for the finances and human resources of the project. I helped manage the office; kept accounts; managed local staff contracts; hired and fired; paid expenses and local staff salaries. I also became the resident computer expert, which amused me. I helped improve data collection, analyses, and reports. In the process I learned a lot about calculating crude mortality rates, malnutrition measures, and epidemic indicators. At one time I also managed a small army of guards and drivers, although I soon reassigned them to the logistics team as security and transport were more their domain. Apart from that I also arranged flights to ferry volunteers to and from the field, greeted them on arrival, and bid them farewell at the end of their missions. We negotiated house and warehouse rentals, processed vehicle and visa documentation, organized domestic staff, and ordered our food supplies. My mass of administrative tasks even extended to organizing the lunchtime meal for the volunteers. Trying my best to balance their diet, I planned the weekly menu. I compiled the shopping lists and gave the team's ever-cheerful cooks, Dona Madonna and Dona Luisa, the cash they needed for the market. Then, when I had done all that, I started all over again.

Of course, I wasn't alone. Julio and Armando were indispensable members of the administrative team. I relied keenly on Julio's knowledge and experience. He spoke fluent French and English and was pivotal to my survival during the first few months, but when he went home to his family in Luanda for Christmas my Portuguese was plunged into the sink-or-swim phase. Armando, on the other hand, had a rather exalted estimation of himself. He clearly loved his position—the authority and prestige. I think he even loved to sit at his desk. I'd watch him arrive each day, immaculately dressed—a colourful tie, shiny shoes, and a blazer adorned with gold buttons. It was quite something for our casual jeans-and-runners-style office. He would saunter nonchalantly through the door and pull out his squeaky chair. With great ceremony, Armando would sit down to begin his early morning routine: shifting neatly arranged papers around his desk. But I soon learned that few could tolerate his smarmy demeanour.

While many of our administrative tasks were tedious, I relished the human resources function. Due to the chronic emergency in which we all operated, the project rapidly outgrew its early structures and guidelines, so I busied myself with re-evaluating job descriptions, organigrams, staffing levels, and procedures.

Kuito was the largest MSF project in Angola, and it was MSF's largest project worldwide at the time. In fact there were three projects in one: the hospital, the nutritional program, and camp health. We had as many as eighteen expatriate volunteers, ninety-five full-time national staff, and more than two hundred part-time workers, including the casual labourers who unloaded planes when supplies arrived, helped dig latrines in the camps, and so on. Some of our home monitors were also engaged under the WFP's Food-for-Work scheme. We also supplemented the salaries of key hospital staff, mainly nurses employed by the Ministry of Health. In the few Angolan hospitals that still functioned then, patients were often left to fend for themselves, especially in the afternoons and evenings, as staff members seldom returned to work after lunch. But, as mentioned, meagre salaries were often not paid, forcing staff to supplement their family income by other means. It was the only way to survive. Nevertheless, in Kuito, the small amount we gave these elite hospital personnel was a highly appreciated bonus and helped to motivate them. More important, the bonus ensured these crucial staff members turned up to work each day and kept the hospital and feeding centres functioning.

Throughout the month of January I reviewed the long-term viability of this bonus system, and each day would wade through reams of salary data for more than six hundred staff at the hospital. This data had been presented to me in boxes stuffed full of handwritten forms. I spent my spare time perched in front of a computer analyzing it all. I was fascinated to discover that, regardless of their position in the hospital hierarchy, a large number of people earned the same salary: US$10 per month. This salary uniformity helped me though, as it kept the numbers simple. A washerwoman earned the same as a qualified nurse. Mind you, she spent her days bent over a concrete tub and washboard with a cake of coarse soap in one hand and a soiled blanket in the other, as there were no washing machines. Qualifications counted for little either, except for the lucky few who had their salary "converted." This happened when the government decided that it had enough money to pay an employee the official salary. The pay for these fortunate convertees then increased as much as tenfold, to $100 per month. But our band-aid bonus system was not sustainable and left me with a big problem. MSF had created an incentive system that kept the wheels of the hospital turning, but how could we extricate ourselves from our commitment in the longer term? How could we take it away? And when? By continuing to support a rotting system, were we absolving the government of its responsibility? I often wondered whether we would ever achieve our goal to hand the hospital back to the Ministry of Health. At the time, I dithered over what to write in my recommendation, short of first solving the chronic economic and political problems of Angola. But in the end, inspiration must have fallen out of the mountains of figures through which I sifted, because I recall being quite pleased with my simple proposal which pegged the MSF bonus to the government's own salary conversion system. As salaries went up the bonus went down. And two years later, MSF finally did hand the responsibility of staffing the hospital with doctors and a surgeon back to the government of Angola.

Preparing dinner for the patients in the hospital kitchen.

Chapter 51
Bombs of Remembrance

Karin continues…

"Oh pátria nunca mais esqueceremos, os heróis do quatro de fevereiro"
(Oh homeland we will never forget, the heroes of February 4)
— Angolan national anthem

February 4 was an invitation for terror. A bomb exploded opposite the police station two days before the national holiday celebrations in an already gutted building just a couple of blocks from *Casa Quatro*. Fortunately, we were both at *Casa Três* for dinner with the team, so we didn't hear the blast, which apparently rocked our home. Inácio from the UN was on the doorstep within minutes to check that we were all accounted for and Roberto set out to locate a couple of teammates who were elsewhere for the evening.

Speculation around town was that it was a mere scare tactic aimed at the police, but as with all stories everything was just one big *confusão*. Security was definitely deteriorating. The week before, about eighty UNITA soldiers had attacked the town of Uïge, some two hundred kilometres north of Luanda. When shelling came within metres of their house, our MSF colleagues decided to evacuate. There were persistent reports of other daring attacks throughout the provinces.

The infamous elite commando troops were stationed in Kuito again, another sure sign that things were coming unstuck. By then we were convinced the commandos had been involved in the ambush of the hospital ambulance that had killed Manuel months before. Someone said the perpetrators had been summarily executed, but others speculated that this was only wishful thinking. I didn't find either thought very comforting. One of our local friends told us that these troops were recruited from another ethnic group, so had less respect for the people of Bié. UNITA traditionally garnered support amongst the Ovimbundu, the dominant ethnic group of the central highlands, while the government heartland was with the Mbundu people, closer to Luanda. People rarely discussed politics, but some alluded privately that Kuito was once loyal to UNITA, opposing the MPLA's short-lived communist leanings. But no one believed in anything anymore. Angola's war could no longer be simply defined as an ethno-regional conflict. Long devoid of ideology the war had become single-mindedly focused on the determination of opposing leaders to assume absolute power. As the political ideology of both sides lurched from one extreme to the other, their obsession with domination remained undiminished. As for the intimidated population, all that remained was steadfast skepticism about prospects for peace.

Trouble at this time of the year was to be expected as the holiday marked the fortieth anniversary of the Anti-Colonial Independence War. Angola's three main nationalist movements (MPLA, FNLA, and UNITA) were founded in the 1950s and 1960s among the different ethno-linguistic groups. The MPLA, established in 1956 amongst the Mbundu and some *mestiço* intellectuals, claims February 4, 1961, as the beginning of its war for liberation, hence the national holiday. On that day, several hundred Angolans, armed with little more than knives and clubs, launched an attack on a jail in Luanda to free imprisoned comrades. They suffered heavy casualties: some forty were killed, sparking further riots. The administration retaliated with summary executions, inciting further vigilante attacks. In the end about three thousand died and thousands more were wounded. For this reason they are remembered in the Angolan National Anthem as "os heróis do quatro de fevereiro"—the heroes of February 4.

During our short stay in Angola we witnessed two significant anniversaries of events that defined the country's modern history: the twenty-fifth anniversary of Independence and the fortieth anniversary of the Anti-Colonial War. But the majority had little to celebrate. There was apparently a ceremony in Kuito, but we weren't allowed to move around in case of further skirmishes. As with most national holidays, this one seemed to generate little spontaneous enthusiasm, except for the days off.

Surprisingly too, on completing our mission, we encountered some interesting reactions, based on misconceptions of colonial history. Some people yearned idealistically—almost romantically—for the grandeur of the colonial past. This was demonstrated by a comment from an elderly gentleman who tottered up to us at the end of a presentation after our return.

"Thank you," he said. "Thank you both so much for such an interesting talk. But tell me..." he said, as if wallowing in nostalgia. "Don't you think they were better off under colonial rule?"

I must have bristled. After all, our presentation was not a debate about the merits of colonialism, but an exposé of life for average Angolans in today's world.

"Well sir," I replied with a warm, gentle smile. "That depends on your view of the slave trade." He turned and tottered off, absorbing the implications of it all, his mouth in motion but inaudible.

But my reply ignored the distinct phases of Angola's evolution. Apart from a brief interlude of Dutch colonial rule between 1641 and 1648, Angola was a Portuguese colony for more than four hundred seventy-five years, longer than Macao.[35] For around three hundred fifty of those years, up to the mid-1800s, over three million slaves were exported from Angola's shores to the New World. They went mainly to Brazil and Cuba, but also to the US. Benguela and Luanda were the main ports for this odious enterprise, which, over time, involved every major maritime nation of Europe: Portugal, England, France, Denmark, and Spain, in addition to Brazil and the US.[36] Underscoring this figure is an additional number of those who died because of maltreatment and disease and some who were reportedly enslaved on their own native soil. Only in Angola did European military forces play an important role in the capture and enslavement of the local populace. The military and commercial slave traders were based on the coast. They made frequent raids on the plateau, capturing thousands of Ovimbundu people for transportation. By the 1800s, some Ovimbundu had been coerced into the trade. Forming huge caravans they became some of Africa's greatest traders, journeying across the country, dealing in slaves, ivory, wax, and rubber.

Preoccupied with lucrative human trafficking, Angola itself recorded little economic progress. Besides, Brazil was the favoured colony until its independence from Portugal in 1822. During this extended period, Portugal made little attempt to settle Angola. Instead it satisfied itself with a pattern of exploitation that persisted into the early twentieth century. But as the slave trade had become outlawed in much of the Americas by the 1860s there were sporadic movements for Portugal to formally abandon Angola. Although it was Europe's earliest colonial power in Africa, firm governance was at best episodic. The administration failed to invest enough in education and infrastructure: basics for economic development. It also failed to control the rugged interior, which held little interest.

Portuguese settler families started to trickle into Angola around the late 1800s. They were not attracted in large numbers, however, until the 1950s. By then Portugal had become a poor country under a brutal fascist rule. Most of the settlers came from peasant stock, many from the islands of Madeira and the Azores. Some even competed with the local populace for jobs in the booming coffee industry. The collapse of coffee prices in the 1960s unsettled the country, leading to anti-colonial revolts. The war for independence ensued. And when it happened, the ultimate turning point in Angola's history came from Lisbon, in the form of a military coup against the Salazar regime in 1974. This crisis (well after the Anti-Colonial Wars had begun) was the most important factor leading to the ultimate demise of Portuguese colonial rule for Angola, Mozambique, and Guinea-Bissau.

Portugal finally withdrew in 1975. Although reprisals by locals were limited, concern for the settlers' futures in the new Angola led to a scrambled mass evacuation of almost the entire settler population. Most of the technically educated left, undermining what remained of the fledgling economy and rudimentary social services. As the economy nose-dived, various factions fought for total control. Some settlers remained defiant and refused to leave their beloved homeland for a Portugal they never knew. But by the late 1970s most had succumbed to the realization that Angola teetered on the brink and drifted away.

> Angola avante revolução, pelo poder popular,
> pátria unida liberdade, um só povo uma só nação.
> (Angola advance the revolution, through people power,
> unified free homeland, one people, one nation)
> — Angolan national anthem

Ruins of Kuito cathedral.

Chapter 52
Peace in a Civil War

Karin continues...

Four new team members arrived in late February and along with them, dozens of parcels. Mail dating back to early November was finally delivered, so Christmas came to Kuito a little later than usual, but it was just as exciting. We all sat on the steps of *Casa Dois*, laughing and chatting as we opened our packages from home. Between us we received Christmas decorations including tinsel, streamers, and balloons, as well as presents and sweets. Wei and I received six parcels including two videos of the 2000 Sydney Olympic Games from my brother, Lloyd. We suggested film night at *Casa Um* and everyone was excited. Someone even admitted to hoarding a stash of popcorn, so we marked the occasion with a special treat.

Brook, Anna, and two Danish training nurses, Lone and Helle, were the couriers of these belated treats and news from home. Brook was a doctor of Ethiopian origins who had arrived along with our new hospital coordinator, Anna. She was British of Polish heritage and had grown up in Brazil, explaining her astonishing fluency in Portuguese. We were all green with envy from her linguistic prowess. Her sense of humour was immediately evident, and, given that we had been without a hospital coordinator for months, we were delighted to have Anna on board. In fact, their arrival made us aware that our own time in Kuito was coming to an end. Such was the strange mechanism of volunteering. Everyone's "End of Mission" date crept up and, one by one, the team started to change. The dynamics shifted a little each time and while it was always nice to welcome new members, old friends were sorely missed. Around this time we learned that our own replacements had been identified, although Wei's wouldn't arrive until early April. But even that was just eight weeks away.

At about this time, we also ran out of propane gas. We rolled technology back two thousand years and resorted to environmentally unfriendly charcoal. I managed to kindle a reluctant fire some days, but it wasn't easy. Don't even think of char-grilled steak or roasted coffee. Steaks were but a fantasy and the only romance I found in the coffee I made over the coals was the novelty of doing it. But that soon wore off. However, this is not a complaint about the privations of life, as by then we revelled in our new lifestyle. The weather was pleasant and although each day was as unpredictable as the last, we had slid into a certain rhythm. You could start a day in a wool sweater, be sweating by mid-morning, get sunburnt walking home at lunchtime, drenched by torrential flooding rains on the return, and end the day with three blankets at bedtime. The Tropics at 1,600 metres was that sort of place.

If I were to close my eyes and peel away the images of the traumatized and the suffering, I felt an emerging primordial love for Kuito. They say Africa really gets into your blood and you never want to leave and I was sensing just that. Perhaps it was because Africa reminded me of Australia. Perhaps it was that sense of ruggedness that I found so appealing—an environment rough around the edges; our own vulnerability pitched against a hardy landscape.

After years in Hong Kong it was striking how easy it was to accustom ourselves to a slower-paced life. Above all, Wei and I enjoyed quality time together: doing simple things like reading, chatting, writing, and (when the power permitted) listening to music. We actually had time to sit on the grass and peruse out-of-date news or a book. How rare it is in life today to find this sort of time to indulge in simple pleasures occluded by contemporary lifestyles.

Strangely, life was tranquil there…well except for those lively *festas*. Not being party people, it was a surprise to us just how often we attended *festas* in Kuito. Although they became a part of our life there, they could be a tad tiresome: same faces, same music, even the same dance. Inger's farewell was in February. Having skilfully avoided dancing until then, I was forced for the first time to learn the *Kuzamba*, a samba-style dance. Without exception, it was the only dance for parties. That night, a young man caught me off guard and adeptly whisked me onto the dance floor, and, before I knew it, I was learning my first steps. I venture to add that the *Kuzamba* is a very close dance. Vertical expression of a horizontal desire[37] is a fitting description, but that has already been attributed to the tango.

But *festas* aside, with a relentless around-the-clock roster, life in

Kuito could easily have resembled more of the same Hong Kong scramble. Looking back I often wonder how we endured those Hong Kong years when Wei's hospital schedule ruled our life, like a ship anchored to the ocean floor. Somehow, the pressures in Kuito were different. Life back home had blurred into a series of obligations and time-devouring commitments. But in Kuito, Wei was energized by his new surroundings. He worked as hard as ever, but it was a different kind of stress. He was challenged by the enormous variety of cases presented: people in need of things as simple as a life-saving lance to an abscess or as rare and complicated as eclampsia. Wei was invariably tired, but thrived on the team spirit with renewed purpose. Work became an adrenalin rush.

I also enjoyed a job without the pressures and stress of the commercial world, not that I shirked either. And for someone whose days were once defined by the indulgent, somewhat whimsical, world of ice cream, I became immensely interested in Wei's work. I took to reading about the various conditions he encountered when textbooks lay open around the house. I also had the opportunity to see him in action, demystifying parts of the hospital that had previously been inaccessible. I marvelled at the way he was so disarming, especially with children. His manner transcended words, and in the stressful environment of the operating theatre, I saw his inherently calm nature cast a spell during intense moments.

The pressure on aid workers was dramatically different. While there is no doubt that we were not as efficient as a well-oiled corporate machine, the environment had a lot to do with that. I found it both refreshing and fascinating.

As the months rolled on I contemplated the collage of life. I know it sounds crazy, but Wei and I found a certain peace in Kuito: peace in a civil war. And for all my foreboding about what life would be like in a combat zone, perhaps our most curious discovery was the way people brimmed with life. It was a life of ebullient colours, gaggles of laughter, and dancing that never seemed to stop. There was harmony and rhythm without end. It was the spontaneity of welcoming smiles from traumatized strangers living in limbo. Toiling in impossible conditions, no one cowered from death. As if imbued with a sense of purpose, life still ambled along. It was this very zest for life with all its energy set against a backdrop of decay that made us want to go on hoping. Their soul-quenching determination, their patience, and their dignity were nothing short of inspiring. At that time I was not sure where life would take us beyond Kuito, but quite frankly, I was scared our months there would not last long enough. In Kuito we were where we wanted to be, doing what we wanted to do, and doing it together. In the evening stillness at the end of long days, we often felt a warm sense of satisfaction: a contentment that transcended everything.

Karin and Wei in front of Casa Quatro.

Chapter 53
Awash with Arms

Karin writes…

My initial perception of war was mingled with stereotypes gleaned from the media and movies. After all, I come from a generation that has never seen war. Before arriving in Angola, I envisaged bloody battles of front line fighting, tanks, and heavy weaponry. By extension, I thought war surgery involved treating those wounded in the line of duty: green fatigues, the battle hardened. I feared for Wei as a war surgeon…to be honest, it scared me senseless. Although I say it with the innocence of one who discovered things from the fringes, I learned—and quickly—that there was another equally ugly side to war. From my vantage point, I was struck by three singular phenomena: the impact when a country becomes awash with arms, the spiritual desolation, and the role of alcohol.

I remember the shock when I discovered the first and last. It was towards the end of an otherwise agreeable weekend. We had been to our neighbour Ranjit's house, for drinks that afternoon. Ranjit was a friendly fellow from Goa, India who was the head of WFP in Kuito. He had taught his maid to cook the most mouth-watering Indian cuisine that was, without doubt, the most scrumptious food in town. Blissfully satisfied, we drove over to join the team at *Casa Um*. We were chatting and laughing in the garden, enjoying a calm evening. Stars sparkled in an inky sky—an immense canopy that spanned the distant horizon. Wei was beginning to unwind and soak up the atmosphere. Suddenly one of his assistants burst out of the darkness. The hospital ambulance was waiting beyond the fence. Within moments, Wei was gone and the party atmosphere evaporated in an instant. I went home to an empty house and lay in bed, listless. I stared up through the mosquito netting and awaited Wei's return.

It must have been after 3 a.m. when he finally slunk into bed, tired and demoralized. He had spent the night trying to stitch together the remnants of a family. The father, a policeman, had attacked his family in drunken rage. A beautiful toddler, her sister, and their mother had all been shot. The mother and toddler died. This wasn't exactly war surgery, but the family was a victim of it all the same. The gun-toting police that patrolled the streets by day went home to the suburbs with their guns at night. Military patrols were on the streets in the evening and everyone lived on edge. There were weapons everywhere. Top this up with alcohol and you had a volatile combination—a savage side effect of war. Years of endless war ultimately broke the spirit; an insidious problem that resulted in other more observable ones and underscored them.

In another incident, a soldier was rushed into the *Banco de Urgência* on a stretcher. A bullet had penetrated his heart. The bulky soldier was of peak fitness, which increased his chances of survival. However, his breathing was laboured and he reeked of alcohol.

"Get him to the operating theatre immediately!" Wei shouted, as he prepared himself mentally for the task of open-heart surgery in rudimentary conditions.

Wei mustered a posse of men who heaved the stretcher off the floor. They felt the full impact of the 120-kilo load as they struggled awkwardly down the stairs. Straining under his weight, they shuffled quickly across the dusty compound, when the soldier took his last gasps and died. Wei felt the all-too-frequent thud of defeat, a sense that lingered until he learned that the soldier had shot himself. In a multiple murder suicide, he first killed his young wife and then his own children. Another case of domestic violence played out between the real battles.

Around town, the commandos were feared not for their hardened battle skills but for their hardened appetite for liquor. I quickly learned to fear the bottle as much as guns. Inebriated, soldiers once threatened the guards at the house of the HALO Trust with hand grenades to get inside, drink, and loot. Pillaging was a big business. Many locals drank a crude, cheap brew of distilled sweet potato, maize, or fruits (called owalende), which rendered them absolutely blotto. Drunk, dangerously drunk! Add a gun and all hell broke loose. We often heard the wild pop, pop, pop of shooting at night and it didn't take long to realize that our greatest risk was not stepping on landmines or being caught in the crossfire from a military assault, but being attacked by an armed drunkard—intoxicated and lethal.

With the war dragging on and their spirits crushed, the unemployed had little reason to hope. "Alcohol is the anaesthesia by which we endure the operation of life."[38] Booze dulls the mind. Drunkards staggered incoherently around town, their eyes the colour of blood oranges. They had nothing to do but while away days of emptiness. Through alcohol-induced oblivion, one day morphed into the next.

I was walking back to the office after lunch at *Casa Dois* some time in February when I saw a drunk stumbling down the street. I attempted to cross to the other side, but it was too late. This very movement ignited his interest and I became a walking beacon. He was upon me within moments and grabbed angrily at my bag. A silly instinct made me pull back in self-defence, as if to guard my worthless possessions. In so doing I unleashed his aggression. There in the middle of the road in blazing sunshine, he lurched forward tearing wantonly at my clothes, grunting incoherently. His breath was thick with the raw odour of rough booze. Suddenly I froze, fearing he had a gun in his ruffled trousers. He swung his arms like a rag doll, launching his limbs at me with all his strength. I let out a shrill scream! Within seconds my rescuers came running from all directions. These angelic townsfolk lunged at him and ushered me to safety, pushing the drunkard on his way. He staggered off.

While that encounter was over almost as quickly as it started, another seemed to last an eternity. After an evening in the operating theatre, Wei and I were intoxicated, not by alcohol, but by the romantic moonlight. It was a clear night and the milky moon glowed to the size of a dinner plate. So balmy was the evening air that we decided on impulse to walk the short distance back home. A pleasant hush had come over Kuito as we stepped out into the still warm air, hugging each other tightly. Arm in arm, we strolled through the hospital compound and into the street. We passed a lone eucalyptus tree that stood imposingly, a wistful reminder of home. Our discourse was peppered with soft laughter as we soaked up the magic of the moment. On passing the second house in the street a voice cut through the quiet. It was an angry voice and one that made us intuitively quicken our pace.

"Just ignore him!" Wei implored, as the stranger called once more.

By now we were directly in front of the house and had to pass his gate. A bulky, dark shadow emerged and it was enough to tell us about his inebriated state. He hurled words incoherently, but his hostility was palpable. My heartbeat shifted into top gear. I tried to suppress my urge to panic and pleaded with Wei to walk faster. I made a beeline for home.

"Don't run!" Wei whispered sharply. I tried to contain my urge to bolt. "He might have a gun!"

Until then it hadn't occurred to me, but from then on it was one of those ineffable situations, like an awful recurring dream where you want to run faster but can't. The drunkard lunged out from behind the bushes and pursued us. Through his shadow we were convinced he had something in his hands and I felt the skin between my shoulder blades go taut with raw, unadulterated fear. I could hear the muffled breathing as our assailant started gaining. Fear poured into us. It sat like a cold stone in my mouth. Wei's controlled steps seemed like no more than a dawdle and my paranoia welled. I waited for the crack of a gunshot to pierce the night. My heart was crashing against my chest, thundering like waves against a rock wall.

Without drawing breath I reached the corner first, having broken three steps ahead of Wei. We wanted to sprint, but were still frozen by fear of the reaction we would provoke. Then we heard him stumble, followed by a heavy thud, but didn't turn back to look. By now I was riven with self-contempt. Rule number one: Never walk at night! We knew that, so why did we take the risk? Miraculously we made it round the corner to home and lived to laugh about it later. Our drunken neighbour had become another victim of the infamous Kuito sidewalks. The pavements were hazardous at the best of times, but in the dark they were an accident waiting to happen. I was never so glad of those gaping holes.

But our stories were piffling compared to the brutality endured by ordinary citizens, which is why we were sickened when in late December 2000, we read how the son of the late French President François Mitterrand had become embroiled in a scandal of trafficking arms to Angola. Jean-Christophe Mitterrand was the African adviser to his father from 1986 to 1992. Nicknamed "Papa-m'a-dit" (Daddy told me), he was also criticized for conducting France's African policy in an environment of excessive secrecy. Allegations about illegal arms sales and corruption in Angola had dogged France's political administration since 1997. Jean-Christophe allegedly received payments, into Swiss bank accounts, as recently as 1998, just as war resumed in Angola.

After more than forty years of war, no one knew how many arms were circulating within Angola. Illicit and conventional procurements kept weaponry flowing from willing and covert suppliers in Eastern Europe and beyond. The main supply lines to the opposition UNITA forces were reportedly managed by nationals of Belgium, France, Portugal, Lebanon, and South Africa, with the majority of supplies coming from the Ukraine. To take one year as an example, in 1999 the Angolan government earmarked the largest part of US$5.1 billion, no less than forty-one percent of the general state budget, for defence and civil order.[39] Yet at just US$6, an AK-47 was almost as affordable as a nutritious meal.[40]

By 2002 Angola was also one of an elite group of fifteen countries that was subject to Article 41 of the UN Charter[41] allowing the Security Council to call on member states to apply sanctions. The list of resolutions on Angola read like the till receipt from a supermarket checkout. Resolution 864 of September 1993 imposed an oil and arms embargo on UNITA. It was followed by resolutions 1127 and 1130; then by 1135, 1149, 1157, and 1164. In June 1998 resolution 1173 decreed that all states should take the necessary measures to prohibit the importation of uncontrolled diamonds from Angola, the so-called "dirty diamonds." This resolution was followed closely by yet more resolutions that tried to trace violations. Finally on April 18, 2000, the Security Council unanimously adopted resolution 1295 to investigate violations of the Council's previous sanctions.

As the net widened, the fish became more slippery. Weapons spilled over the borders from neighbouring conflicts and circulated virtually uncontrolled. Yet consider this: the equivalent of one day's global arms expenditure would more than meet the annual investment needs of the agriculture sector in Africa today. Only a modest investment in seed and tools would be required to avert the need for emergency food aid.

Abandoned tank in suburban Kuito.

Chapter 54
Chez Augusto

Wei takes up the story...

One day in mid-March Karin and I were honoured with an invitation to Augusto Silivondela's home for Saturday lunch.

His house, about two twisting kilometres from ours, was difficult to find without local knowledge. Even though I had been there before, I was very relieved when he insisted on picking us up. He led us through the maze of rutted streets and crooked lanes that defined suburban Kuito. A pall of lead-grey clouds hung overhead and drizzled intermittently, ensuring the mud was slippery underfoot. We passed a house that had been reduced to a pile of rubble, prompting me to think of poor Bento. He had been late to work the day before because his grandfather was killed when the house collapsed on top of him. I was surprised he came at all, but such was the dedication of my team. The collapse of an adobe house was not unusual. Misshapen residences were a feature of the rainy season. For months the orthopedic ward had been filling up with patients who sustained fractures when their mud homes disintegrated after heavy downpours.

We pushed on past the rubble, past the gutted flourmill and into Augusto's neighbourhood. I didn't recognize it at first. With the arrival of the wet, everything looked so different from the crackling September day when I first visited. In those days, Augusto was delighted just to accompany me on a jog around town, but the novelty soon wore off. Back then we jogged to his home so he could proudly show me his abode. He had recently completed it for his aging parents and young family. A well-manicured pathway lined with stones led up to the door of the modest mud construction. Even back then, it was deserving of hearty admiration. He had also bought a shiny new bicycle, but soon learned that this attracted more attention than it was worth. The police often stopped him and demanded fines, claiming an infringement of one vague law or another.

Although I didn't realize it at the time, Augusto's fortunes changed considerably once I arrived in Kuito. He still taught a few hours of English at a local school, but my constant need for a translator—firstly for Portuguese and then for Umbundu—guaranteed him an uninterrupted stream of work. He was surely one of the better-paid individuals around town, earning $6 a day and feeling eternally indebted to my linguistic ineptitude. He wanted to show me the home improvements that were enabled by the fruits of his labour for me—he had been badgering me for weeks to come and visit again. Unfortunately, life at the hospital always seemed to get in the way.

We hadn't seen Augusto's family since they came to our place to celebrate International Women's Day. Life in surgery was demanding and I really appreciated the commitment of the wives, so Karin and I hosted a party to acknowledge them. I have often wondered why this auspicious occasion is rarely acknowledged in the West. International Women's Day was always a special event in China, so I was pleased to see that Angola publicly recognized the contribution of women to society with a holiday—a connection to their socialist past no doubt. Mao used to say: "Women hold up half the sky," and I wholeheartedly agree. I helped Karin prepare a slap-up meal, but could never surpass her culinary skills. It was a veritable feast, despite the limited ingredients and utensils. At first everyone was quietly restrained, but as the afternoon drew on the true Angolan spirit sparkled.

Upon arriving at Augusto's house everyone was there to greet us, dressed in their Sunday best. Grandpa sported a baggy, grey suit, tie, and bright white jogging shoes. Grandma, once my barefoot patient, had new black shoes. We were guided through the four-roomed house. It was impeccably, if not simply, furnished. The living room was adorned with several displays of empty soft drink cans, neatly arranged in small stacks mounted on special niches in each corner. A portable stereo with detachable speakers was wrapped in cloth and positioned on a roughly hewn sideboard. Augusto proudly unveiled it and marked the occasion by playing some music. I asked with genuine curiosity why he had forgotten to connect one of the speakers, wherein he explained that the battery would run out too quickly if he connected both simultaneously. There was no electricity and even the poorest quality batteries were expensive. I felt embarrassed by my own city-bred assumptions. It also forced me to reflect on the same sense of pride I felt as a young child nestled next to a crystal-set radio as I secretly tuned in to *Voice of America* during the height of the Cultural Revolution. Scratchy as the reception was, it was exhilarating to listen to my first words of English on the magical technology that fascinated my curiosity beyond comprehension.

Augusto's wife, Elisa Raquel had prepared a delicious meal with eggplant, chicken, and maize *funge*. Karin and I shared a small glass of soft drink, which they had bought especially for the occasion. Knowing how expensive they were, we were hesitant to partake, but Augusto was insistent and we didn't want to disappoint. This was no ordinary meal. Prices for chicken had been spiralling in the market and Karin calculated that the meal would have cost about US$12, the equivalent of Elisa's weekly pay. We were genuinely humbled by their generous hospitality.

After the meal we sat in the backyard and met neighbours and members of the extended family. Karin showed the children how to play with the toys we had brought. And all the while, Grandpa sat in the shade of a nearby tree, smiling broadly as he observed the theatre before him.

I have no idea how he found me, but before long Eduardo arrived in the ambulance with news that more wounded had arrived. We had just enough time for a family photograph as they assembled to wave goodbye and we were off. It was the most memorable of meals.

The wives together on International Women's Day, Casa Quatro.

Augusto's family including Augusto's father (second from left), Augusto (third from left), and his mother (fourth from left). Augusto's wife, Elisa Raquel (far right) holding baby Berit.

Chapter 55
Disaster Dawns

Karin writes…

Luanda was an awful place. When we were away from it, we all talked about how awful it was. When we went back for another visit, we braced ourselves for its awfulness. Imagine the debris that a flooded river leaves after the water recedes; when branches and rubbish have been washed downstream for miles and ungraciously dumped, snarled and twisted, in one chaotic mess. That was modern-day Luanda. It was as if the whole country had drained into one city, which was not far from reality. I shouldn't blame Luanda as the city was a victim of the endless war. It was seething with the homeless and displaced, swollen by hundreds of thousands who had escaped the misery upcountry to settle in the safety of a lesser misery. At independence, Luanda was home to 500,000 people. By the time the war had ended the population was close to four million—over thirty percent of the country's population. However, the infrastructure was limited to the pre-independence "concrete city": home to the more affluent sector of society. Vast and densely built shantytowns, known as *musseques*, surrounded the downtown, and the *musseques* were overflowing.

In the wet season Luanda was steamy hot, something akin to Hong Kong in July but with no chance of escape to into air-conditioned comfort. Luanda was just oppressive—day and night. We went to Luanda on February 21. Looking back at some of my correspondence from this time, I talked of a "pleasant break in Luanda." Perhaps I was stretching the facts, trying to smother worry with cheer. I cannot remember much about our visit except for the anxiety. I wrote of hearing the constant drone of military aircraft as we arrived. They were laden with troops destined for Kinshasa in neighbouring Congo to help stabilize the capital following the death of President Kabila. We also met up with friends at the Dutch consulate and I described it as a very social time. But in reality our visit to Luanda was for unpleasant reasons. Outwardly confident but secretly scared, we were taking a three-day break to collect the results of a blood test; the last in the protracted process to confirm whether Wei had been accidentally infected with HIV.

HIV is always a concern for MSF volunteers, especially in Africa. Nearby countries like South Africa and Botswana lay at the heart of this cataclysm. Not limited to specific high-risk groups, nor properly controlled, AIDS now blights the lives of more than thirty million people in sub-Saharan Africa alone. Health workers, particularly surgical staff working in rudimentary conditions, face considerable risks. Although Wei rarely voiced his reservations, Angola's HIV infection rate was one of the first things I asked about when we discussed our impending mission. Having just read about the tragedy of nearby Botswana, where a shocking thirty-nine percent of adults are HIV positive, it was with a sense of disbelief that I learned of Angola's claim of infection rates as low as 3.4 percent.[42]

Wei was always more positive, quietly admitting that it was a risk for a surgeon, albeit a small one. When I persisted, he mocked me lovingly with statements like "So, what are we going to do? Sit at home for the rest of our lives to ensure we are safe?" His scientific mind eventually won over my emotional concerns and I accepted that the risks of contracting malaria or stepping on a landmine were possibly greater than contracting HIV through surgery. Eventually I put the fear of AIDS aside, but it was never far from my thoughts.

I also remember the day of Wei's surgical accident as vividly as if it were yesterday. He came wandering into the study at *Casa Quatro*. It was lunchtime on a Tuesday in late November. I was lying on the sunken bed in the spare room, immersed in some mail from home.

"Guess what happened at work today?" he said in a nonchalant tone that masked his true concern. It was a rhetorical question that he answered in the next breath. "One of my staff dropped an instrument on me." It sounded innocent enough and I wasn't sure how I was supposed to react, so waited for Wei to take the lead.

"I had my hand in the patient's abdominal cavity. My surgical glove was covered in blood and then the instrument cut right through!" he explained, pointing to an innocuous cut in his middle finger. In any other circumstances the conversation would have sounded trivial but the seriousness of the situation soon sunk in.

Wei didn't want to overreact, but protocol required him to report it to Bertrand, the doctor in charge of health for volunteers at the time. The next few hours passed in a whirlwind. An official assessment determined the risk of infection to be "moderate." This was higher than I had expected but mainly because the patient on whom Wei had been operating was suffering from tuberculosis (TB). TB isn't AIDS, I reassured myself, but Wei explained that an AIDS patient is more vulnerable to TB, so the two diseases often occur concurrently. In Angola, TB is rife and it was estimated that at least twenty-two percent of these patients were also infected with HIV.[43]

Although Wei considered the risk to be low, he anguished over what to do. In the end he chose to be conservative and followed the protocol: an immediate course of AZT. It was a precautionary measure, he explained, but declined the more standard option of evacuation to Belgium. I was outwardly supportive, yet secretly shell-shocked! I don't remember the rest of the day, but somehow managed to go back to the office and focus on my work. When news of the accident ricocheted its way through the team, everyone around me seemed to whisper, as if quietly respecting the privacy of the afflicted. No one was supposed to know. Everyone did. In reality we all knew it was our worst fear realized through a fellow colleague's misfortune.

If taken within hours of a suspected infection, AZT can significantly cut the rate of infection. But it is an aggressive drug that needs constant monitoring and no drug is without side effects. AZT's included nausea, headaches, insomnia, vomiting, diarrhea, and muscle soreness. Wei was soon suffering from nausea, sleeplessness, and constant lethargy. More disturbing still, he began to lose weight.

On December 13, careful not to raise the alarm, I wrote to my mother, a clinical dietician.

"Mum, can you give us some ideas on how to increase the protein in our diet? Wei is losing weight quite rapidly. I am a little worried, but he insists he is OK. He thinks it is just the change of diet, which is much lower in fat and protein. We can buy meat, but I don't like cooking it, as it is so tough. We can get some beans and we eat them once or twice a week. There is an abundance of tomatoes, onions, and avocadoes, but no soy. Our diet consists mainly of vegetables and carbohydrates like pasta, rice, and corn meal. Any suggestions?"

Mum wrote back with various ideas, all of which I tried, but Wei continued to waste. He persisted with AZT for a while, but the drug really knocked him around. He was finding it difficult to keep up the pace in the operating theatre and was constantly drained. In the end he became more concerned about the effect of the drug on his health, especially in that unmonitored environment, than with the risk of AIDS itself. By this time the first test had come back negative, so together we took the bold decision to abandon the medication and hope for the best. Wei remained calm, composed: my rock, my strength. He spoke logically, borrowing heavily from medical statistics. He talked of odds and of the two tortuous months we still had to tread together in the middle of nowhere until we could be certain of the outcome. With Wei snuggled up beside me in deep slumber I used to lie awake those first weeks, galvanized by fear, imagining how our lives would change if he tested positive. I could not imagine life without my darling.

The weeks passed slowly. I fretted about Wei's health, but did my best to maintain a cheery disposition. Evenings alone at home were hardest. Wei was always in the operating theatre, giving my brain plenty of time to churn. Images of Wei's father played heavily on my mind. I was convinced he thought that I had instigated this adventure and enticed his beloved son away from a successful career. And for what? This? I remembered the family's reaction with clarity.

"But why?" Wei's father asked, exasperated. "Why Africa?"

"I can't believe that you would give up your job," added his brother incredulously.

But they also knew that for more than ten years, weekends had blurred into workdays and Wei had been constantly on-call. The demands of his schedule compromised the essence of life. Still, I knew that if anything happened in Angola Wei's family would never forgive me. Fear and dark thoughts, tinged with regret, regularly gripped me. I wandered through memories of our visit to Jié Yáng county and the ancestral hometown of the Cheng family, in the heart of rolling farmlands of northern Guangdong. I was spellbound as we explored the village steeped in the history of the early Ming dynasty. We soaked up the warm hospitality of the Cheng clan before we paid homage to the ancestors. I lit incense at the ancient matriarchal tomb, marked by a pile of ancient stones. It was a plain, unremarkable grave set among hundreds of tombstones that dotted the hillside. It had been there for five hundred years and I felt humbled as I approached to pay our respects. These images often came back to haunt me with an ethereal quality as we waited for these weeks to pass.

Slowly I developed a mechanism to push fears for Wei out of my mind. Twice over that three-month period Wei's blood samples were flown to Luanda for testing and once we flew in, so he could give blood in person. On that occasion we were en route to South Africa. The driver pulled up outside the clinic. It housed the only laboratory in Angola capable of reliably conducting the test. Nestled in middle-class suburbia, the oversized garage was clean and modern. The modest clinic belonged to a French oil company and was used exclusively for employees and their families. Wei and I balked at the irony of being treated at the clinic of the same company allegedly embroiled in corruption allegations. But it was this or certain evacuation to Belgium and a premature end to our time in Kuito. We had little option and were truly grateful for the service.

Each time we would wait anxiously for the results and throw ourselves ecstatically into each other's arms when they came back negative. But we also knew that nothing was certain until the third month. For confidentiality reasons the results of the final test had to be collected in person. On this occasion we had to see a doctor at the French embassy clinic in an exclusive neighbourhood. It was a hot sunny day and the warm tropical air was moist against my cheeks as we stepped out of the taxi. As we waited in the cool of the waiting room, Wei and I exchanged silly jokes in an effort to suppress our collective concerns. To our surprise the doctor was a young Vietnamese-Chinese who was keen to practice a few words of Mandarin. His relaxed demeanour calmed the butterflies in my stomach as I braced myself for the final outcome.

"See...I told you so! Negative!" Wei claimed triumphantly. But his facial expression divulged deep relief as he wrapped his arms around me. It was a strong, loving hug that expunged the anxiety that had clouded our lives since November. Wei was lucky and now insists lightheartedly that we had overreacted. Brave words proffered in retrospect! How were we supposed to react?

However, I know for sure that in Angola AIDS is a disaster waiting to happen. Ironically the ongoing war impeded the disease's progress because all transport routes had collapsed. But as large numbers of people gravitated towards urban areas to escape the war, this hiatus has not lasted. The education and health care sectors are in an appalling state and AIDS awareness barely registers on the agenda.

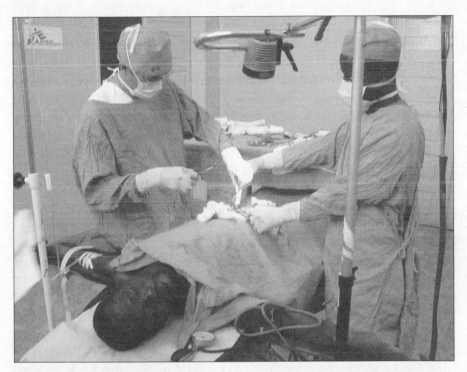

Wei in the operating theatre.

Chapter 56
Os Deslocados

Karin continues...

What transpired in late February will remain indelibly etched in my memory as one of the more moving images of Angola. We were out at the Kuito airstrip for the final farewell to Bertrand and Bérengère, the doctor-nurse couple that had been so much a part of our team's personality. We were all sad to see them go and everyone who could make it turned up for a final goodbye.

We stood on the tarmac as the cargo of drugs, essential supplies, and the team's long overdue food order was unloaded. We were hugging, kissing, and saying all those philosophical things one does on such occasions when Armando calmly remarked, "Ai, ai, ai! Ohla Karin. Olha lá. Deslocados! Muitos novos deslocados!" (Oh, oh, oh! Look Karin. Look there. Displaced! Many new displaced!) I couldn't tell whether genuine compassion lay behind his remarks, as he said it with that sigh of resignation one heard so often...as if to say, "And here comes another lot."

I turned to look in that direction, through the heavily guarded gates of *Aeroporto de Kuito*. And there, some one hundred metres further on, they marched on a thin, well-worn track along the airport perimeter. The area just beyond that narrow path was known to be mined and treacherous.

Os deslocados, the displaced, the dispossessed. In any other context, they would have been called refugees. But because these *deslocados* were stuck in the middle of central Angola, hundreds of kilometres from the nearest border, they were officially labelled Internally Displaced Persons. They remained unprotected by the UN convention for refugees until they crossed an international border. Physically unable to cross to safety, any way they went, they passed unnoticed by the world at large. Harangued by marauding armies, survival meant moving, yet they had nothing more than their bare feet to carry them. Since the conflict resumed in 1998 a further 2.6 million Angolans were displaced. In fact one-third of Angola's population was uprooted by the conflict, placing it second in the world to Sudan for the sheer numbers.

It was a long snake of humanity: bare-foot, single-file, and silent. They were all headed somewhere with apparent purpose. Women and children, a few men, more women, more children—one after another. There was no doubting they wore all the clothes they owned and carried the rest of their belongings atop their heads. Bundled together in dirty rags were their worldly possessions and basic essentials: cooking pots and charcoal. In addition to the head loads the women had infants strapped to their backs. Some carried old hand-woven baskets, uniquely woven in a style I had not seen in Kuito. Children carried water gourds and occasionally a farming tool.

We waved Bertrand and Bérengère goodbye and watched the plane take off into the vast blue skies before we piled into the Land Cruiser to head back to town. The road to the airstrip was long, straight, and undulating with one large dip that stretches out and rises again to the flats of Kuito. The *deslocados* marched silently along the right-hand side of the road. There was a stream of people as far as the eye could see. Negotiating the gaping potholes, we drove past slowly. The entire, normally animated, team was completely silenced by what we were witnessing. Motionless and mute, our eyes followed them.

Someone finally broke the silence with a silly joke about stopping to do a roadside MUAC screening for malnutrition. No one reacted. Our eyes were fixed in one direction, mesmerized by the quiet kinetic energy that propelled the *deslocados* forward. It was like watching an old sepia-coloured silent movie—all black and white with shades of brown-grey. It was a dull brown-grey set against the lush tropical vegetation, as if superimposed by some modern video technique.

Angolans are usually a very colourfully dressed people. But these *deslocados* were colourless. Everything was parched and faded—dirty beyond recognition. To use the word "filthy'" in English brings with it all the negative connotations of disgust, but here I am stuck with it, as I find no other word better suited to describe their condition. They were absolutely filthy. From head to toe they were the same colour. Weary, grey-brown, lifeless rags clung to weary, dusty, brown bodies. Dirty. Dusty. Filthy. Filthy dirty.

How can one not have the greatest admiration for the stoic women of Angola? It was they who fetched the water and carted it atop their heads. They carried the children, the wood, and the charcoal. They cultivated the fields, pounded the maize, and cooked the meals. They earned extra income by hawking home-grown vegetables from basins balanced on their heads. We brazenly talk of multitasking, but Angolan women made it an art form. And it was these same women who were forced to leave their husbands to struggle alone and to walk their families to safety. Women and children comprised the vast majority of Angola's displaced.

Christelle, the nurse who coordinated our nutrition project, had been in Angola the longest. She served in both Kuito and Luena. She told us that she had never seen anything like this. We radioed ahead to the UN OCHA office and encouraged Inácio to look out his window. But he already knew of their plight and was frantically trying to arrange a place for them to camp. By now they were already streaming through the main street of Kuito towards the camps on the other side of town. With them they carried their wounded and Wei received a small five-year-old boy who claimed that government troops shot him in the face. He had been scared and was merely trying to run away. The bullet penetrated his cheek and exited through his ear. Fortunately it was a fairly superficial wound, but his young brother was not so lucky. He was shot dead at close range by the same soldiers.

Later that day we learned that these people had been walking for six days, resting at night. Over one thousand arrived in two days. They came from the region near Umpulo about one hundred twenty kilometres southeast of Kuito. They had managed to cross two rivers. We also learned more about the government's *limpeza* campaign. Unable to thwart guerrilla warfare with conventional tactics the government was reportedly engaged in successive *limpeza*s. The local population was "encouraged" (forced) to move. Their crops were looted and destroyed. Houses were often burned. Nothing was left unscathed. This action was aimed at annihilating any means of support for UNITA soldiers. Slowly the countryside was emptied in the hope that Savimbi's men would be starved into submission. What happened to all the village men during these brutal raids remained unclear. Moreover, there were persistent reports of killing, looting, burning, and men forced to work as porters, participating unwillingly in the *limpeza* or worse. Who knows? Scared and with little time to prepare, the village elders, women, and children were herded off in the direction of government "safe zones." The government recommended Umpulo township, but with no food or medical care more than one thousand decided to head for Kuito while roughly three thousand stayed behind, many too weak or elderly to attempt the journey. While these new arrivals were dehydrated, they were not malnourished. They had been farmers but arrived without food, leaving their soon-to-be-harvested crops behind as rich pickings for one army or the other.

We received large numbers of IDPs at that time. More than twelve thousand arrived after the New Year, the direct result of these *limpezas*. The camps were stretched to bursting point and we moved into emergency mode. Tents were hastily pitched to accommodate the new arrivals in appalling wet weather. Together with the provincial government and other NGOs we busily prepared kits of essentials like soap, blankets, plastic sheeting, clothes, and cooking pots. Oxfam drilled for more water. The International Committee of the Red Cross and MSF dug more latrines. Diarrhea was a problem and scabies was rife. All the while, we endured torrential down pours turning the camps into quagmires. Yet every day, they continued to arrive—*muitos novos deslocados*.

Os deslocados at Chissindo camp.

Chapter 57
Hollow Eyes,
Diffident Expressions

Karin continues...

Wei called it desensitization—the way you stop seeing, stop noticing. He felt it was happening to him just two short months after he arrived and warned me about it. And how true it was. It wasn't long before I felt it was happening to me. I soon reached a point where I had stopped seeing in many ways. Everything became so normal.

I stopped being surprised by children in much-mended clothing held together with string, the battered shoes, and the bare feet. I stopped noticing the children toil at the communal water pump. That too became normal. Everywhere I looked, water was being carted on the heads of women and children. Small children were endowed with family responsibilities that others could not antici-pate for a further twenty years. Normal. I became accustomed to the appalling living conditions, the grinding poverty, and the everyday struggle of people aged beyond their years. The sickness and death, the wailing mothers with their hollow eyes and diffident expres-sions—normal. One day I passed an anguished man in the street as he cantered by with a wheelbarrow—his emaciated child curled up inside like a lifeless kitten. The front wheel wobbled as he navigat-ed the potholes and headed in the direction of the hospital. In a kind of languorous despair, I let him pass like any other, barely flinching at the gravity of his situation.

Even the police in their boiler-blue uniforms with their charcoal AK-47s slung lazily over their shoulders became altogether normal. The explosions that shook my office desk failed to evoke any sense of alarm. When I had arrived all these things heightened my sense of anxiety. Then they started to melt into the background with a sense of tired resignation. Perhaps desensitization is just a process of integration or maybe a defence mechanism that stops us from falling apart.

Amongst the throng, I didn't see the polio victim until he tugged at my shirttails while I was shopping in the market. I cast my eyes downwards and caught sight of his sooty face. His blackened outstretched claw defined his state of wretchedness. I slipped him a few Kwanzas and his eyes sparkled. He threw me a toothless grin before scrambling off through the dust, dragging his shrivelled limbs behind him. I watched as he negotiated his way through the forest of legs from where he viewed the world and, for a moment, he rattled my senses back into consciousness.

For a disease that has almost been eradicated worldwide, I found the victims of polio particularly woeful. There was a misshapen boy, perhaps ten years old, who lived not far from us. I often passed him in the street. He crawled sideways like a crab with such speed that at times I had trouble keeping up with him. He seemed completely oblivious to his misfortune. Fortune is relative, I guess, for in those surroundings he was just part of the fabric of normality. There were others who moved about in simple homemade wheelchairs pushed by able sons. Their tough encounters with the rubble sidewalks went unnoticed. Some ingeniously inverted bike frames, attached carts, and converted them into primitive wheelchairs. Using the pedals to hand-power their contraption, they gained some form of independence. I also often saw a boy leading his blind grandfather about the streets. Each held the opposite end of a stick, and, with the young boy in the lead, they negotiated the streets together. It was the most touching scene of filial piety I had ever witnessed.

But the most prolific were the amputees. You saw crutches on every street: a trouser leg tied in a knot where a knee should have been. I had never seen so many. Imagine the ones I couldn't see—the three hundred or so that the International Committee of the Red Cross fitted with artificial limbs every year in Kuito. They still limped but at least their debilitating handicap could be disguised under trousers or a long skirt. In another society we would have been outraged by these conditions. Yet there, out of sight, all this was no longer a story in the media sense of the word. I knew all about PR, but there were obviously more relevant media opportunities to be had elsewhere.

Wei's daily reports about his patients had also slowed and I had to coax the stories out of him. "Nothing unusual," he would report, before blithely rattling off a laundry list of appalling life stories. Shocking as they were, even these atrocities became everyday occurrences. One ordinary day Wei received a young boy who had been the victim of police brutality. After being spotted selling charcoal at a roadside stall he was stopped by two policemen who demanded money. "But I have none," the boy pleaded, clenching a few precious cents in his fist. Mercilessly, the policemen awarded his little white lie with a disability for life: a bullet to the hand, which Wei amputated the next morning.

Things like this were regularly reported in our Friday evening staff meetings at the office. It was a list of wanton destruction and killing that had swirled on around us. In the absence of news, we also exchanged rumours we had heard, as these were also valuable. I always watched the reaction of our local staff when we read the list of reported incidents. Week after week their reaction was the same—stone faces. They sat glumly in lethargic despair. No surprises. Little feedback. Nothing elicited a reaction. They had heard it all before. They were totally punch-drunk. Tired and fed up. How could they influence anything? What help was knowing? They couldn't escape and could do no more than look after their own families for another day.

As UNITA pushed further away from strategically important cities like Kuito, the tactics started to change. Attacks against civilians became more frequent and indiscriminate. The military objectives became more obtuse and the government forces responded in equal fashion. We often heard reports of soldiers raping civilian women. *Batidas* (a favoured military strategy that came to symbolize forced labour and pillaging) were on the increase. An unsuspecting village would suddenly become geographically important to one side or another. The mere presence of village residents was used as "evidence" of their support for the other side. Their act of betrayal was simply to stay at home.

The citizens of rural Angola suffered not only from continual deprivation, but were also forced to live in a perpetual state of acute anxiety. Escaping into the *mata* (bush) became their only means of survival. They were always hiding, on the move, often displaced more than once. Each arrival of IDPs brought more stories of attacks, killings, abduction, rape, looting, pillaging, torture, mutilation, villages burned. Unconscionable acts of brutality that exemplified the deliberate targeting of the civilian population by both sides.

Among all the patchwork of imagery that drifts through my mind one woman's face looms large. For me she captured the very essence of the daily struggle suffered by those around us. It was during my first weeks in Kuito, when I was still able to "see." I passed her on my way to work. She was in her twenties perhaps, although her face was chiselled by a hard life. A child, strapped to her body with a colourful cotton shawl, suckled from a saggy breast. It was food-on-the-move. Atop her head she balanced a laden basin, which was set against the blue sky. A plastic bag with a few vegetables hung from her bony fingers. She moved forward stealthily, clutching her crutches. She was also victim of a landmine: an above-knee amputee.

I never sent stories like this back home as they sounded too melancholy. But I recorded my feelings when I felt my powers of observation were being numbed. But it was also about this time that we were deeply touched by the actions of Hong Kong donors whose Chinese New Year greetings we received belatedly in the field. Two parcels arrived from the office of MSF Hong Kong containing over four hundred uplifting wishes and touching words of encouragement from donors. Children sent us drawings, poetry, and adages. Others sent words and music to a song. A teacher forwarded us a drawing by students of her slow learners' class. Two gentlemen wrote movingly about how they had always wanted to be doctors but couldn't realize their dreams and now lived them through Wei. People genuinely poured out their hearts.

Some have ventured to say that Hong Kong is too commercial and doesn't have a heart, but we beg to differ. We were deeply moved.

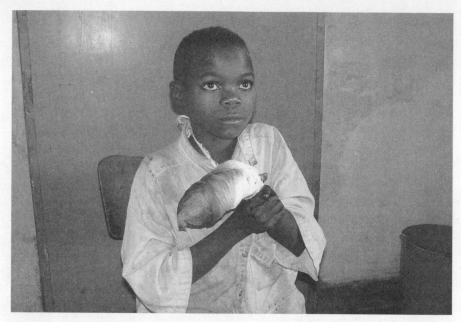

Young victim of police brutality, shot for a little white lie. Wei amputated his hand the next morning.

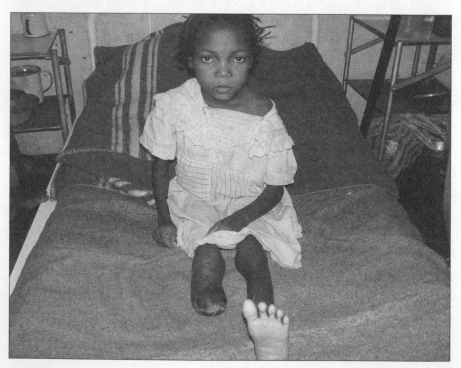

Hollow eyes...

Chapter 58
Carnaval de Kuito

Karin continues…

It was carnival, the holiday preceding Lent. The entire fabric of Kuito's society turned up to celebrate with all the vibrancy one would expect of carnival. Armed police mingled amongst wheelchairs, crutches, amputees, and groups of reluctant soldiers. Think not of the carnival in Rio de Janeiro, as *Carnaval de Kuito* was poles apart. It lacked the paraphernalia that goes with festivities elsewhere—there was no Coca-Cola sea of red, no balloons, no ice cream, or candy floss. There wasn't even much glitter as this was the poor man's carnival.

Groups of revellers assembled in the main street and danced rhythmically past the judge's podium, a simple lean-to erected in the town square. The dancers had made inventive skirts from grass or those infinitely versatile WFP corn sacks. Others daubed themselves with paint and crowned their heads with chicken feathers—a panoply of creativity. Like an ambulatory magnolia, Kuito's own incandescent Carmen Miranda glided by. She was resplendent in a mauve wraparound set against flawless ebony skin. A huge wicker basket brimming with a dazzling array of fruit was perched effortlessly on her head. Others danced alongside balancing huge gourds in apparent contempt for the laws of gravity. They danced with handwoven baskets laden with vegetables: sugar cane, cobs of corn, avocados, sweet potato, and pumpkins—all wishful symbols of abundance.

Others seeking to be elected kings and queens for the day turned to their basketry skills to create elaborate headdresses that crowned their vibrant faces. Cross-dressed men touted lumpy breasts and overstuffed bottoms. They pouted their lips and batted their eyelashes at passersby with exaggerated enthusiasm; quite a revelation in gay-shy Africa. I had read something of African soldiers and cross-dressing. Apparently some believed that by taking on the identity of another person (particularly a woman) they protect themselves from evil and shield themselves from bullets. There were others who thought their opponents would be frightened into believing that an evil spirit had overtaken the opposing forces and would run away in fear. But there in Kuito I was not sure whether this was the case. The carnival was a fascinating, eclectic mix of Christian, pagan, modern, and tribal traditions.

We stopped for a while to watch a group that had distinguished themselves with turbans woven from black plastic bags. They had tied them on their heads with jute and daubed their black skin with white paint. As they danced their grass skirts rustled to the rhythm of the papaya-seed rattles strapped to their ankles. Bent from the waist, faces towards the ground, their breasts swung like bell clappers around the drummer in a tribal trance. Crowds packed the footpaths and every possible vantage point. Dozens of children clung to high branches in every available tree, exhilarated by the fun. Others clambered atop the remnants of the gates of the provincial government. Like an hour hand at one o'clock the posts leaned precariously and a scene at *Banco de Urgência* flashed through my mind. Our role was hardly passive. We attracted an entourage of curious children, many of who followed us for the entire event. They were completely enthralled by the digital screen on our camera. I was beguiled by their naïveté and charmed by their innocence, a rare quality in today's overstimulated world. Their fascination clearly outweighed the desire to grab and run, even though I sensed their raw desire to behold, if just for a moment. The beady eyes of one admirer peered out from behind a homemade mask fashioned from a WFP oil can. Taking advantage of the sidewall's natural curvature the ingenious child had cut a mask with square eyes and martian ears. A bushy moustache completed the caricature. Every time I looked around, the masked boy was just two paces behind me. He followed us religiously for more than half an hour before melting into the crowd.

All of a sudden the children were running and screaming in mass hysteria. They streamed past us like an outgoing full moon tide. Perplexed to the point of alarm we turned in their direction to discover that the monster *Palhaço* had arrived. Looking like a mini haystack gliding by on two feet, *Palhaço* is a festive monster with a mystical reputation for scaring naughty children. We soon learned that the objective of the game was to taunt *Palhaço* and see who dared to get closest to the demon. As the taunting games began the euphoria of the day kicked up a notch. It continued like this all afternoon, eventually dissolving into smaller theatrical groups that entertained from house to house. We were utterly charmed.

Carnaval de Kuito.

Chapter 59
Nature's Way

Wei writes...

During my first weeks in Kuito, early September perhaps, I remember having my Portuguese lesson interrupted by a knock at the door. The hospital had sent the ambulance to fetch me for an urgent case. I went to *Banco de Urgência* where I saw a little nine-year-old girl, although she looked seven by Western nutritional standards. A soldier had apparently shot her in the chest the previous night. She had all the classical signs of shock: she was pale, breathing rapidly, and murmuring for water. She was literally dying of thirst. Her pulse was weak and rapid. We inserted a chest tube and a drip. The hospital had no blood, but she needed some badly. Her hemoglobin was only half the normal level, so we asked her father to test and donate. Although he had carried her from thirty kilometres away, he categorically refused.

"What kind of father is he?" I thought, in spontaneous rage. In those early days I didn't understand and had little time to find out what was going on. As she lingered on the threshold of death, her physical state became my obsession. We had no blood, and I could not find a suitable donor. What more could I do? I fretted about her and struggled to reconcile why a father who loved his daughter enough to carry her many kilometres through treacherous terrain would deny her life-saving blood. It didn't add up. Worried and confused, I wrote in my diary that I was not there to judge. I reminded myself that I could not apply my own logic to a society with no material wealth and little understanding of medical science. "After all," I rationalized, "life's priorities are moderated by one's environment. If you have something, you might be willing to donate, but if you have nothing how much can you afford to give away?"

In fact, my logic was wide of the mark. Finding blood was futile as the father continued to refuse. I later learned that it was the cultural belief of their people not to give or receive blood. Blood transfusion had never been practiced and, perhaps like traditional Chinese, these villagers believed any loss of blood by the donor compromised health. Yet, as if in defiance of modern medicine, his little daughter survived. The more she recovered the more awestruck I became. In another hospital, at another time, I would not have thought it possible. Stressful as it was I had been forced not to interfere and was left hoping. I watched my patient teeter on the abyss and finally she won. It was an exhilarating outcome.

With alternative medicine de rigueur in the Western world, I am often bemused by blanket assumptions that natural alternatives are always the best. To my mind there is still much to be learned. But pharmaceutical companies find little incentive to develop anything for backwaters like Kuito. In the absence of Western medicine people were forced to rely on natural herbal remedies as they had done for generations.

About a month or so after that first encounter with traditional beliefs a woman arrived with chronic mastitis compounded by a severe caustic burn. A poultice of natural herbs had been applied to her lactating breast to treat the mastitis. The herbs were so potent that they had burned through the entire thickness of the skin, denuding fifty percent of the breast tissue. It was a frightful sight. I never did discover the name of the herb she had used, but there was no doubting its potency. The surgery to remove the dead tissue was extensive and when complete I was faced with a real dilemma. While her breast required skin grafts, her newborn child needed to be fed. A lactating breast would prevent the skin graft from taking, and with no infant formula the operation would surely have caused the death of her child, so we could only help the skin to heal itself. The unadulterated pain this woman endured on each change of bandage was so excruciating that I could not bear to inflict it myself. Each day I asked her to assist in the dreadful process. Slowly…ever so slowly…her wound recovered and she and her baby were discharged.

Thankfully some treatments were more benign. Puzzled by the string tied around a lady's big toe on my operating table, I asked my staff whether it was a new sort of patient labelling system. "Oh no," they laughed. "It is to stop her diarrhea!" They were surprised by my ignorance. Diarrhea? Sizing up my position at the operating table, I immediately hoped it was working. I also had good reason to try this technique some weeks later and can report it doesn't work, at least not for me. Perhaps I tied the wrong toe.

I took all of these beliefs as a learning experience, but some continued to confound. At the end of January I received a patient who had fallen into a charcoal fire in her hut. Her name was Constança. This was not the first burn case I had received but, in this instance, both her hands had been carbonated beyond recognition. Given the severity of the burns to both limbs I couldn't understand how she had sustained such grave disfiguration without a fight. It was then explained that she had fallen into the fire during an epileptic fit. I learned that locals thought that it was bad luck to touch someone during a fit, believing the victim to be momentarily possessed by a spirit. Quick action could have saved her, but traditions endure. I had no option but to amputate both her hands in their entirety and it sickened me to do so.

But there are undoubtedly cases where nature does a better job. At about the same time I received a patient with a massive chop wound to his head. He claimed UNITA soldiers had inflicted a machete blow to his skull. His grey matter was exposed and he had brain damage akin to that of a stroke. Quite frankly I was scared to do anything to the poor man as I am not a neurosurgeon, after all. The wound was deep and verminous, and, despite our best attempts, it refused to heal. A week later, while checking him once more, I was confronted with maggots in his cerebral matter. Overcoming my revulsion I hypothesized that the maggots were better than any invasive attempt by me to clean the wound. Indeed, the maggots did a great job, eating away much of the dead tissue. And when they had finished the wound healed naturally. Such were the rudimentary conditions in which we administered medical care.

One of my last cases was infinitely droller. At first I was alarmed when a young woman arrived from the countryside with one metre of dead intestine hanging out of her anus. Astonished at the sight and the severity of such a condition, I was bewildered when she had no other symptoms. A prolapsed bowel or a rare case of intussusception? Given her condition it couldn't be! She looked remarkably well. But without a moment to lose we spun into emergency mode and raced her to surgery. I lifted the protruding intestine for further inspection when the dead gut suddenly broke off in my hands. Standing there in the middle of the operating theatre with a metre of muddy intestine draped across my arms, I panicked momentarily. I looked at my patient, but she had hardly flinched. She just gazed back at me in wonderment as I stood stupefied with the specimen in my hands. How could this be? I was completely stumped.

On further examination I thought it best not to operate and decided to observe her condition. I was thoroughly perplexed, but it took me days to understand her full medical history. She spoke a native dialect rare to that area and when we finally located a translator the story unravelled. Unable to become pregnant within six months of marriage, she had endured various natural remedies to assist with conception. The traditional healer had prescribed a suppository of natural herbs. It was so natural that the poultice was encapsulated in a metre of animal gut and inserted in her rectum to be close to the womb. It was this gut (of a sheep or goat) that I had held in my arms, baffled by how it had broken free from her body. Relieved to finally understand the full story, I chuckled to myself. If only her husband had been forced to endure the same treatment, perhaps they would have stuck to more conventional means of procreation!

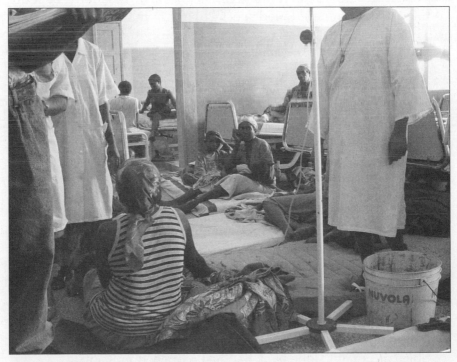

Surgical ward.

Chapter 60
Social Security

Karin takes up the story...

In the middle of obscurity the government of Angola decided to reopen the Department of Social Security. When Julio first explained this I found the concept unbelievable, but that was part of the riddle of modern day Angola. I was awestruck that someone should have seen it as such a priority.

As aid agencies were the main source of formal employment in Kuito, they were doubtless a welcome source of foreign exchange. We paid our employees in the useful hard currency of US dollars. We also paid government social security for each full-time employee, ostensibly for their retirement, sickness, or disability benefits. While the government failed spectacularly in many aspects of good governance, its labour laws were befitting the most advanced economies. As *administradora de finanças* I took my responsibility for human resources as seriously as my accountabilities for cash. On several occasions I laboured to read a document that attempted to summarize the labour laws of the country. The language of the booklet in question was akin to a merger between the verbosity of bureaucratic Hong Kong English and the convoluted words of the government of China. I read the abridged version, but the legalese tested my Portuguese to the limit.

For weeks Julio and I tried to visit the office in question. We wanted to change the way we directed these payments. Until then we had dutifully paid them to an office in Luanda. But Kuito was hundreds of kilometres from the capital, and, not surprisingly, the residents of Bié province were suspicious of their masters down there. How could we, their employer, guarantee that as residents of Bié province they would receive the accrued benefit when the need arose? The sheer logistics of moving cash from one city to another was a major undertaking. No electronic transfers there. The banking system had been hobbled although a lone bank had just reopened in Kuito.

Julio was among our longest serving employees and his determination to change the locality of our payments took on crusader-like proportions. The reopening of the Department of Social Security was cause to celebrate. The plan, to which Julio was resolutely attached, was to have the provincial government of Bié take responsibility for social security locally. Otherwise, what with endemic corruption, no one expected their contributions to see the light of day. I understood the sentiment.

I had been a bit concerned about Julio, as his second wife had recently died. She was still young and it was all very sudden. I was shocked but everyone seemed to accept the death in a more matter of fact way, or perhaps they just churned on the inside. Granted, he and his wife had been separated for some time, but Julio seemed quieter than usual and I suspected he was worried about their young child, whom he had brought to live with the family of his third wife.

Rain pelted on the windshield in staccato fashion as we made our way to the office on the east side of town. All previous attempts at an audience with the director had failed. We knew the routine by then. We had been greeted on each occasion by someone who, regardless of the time we showed up, always gave a disinterested shrug before explaining that the director was on vacation, in Luanda, gone for lunch, or simply not there at the moment. Julio, ever professional, managed to look respectful, but that day I sensed his exasperation as we approached the office once more. We leapt out of the Land Cruiser and squelched through sticky mud to get to the front door of the neat stucco bungalow. We were shepherded into the waiting area, a freshly painted room with three wooden chairs. I was immediately captivated by a sound I had not heard in years. It was the melodic high-pitched "ding" of a typewriter carriage heralding the end of a line. "Clack, clack…clack…clack, clack…ding!" Redolent of another age, the sound echoed throughout the room.

Julio cast a reassuring nod in my direction as it became evident we were getting somewhere and soon the director's assistant was rattling instructions at us. With excruciating tedium he continued without drawing breath, "Give us this document in duplicate and copies of this one in triplicate. A rubber stamp from your organization is required here beside the line that says 'Name of Organization.' And sign here and here. Take a cheque to the bank for the designated amount, but make sure this document is stamped first by the director and ensure each employee signs their contribution statement each month on pages three and five."

I made an appropriately appreciative face, but the Portuguese words rattled around in my brain with random association and I hoped Julio was catching the finer points of their requirements. One rubber stamp in the wrong place and I knew we would be back to square one. The assistant inhaled deeply as we gathered up the paperwork. "We can't stamp or sign anything until you have completed all the forms correctly," he insisted, before breaking into a magnanimous smile that indicated the meeting had come to an end. We were dismissed and sent outside into the pouring rain.

Angolan government officers revelled in officialdom. The more there was, the more they justified their existence. The similarities with China seemed too close: their love of forms, carbon paper, duplicate and triplicate. If Communism taught Angola anything, it was the venerable art of hiding behind the rubber stamp. How hard was it to let go? As if scared the story would change before we returned, we kept moving and paid our first cheque directly to the government of Bié. It was a proud moment and I could tell from Julio's triumphant smile that this truly was a breakthrough. Word spread back at the office and with everyone abuzz I soon realized just how significant it had been. Progress…in a land where, ironically, there was little social security at all.

Julio Domingos Mbumba, MSF's local administrator.

Chapter 61
A Walk in a Minefield

Karin continues...

One morning we went for a walk in a minefield—quite deliberately. I remember the first time I was struck with the sobering reality that we lived so close to minefields. It was early October, not long after my arrival, and I was out at the airstrip. I bumped into a fellow Aussie called Damian from the HALO Trust. We were casually chatting. He was telling me about his disappointment at having left the Australian army just before his regiment was sent to Timor. Sensing that he would be in the know I coolly asked him where the closest known mines were. I expected an answer like: "Well, you know that police checkpoint out near Chissindo camp? If you go out on that road for about seven kilometres...turn left, then..."

But he just swung around 180° on his heels and with his index finger extended, nonchalantly replied: "See that lady over there, the one with the big bundle of wood on her head?"

"Yes," I replied, feeling the blood rush.

"She is walking right on the edge of it!"

She was a mere two hundred metres away. I knew that the minefields were close, but somehow there is a difference between not knowing exactly and knowing precisely. It put a bit of a spring in my step. I was probably overreacting, but for a while I became conscious of where I was placing my next footprint. Bitumen and concrete, so often symbols of overdevelopment, never felt so reassuring. The next best source of comfort was a well-worn path and when I walked on loose soil I trod lightly. Ridiculous, when you think about it! After all, sixty-five kilos is sixty-five kilos. Any landmine knows that!

With two or three landmine victims every week, Wei and his team had performed their hundredth amputation just days before our tour of the minefield. One hundred amputations were hardly a reason to celebrate. It was, however, enough to make Wei curious to learn more from the professionals and see the work of another NGO whose efforts we have come to admire: the HALO Trust. In fact, as we were to learn, it was in Kuito where Princess Diana took her famed walk in the minefields. She flew in with her press entourage in January 1997 and, although her visit was extremely short, the attention it brought to the plight of mine victims still lingers.

Angola is awash with landmines. It was said that one mine existed for each of the 13 million inhabitants. That makes roughly one mine per 100 square metres of the country. HALO believed this figure to be overstated, but, even if there were a few million less, Angola would have still maintained its ugly reputation as the world's most heavily mined country. And Kuito was the world's most heavily mined city. Road access in Angola was poor and thick vegetation encroached on areas where mines were once laid. Frequent population movement and the shifting of front lines made the situation worse. Thus, records and local knowledge of mine distribution were lost.

Mining (not for the mineral variety) in and around Bié province had been going on for as long as the war itself and continued until its end. On February 26, a car from the charity Africare drove over an anti-tank mine on the way back from the fields, just nine kilometres from town. I remember the day clearly, as I had been assigned the task of asking all NGOs to volunteer drivers and cars for a nutritional survey. Armando and I arrived at Africare's office just moments after they had received the shocking news. We felt compelled to leave and backed out the door, gesticulating in sympathy. The mine had been planted on a road they used every day. The International Committee for the Red Cross had travelled the same road with them in the morning without a problem. But when the Africare car returned—boom! Remarkably, as I learned later from Wei, the driver sustained only minor injuries but our own drivers talked of nothing else for days.

For our walk in the minefield, Wei rousted me out of bed early. We questioned each other's sanity before heading off to HALO's office at the edge of the city. We were already out on the road towards the airstrip as dawn peeped through the rain-laden clouds. I was greatly comforted by the driver's proud boast that the underbellies of all their Land Rovers are specially modified with several millimetres of reinforced steel. It was not far from the city centre to the minefields, so we arrived at our destination within minutes, parked the vehicle by the roadside, and followed our guide into a clearing. We were introduced to Francisco, the minefield supervisor, who gave us a military-style briefing. He presented the statistics using a hand-drawn map and explained the inherent dangers and the safety procedures.

Cuban forces had originally placed the minefield around the airport perimeter. They had also dug the trenches, which Francisco proceeded to point out. During the first stage of the civil war (from independence to 1991) the government and Cuban forces planted defensive minefields close to key installations, while UNITA mined roads and approaches to their rebel bases. The Cubans cleared much of their own defences before pulling out. However, after the collapse of the 1992 elections, the fight for provincial capitals led to further indiscriminate mining.

This particular minefield was called Cavanga. For 246 days HALO had been working it painstakingly and at 52,534 square metres it was one of their largest active sites. They had already cleared 35,712 square metres, found twenty-one assorted mines, and detonated one large UXO. It was a tedious process. Mines are most often planted in rows or clusters, along roads and footpaths, or around anything that can be used by the enemy to take cover. Trees, abandoned buildings, fences, and trenches are favourite locations. The mines they found were mainly of Russian and Romanian origin. But Angola harboured the world's most diverse array of mines originating from the largest cross-section of countries. They say there were seventy-five different types of anti-personnel mines originating from twenty-one countries. HALO's own chilling collection on display at their Kuito office included mines from the USSR, North Korea, China, Hungary, Israel, South Africa, Italy, Germany, Belgium, France, Britain, and the US.

Working with local information and a chequered history of mine accidents, Francisco explained that the mines had been placed in a line about ten metres from the road. But a line in which direction? I looked back towards the road, noting with consternation that we were now more than one hundred metres from the bitumen. Observing my hesitation Francisco reassured us that we were standing in a "clean" administration area, and I figured that he was referring to something more serious than litter. In fact, Francisco instilled confidence, so we donned our protective gear: an extra thick bulletproof jacket and a cylindrical Perspex mask. I felt like a riot policeman. I looked down at the curious bulletproof wad that dangled between my legs. It was something akin to a sporran and I surmised that these were essentially designed for the male of the species. Did

Princess Di wear one of these? I suspected that she probably had a more photo-friendly model made up for the occasion.

I then asked Francisco about that widely held belief that a mine doesn't explode when you step on it but only when you step off. He thought that was a great joke and laughed heartily. When I heard him mention Hollywood, I got the general drift.

As we set off I tried to remember the jumble of details from the briefing, in particular the all-essential colour coding system. "Vermelho—that's yellow isn't it?" I challenged myself. It was one of those Portuguese words that never seemed to stick. "Vermelho…yellow…or perhaps that is amarelo?" After a moment's befuddled hesitation, I hastened my pace to check with Wei.

Wei looked at me fixedly through his Perspex mask. "No, vermelho isn't yellow! It's red!" Wei explained, sounding a tad exasperated, before reminding me of the rest. "A white marker defines the edge of the cleared area, a red stick the location of a previous mine, and the yellow and green ones denote active clearance areas and are used by the sappers and their supervisors to check every centimetre cleared," he recited urgently, trying to drill it in my head for the last time. Unlike me, he always had a great memory for facts and figures, so I felt reassured as we set off.

But this marker system wasn't foolproof as villagers often stole the sticks for firewood. When that happened, HALO resorted to painted white stones. I knew that fact clearly enough from an incident that happened when one of our nurses was out working in the camps. I was in the office listening to the day's events over the two-way radio when suddenly there was a call.

"Roberto para Anne-So."

"Yes, Anne-So, go ahead."

"I am out here near the limit of Campandua camp and I have come across a painted white stone. Do you think that is a white stone from HALO Trust or something else? I can't see any more white stones around here," Anne-Sophie said.

"Where are you?" queried Roberto urgently.

"Right at the edge of Campandua camp," she replied calmly.

"Don't move! Please stay where you are! Tell me your exact location. I am coming to get you. Please just don't move!"

Julio and I exchanged anxious glances as Roberto rushed off. However, the story ended happily enough as both Roberto and Anne-Sophie came home for lunch, laughing and full of their tale.

But I digress. Back at Cavanga, we followed Francisco single file along a crooked path into the middle of the minefield. Recent discoveries indicated that the path tracked the general line of mines. Several sappers worked each field at any one time, keeping a clearly defined fifteen metres from each other. For a closer view, we approached one sapper working with his metal detector. Francisco pointed to an ominous fuse they had found nearby, evidence that there was definitely a mine about a metre from where we were standing. He commented that it could take weeks to unearth it. They were in no rush. Nor was I.

The steely-nerved sappers were all local Angolans trained by the HALO Trust. Sappers work on their hands and knees, one square metre at a time. Each small plot was measured and marked with string and the colour-coded sticks. Sappers gingerly checked the surface vegetation with a thin probe looking for trip wires and booby traps. If they found nothing, they gently clipped the vegetation away with secateurs, removing each cutting by hand. After first testing their metal detectors, they waved these wands over a twenty-centimetre strip before creeping forward with their markers and repeating the process. Calibrated to detect metal up to twenty centimetres deep, the alarm sounded with frightening regularity, so it wasn't long before the shrill warning sent my heart racing. But the sapper remained calm and marked the spot with a white plastic "X." Mines have to be approached from the side as they are designed to explode from direct pressure from above. We watched as the sapper retreated to the safe zone from where he started to dig. Using a small trowel, he dug to a depth of twenty centimetres. Making a trench forty centimetres wide and twenty centimetres deep, the sapper dug unhurriedly towards the white X. He tenderly inserted a needle probe into the exposed soil wall of his hole at five-centimetre intervals. If he hit nothing hard or metallic, he uncovered another five-centimetre shaving of dirt. Bit-by-bit he crept forward until he unearthed the metal in question. On this occasion it was no more than a harmless piece of shrapnel, which he cradled in his palm like a trophy. But it could well have been a deadly rusting mine.

And thus they emptied entire minefields, centimetre by centimetre, of every piece of metal, no matter how small. It was a painstaking, dirty, and tedious process. No machine can do it as effectively as humans. The armoured earthmover was only used when the risk of unearthing a mine was low. It was a far more invasive procedure and detonation was still dangerous, even to those huge, lumbering machines.

A sapper usually clears just fifteen to eighteen square metres per day and works a strict regimen of thirty-minute intervals, punctuated by ten-minute breaks. The whistle soon blew. It was break time and time for us to go as Wei had to get back to the operating theatre to attend to another amputee-in-waiting.

There were said to be some two thousand military amputees in Kuito alone, to say nothing of the civilian victims who bore the brunt of those insidious weapons. Some days as I moved around Kuito I tested my theory that you saw an amputee on every block. It was invariably true. In fact, you usually saw two as they seemed to stick together like a flock of defeated flamingos poised on single legs. It was heart wrenching. On any day around ten amputees would congregate along the road that approached the market where they sat glumly in exalted squalor. They had become the town's shoe-shiners and I am sure the irony of being forced to earn a living from shining shoes was not lost on the limbless.

The evening after our tour of the minefields I was sitting at home, taking stock of the day and writing a letter home when the phone rang for Wei. Another mine victim had arrived at the hospital on a truck from Camacupa. It had taken him a week to get to Kuito, but he had made it, gangrene and all.

Just after we left Angola, sometime in June, we learned that the Director of an NGO called *Fundo de Apoio Social* had been killed, along with several others, when her car hit a mine three kilometres from the neighbouring city of Huambo. It was claimed to be a mine placed recently by the government to protect a military installation.

Angola signed a treaty to ban the use of anti-personnel mines in April 1997, but went no further. Even though the war has ended, Angola's deadly mine legacy will remain for generations.

A Halo Trust sapper digging for a mine.

Wei and Francisco in Cavanga minefield.

Chapter 62
Mistaken Identity

Karin continues...

A certain amount of cynicism pervaded the air. We sat in the wings like actors waiting to perform on stage. It was a typical wet-season day: sauna-like one minute, drizzle the next. We sat in the sticky cabin of the Land Cruiser, restlessly waiting for the motorcade to depart from OCHA's office. The UN delegation was behind schedule.

"How could they send McNamara?" Katelijn scoffed. As I was grappling with the significance of her question, she hissed contemptuously: "He, an ex-Secretary of Defence from the United States!"

I was astonished. A man who had served the Kennedy administration during the Vietnam War out here in Kuito? Why? To me it was implausible that anyone of his stature would be in this forgotten part of the world, let alone representing the UN. But, I said nothing and settled back to marvel at the irony.

By coincidence I was an afterthought in the day's event. I had responded to Katelijn's invitation to come along for the ride. In her role as field coordinator, she found these functions tedious, but to her credit never missed an opportunity to lobby appropriate visiting dignitaries. We always prepared a document containing our latest statistics about the health and nutrition status of the people of Bié, for which I was the English editor. She clutched our latest dossier and we intended to present it to McNamara when we had the chance.

It was the usual circus. Everyone was tripping over themselves to be polite. A fleet of white cars with blue UN flags flying snaked in convoy on their whistle-stop tour to some of the camps. The first stop was Campandua camp. Lush verdure, stringy maize, and bursts of sunflower concealed the thatch huts of the camp, unwittingly built in the middle of a minefield. It took the government months to have the villagers moved to allow de-mining to take place. This was also the camp where, just weeks before, the village *Soba* was killed by a land-mine while cutting grass for thatch by the river.

McNamara climbed out of the vehicle and took a short stroll to look around. He nodded knowingly as a bevy of officials detailed the situation and pointed to the proximity of the minefield which was clearly delineated just a few metres away. I loitered in the background, eyeing this seemingly affable man. He was much younger than I expected—barely old enough to have served under Kennedy, I thought. Inácio soon interrupted my thoughts and called us forward to be introduced. I stepped up and McNamara offered a firm handshake. His warm greeting quickly revealed his true origins.

"Hel-lo! Din-nus McNim-arah." he said confidently in a broad antipodean accent. I knew of no American who could fake a New Zealand accent so well. He was neither American, nor a politician. Dennis McNamara, the UN special coordinator on Internal Displacement and a top official at the UNHCR, was clearly not deserving of our earlier scorn. We exchanged pleasantries about how an Australian and a New Zealander chanced a meeting in a muddy minefield in central Angola before we were ushered on to the next camp.

Back in the car, I teased Katelijn about her presumption. I assured her that Dennis McNamara and Robert S. McNamara were two very different people. We chuckled at the case of mistaken identity as the driver followed the entourage to our next destination. McNamara's delegation was in Kuito to assess the needs of the IDPs. His particular interest was the protection of displaced women and children who constituted over eighty percent of those fleeing the conflict. As highly impoverished heads of households, the situation for these women was more precarious than most. What's more, a full one-third had suffered from physical violence.[44] Yet these women received infinitely less attention than international refugees. Internal displacement remains hard to define and difficult to address. In the case of Angola, the very government responsible for the phenomenon downplayed it. The international community and the media also paid little attention, even though these IDPs were far more numerous than Angola's international refugees. I was not sure what difference McNamara could make to the lives of Kuito's displaced, but I was glad he was there.

The motorcade snaked onwards to Chissindo, a new camp where many of the recently displaced were being resettled. MSF played a key role in the camp's design and we called it "Roberto's Roman camp." As a proud Italian, Roberto claimed to have modelled the layout on an ancient Roman military camp. The sea of thatched roofs formed straight lines as far as the eye could see. Each family had been allocated a certain square footage on which to construct a grass hut and plant a small vegetable patch.

McNamara wasn't shown the hastily erected tents that sheltered dozens of families in appalling conditions from the driving rain. Nor was he shown the IDPs camped overnight in MSF Health Post or school buildings—the places where people ended up when there was nowhere else to go. He wasn't asked to endure temperatures that soared to 40° inside the tents—the ones that overflowed with destitute mothers and children. I had watched these remarkable women sit in the dirt, bent over charcoal embers stirring a vile-looking slurry in blackened cans. It was an arrestingly dire scene. Instead, with white and blue UN flags flying, McNamara was welcomed with a spontaneous chorus, as hundreds of women and children lined the road to greet the motorcade. They clapped with gusto and sang harmoniously, as if choreographed to perfection. It was a rousing Angolan welcome that warmed the heart. In another land women may have hurled abuse, angry at their misfortune. There they just sang from the bottom of their hearts.

I fell back from the entourage. They forged ahead to inspect MSF's newly installed water system that provided chlorinated water to the entire camp. Nigel, a British chap, wandered up to me, introducing himself as an assistant to Mr. Deng. He was sifting for information.

"What are the most common forms of illness in the camps?" he queried, with an Englishman's politesse that seemed so out of place in the harsh surroundings.

Angola's health and nutrition indicators were among the world's worst, so I have no doubt my reply confirmed what he already knew. "Malaria, diarrhea, tuberculosis, abscesses, acute bronchial infections, and just about every vaccine-preventable disease known to these parts of the world."

"And malnutrition?" he quizzed, as if this wasn't enough.

"10.4 percent at last count,"[45] I added perfunctorily.

Nigel listened intently, but clearly had his own agenda.

"During a visit to Angola last year," he ventured, "The UN was advised of several reports of forced conscription of children into the army. Have you of heard anything more out here in the field?"

There were reportedly seven thousand child-soldiers under the age of eighteen in Angola, some as young as eight years old.[46] While

I didn't doubt the shocking reality of this well-documented phenomenon, I couldn't help him with any new specifics. I spoke instead of Jaime, the child-soldier whose leg Wei had amputated several months before. He was still in the hospital recuperating. Wei often talked of how he howled for his mother every morning when enduring the agonizing pain of a bandage change. We couldn't imagine that he had joined the army willingly. Nigel winced sympathetically in disgust and seemed to be making mental notes as we climbed into our cars for the last leg of the tour.

The convoy of Land Cruisers headed eastward across town, traversed Rio Kuito, and chortled up the embankment. There they veered left along the hilly ridge, so the delegation could observe the precarious situation on the slopes of Nharea camp. Hastily constructed, the huts were sliding down the muddy slope as the wet season progressed. Similar things were happening out at Chinguar camp, where Roberto had recently taken us with Helle and Lone. He had wanted to show us all the new huts that had sprung up to form a new camp. They were tucked away on a slope on the northern side of town, an area that I had not visited before. The Land Cruiser struggled to negotiate the steep incline down the embankment and across the creek. The road was rutted. Vehicles had dug deep in the slushy mud, now baked into hard ridges by the scorching sun. We hung on tight and after a bone-jarring ride, a sea of thimble-sized grass huts came into view. They blanketed the hillside, hundreds of flimsy, frail hovels hardly large enough to sleep in. There were no latrines and no water pumps. Yet the strangest thing about Chinguar camp was the scarcity of people—just a gaggle of old women and few squealing kids. Roberto had his theory. Rumours were rife about the WFP's plan to cut food supplies. The IDPs (both new and old arrivals) had been rushing to new locations to build additional huts. They hoped to confuse the authorities into registering them again for a second ration of food aid. I was annoyed when he told me, but that self-righteous reaction lasted only for a moment. In that sea of deprivation, who could begrudge them? I had no doubt that were I irremediably stuck in a place like Chinguar camp I would have been doing the same. We were strolling around, marvelling at their ingenuity and determination, when we came across something that—even after all those months—captivated me. I might not be religious, but the sight of a tiny church, just six metres long and three metres wide, drew me closer. From a distance it looked like no more than a pigpen.

This holy place of worship was full, overflowing in fact. But it had neither floor nor roof. Waist-high thatch delineated the walls and a forked branch pointed to the heavens like a church spire. The parishioners knelt on stones in the oozing mud in praise of the Lord, a poignant scene of religious devotion.

But again, I digress. Back in Nharea camp, we waited another restless half-hour. We slipped McNamara our dossier and then he and his entourage sped off in the direction of the airport. The IDPs went back to their daily routines of pounding maize and cooking gruel over charcoal embers.

Less than a month later the secretary-general of the UN appointed Dennis McNamara as his deputy special representative for East Timor. I read McNamara's report on Angola on my return. It detailed dozens of recommendations for the Angolan government to assume a greater responsibility for its own people, particularly in the areas of health and sanitation, education, protection of the IDPs, and the general rule of law. Among other things, it also called for UNICEF to help in the demobilization of child soldiers. A veritable laundry list that once again exposed the government's neglect of its own, impoverished citizens.

Church at Chinguar camp.

Chapter 63
Walking Shops

Karin continues...

She was a walking shop, one of thousands who paraded the streets of Angolan towns with basins skilfully perched on their heads. Like ambulatory statues, they sauntered around, eager to sell anything to supplement meagre incomes. Adelina was four months pregnant and was walking in the cool of the morning from her village to Trumba, the nearest market town. She was hoping to sell some stringy maize she had harvested from her garden. Before reaching her destination she was apparently accosted by government soldiers who were out on patrol. Without explanation, the corporal of the platoon ordered her to return to her village. Frightened by his angry demand, she hesitated before turning to move away. Then, for reasons we could not fathom, he returned her reticence with a bullet to the back before ordering his men to move on. The bullet ripped straight through Adelina's body and exited, leaving her clutching her bloody breast. The soldiers disappeared into the bush with lightning speed. She dropped her shop on the spot, but retained her composure. Adelina decided on impulse to head directly for Kuito. It was a long, arduous walk, but she hoped to hail a passing truck. Much later, on the camp fringes, an MSF driver spotted her. By then she was dizzy from blood loss. Through the trauma of it all, Adelina suffered a miscarriage and soon after she was on Wei's operating table, gasping for breath. The bullet had collapsed her left lung.

With the decline in Angola's formal economy, most people turned to the informal sector for survival, selling anything they could. Known as the *candonga*, it was born out of necessity during the disastrous years of central planning in the 1980s. The informal market boomed as the rest of the economy (oil and diamonds aside) collapsed. Walking shops mushroomed. For most households it remained the only option and became the lifeblood of the nation with informal market estimates suggesting it was up to three times larger than Angola's GDP. Probably more than half the households had a family member employed in this way in the cities alone.

Investing no more than a plastic basin from which to peddle their produce, the walking shops were readily in business, trawling the streets. Although largely a female phenomenon, in Luanda thousands of unemployed men weaved in and out of the traffic. These inexorable purveyors hawked a cornucopia of goods. Extending their arms towards the passing traffic, they held batteries in one hand and a clutch of bras in the other. In some areas they were so prolific; the streets were like drive-through supermarkets. On the left hand side there were wheel-rims, toilet paper, and plastic flowers for sale. On the right there were padlocks, picture frames, and smelly fish. Garments were displayed on sticks, single cigarettes, soap, sink-plugs, and cheap diapers on outstretched arms. Once we slowed down and a new toilet seat appeared through the window. Intended to entice, it was direct marketing at its most random.

But where poverty was more pervasive, women and their mobile vegetable shops were a feature of daily life. After a morning trudge to the well to collect water, they set off door-to-door, babies strapped to their backs. They sold little more than a few avocadoes, tomatoes, onions, or corn. When business was slow, they chatted to friends, leaning against fences, whiling away the daylight hours before starting over again. It was hard to believe that Angola was once so agriculturally rich or the world's fourth largest producer of coffee. Quite aside from its minerals, in the early 1970s it was self-sufficient in food and even exported maize.[47] Angola grew oil palm, cotton, tobacco, sugar cane, and citrus fruit. Livestock was raised and the fishing industry flourished. Had things progressed, Angolans would now be amongst Africa's most privileged and prosperous. Instead, commercial agriculture collapsed: farms had been laid with mines, abandoned, and overgrown. The ongoing insecurity and displacement jeopardized subsistence farming and pauperized a nation. Over fifty percent of Angolans are engaged in agriculture, but I was told they generate just eight percent of the nation's GDP.[48]

I visited Adelina again in the days before we left. I always found her sitting on her hospital bed mourning the loss of her child. Although her breathing was shallow and laboured, Wei assured me she would survive. Fortunately, she lived to ponder the motives of the soldiers who were supposedly there to protect. Despite a collapsed lung and permanent shortness of breath, she has no doubt gone back to her walking shop.

Walking shop with child.

Amputee observes firewood vendors en route to market.

Chapter 64
The Grey Zone

Karin continues…

My last days in Kuito were blurred and I felt that I hardly had time to say a proper goodbye. Endless confusion about the arrival of the replacement surgeon only made things worse. We cancelled our holiday to Botswana and were left wondering whether a short break to the Namibian desert was possible.

Those final weeks, however, probably flowed like the others before—bustling between home and work, back and forth between emergencies. I also became close to Anna, our new hospital coordinator. Her ability to see the wry side of life brought us together for hours each Sunday. Curled up out of the rain, we laughed and gossiped over glasses of wine. To my amazement, she found flagons of rough plonk for sale in a local store. I realized how much my taste buds had changed when, like two refined vignerons, we concluded that the wine was "not bad." In reality it was more akin to paint stripper.

Our last Sunday started idyllically. How sunshine lifted our spirits after months of steel-grey clouds! We felt re-energized after the monotonous rain that had punctuated our days. The light streaming through our window, beckoned Wei and I to enjoy an early morning stroll in the *bairro*s (suburbs): to soak up the last of Kuito life. I thought back to when we first arrived when I was too scared to venture through those back streets. By the end, however, those same dirt tracks defined so much of what we had come to love about life there. They had become as familiar as the roads in any other city where we had lived. We encountered our friends en route, stopping to chat to staff from the office or hospital, or patients and friendly strangers who were, by then, such a part of our everyday life.

Early that same evening the heavens opened just as we were hosting our own farewell at home. We had already been to so many goodbye parties for others that we kept ours low-key. We had hosted several garden gatherings for Wei's staff, friends from the office, the cooks, maids, and house guards who made our stay so memorable. So, for our last party we gathered our friends for a barbeque in the garage, to shelter us from the driving rain. With candlelight creating a soft ambiance we were swept up by throat-knotting feelings of camaraderie tinged with the sort of foreboding that lurks before departures. It was April 1, 2001, Wei's 42nd birthday. It was a day of some significance as it also marked twenty years to the day since Wei and I first met. We were able to celebrate our special moment with great friends with whom we now shared a unique bond. It was also Tanguy and Emilie's last evening. They were to fly out the next day, their romance already blossoming.

I was scheduled to leave a few days before Wei as couldn't secure seats on the same flight. During my last days at the office, I rushed to complete some reports, helping Katelijn to put the finishing touches on her recommendations from the Camacupa visit. Just a few days earlier a small team had set out on an exploratory mission to Camacupa. The town was east of Kuito, the so-called "grey zone." We had been consistently hearing bad reports about the humanitarian situation there. The government had just reopened the hospital without doctors or even the very basics. Despite unanswerable concerns about landmines and insecurity, Frederico, Roberto, and Katelijn pushed off in a convoy assisted by two experienced drivers who had local knowledge of the area. We monitored every move by radio and anxiously awaited their return. It was the first such trip to Camacupa since MSF's program was halted there in 1998, when war had resumed. The assessment team was gone two long days. The 160-kilometre journey took six long hours in each direction.

Their findings surpassed our worst fears. The nutritional situation alone justified an emergency intervention. There were estimates of more than fifty-five thousand additional IDPs in Camacupa municipality. Nutrition and mortality rates were startling. At twenty-eight percent (almost three times higher than in Kuito), malnutrition was just the beginning. The condition of many patients at the hospital was so shocking that they immediately organized an evacuation for the most needy and malnourished. These vulnerable patients arrived by truck on the Tuesday before we left. Nine children of the eighty patients died en route and the emaciated that survived could be described as the living dead. I saw one survivor waiting for Wei outside the operating theatre on my last visit there. I drew a horrified breath when I set eyes upon her skeletal frame. A wasted figure, she was bent double in a breathless struggle to sit on a chair. She looked like a walking cadaver. Lanky and gaunt, her skin clung like tissue paper to the contours of each bone. My stomach churned.

On the day of my departure a bomb exploded in one of the local churches. Fortunately no one was hurt. The security situation continued to worsen, and yet I didn't want to leave. I packed reluctantly and bundled up all my clothes, apart from those I was wearing, and gave them all to Frederico. I knew he would distribute them to needy people in his parish.

In fact, my own departure was one big *confusão*. I hardly knew until the last minute which plane I would catch and when. Goodbyes were fleeting and even Wei could not make it. With everyone listening, we said our farewells over the two-way radio as the propellers started to drone. There were jibes about us being the last of the great romantics, but it wasn't what I had imagined for our final departure. For one thing, I had hoped Wei and I could leave Kuito together. I hugged and kissed my friends goodbye, not knowing when or if I would ever see them again. I boarded the plane with one of those lumps in my throat that had become common in those last few months, and the door was closed tightly behind me. The tears came as we taxied onto the runway, just as Wei's Land Cruiser came hurtling through the gates. As the plane lifted off into the grey sky, I saw his tiny figure join the sea of arms, waving like fronds in a gentle breeze.

Suburban Kuito.

Chapter 65
Farewell Kuito

Wei writes…

I had no idea it would be that hard to control my emotions. Decades of Chinese culture and self-discipline simply failed me. The WFP flight did not wait for stragglers, and we had been told not to be late. At the last minute, almost the entire team rushed to the airport, but regrettably we had to leave without Jesus, one of my most talented trainees. Even Augusto would have missed us if we hadn't spotted him en route, running towards the airstrip. He was out of breath, but we bundled him in the back of the vehicle for my last ride to *Aeroporto de Kuito*.

My replacement, Rosemarie, had finally arrived, and I completed my handover in a rush. I checked on young Estevão one last time. He was one of my last patients and I felt a strong attachment to this brave boy. As I concluded my last ward round, he waited for me on his bed, unable to contain his beaming smile. I checked his wounds. He was recovering well and there was enormous satisfaction in that. At just six years of age, he had been the victim of a grass-hut fire. He had sustained shocking burns to his head, neck, and back, covering more than twenty percent of his body. At the time, the raw pain must have been intolerable and that he survived at all was remarkable. With no medical care, his scars had contracted, pulling his head taut against his shoulder. His head was locked in this horizontal position for four long years, forcing him to view the world at a 90° angle. Estevão was thin, but well enough to undergo the tricky operation to release the contracture and straighten his head. We grafted skin from his thigh to his neck and the operation went smoothly. Then, he could look the world straight in the eye. That day he was cheerful, but tears welled up in his eyes as I bade him farewell.

I was still reeling from the goodbyes when I finally touched down in Luanda. At the final weekly surgical meeting the hospital director had made a speech. He was a local of Kuito, a hearty authoritarian. His parting words were full of the usual formalities and pleasantries one would imagine on such an occasion. Then, to my surprise, he added a comment that went well beyond the expected.

"Doctor Wei," he said. In Kuito they always called me "Doctor Wei," never "Doctor Cheng," and I loved their unceremonious term, although I never could get them to call me by the name I really preferred, simply "Wei."

"Doctor Wei has treated everyone, Angolans and foreigners alike, without arrogance or superiority. He has treated us all as his brothers and sisters. Your home, Doctor Wei, is in China, but there is always another home for you here in Kuito."

I was deeply moved by his words that mixed ceremony with sensitivity and was overcome with sadness. I took comfort in knowing that, even so far from home, it was possible to reach out and form strong bonds across cultures and borders.

At the airport, Roberto urged me to start saying goodbye as soon as we arrived. I walked over to Bento, Eduardo, Malaquias, and Augusto—my indomitable team. I reached out my hand, but no words came from my mouth. They too remained tongue-tied. Not a syllable was uttered. Instead, tears welled in our eyes. Our throats hardened. These were the people alongside whom I had worked day and night for eight months. Hours earlier we had been laughing until tears streamed down our cheeks. By then we had become emotionally hamstrung.

On the way to the airport, Karin's replacement, Stephane, joked about whether I had prepared a speech. I said I hadn't, but remarked that I wanted to say something meaningful to them. However, as it turned out, I couldn't say anything. Not a thing. We just hugged. It was a hug that said everything and expressed the emotion we couldn't put into words.

Almost the entire crew was there, with the exception of Daniela and the nutrition team. They were preoccupied with the Camacupa emergency. Olivier, Laurence, Elizabeth, Lone, Helle, Anna, Stephane, Roberto, Tanguy's replacement, Francis, Anne-Sophie, Emmanuelle, and Julio—they were all there. Sadly I couldn't say much to them either. Eight months is a short time in a life, yet these people had left an indelible mark.

I climbed aboard the small twin-prop plane with another visiting colleague. She pulled off a few sheets of toilet paper for herself, before throwing me the roll. I wiped my eyes. Even she had been moved to tears by the departure scene. I looked down through the little round window at Kuito, probably for the last time.

Left to right: Malaquias, Bento, Wei, Jesus, Eduardo, Augusto, and Loló.

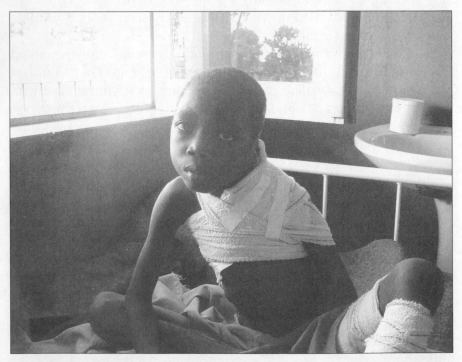

Estevão looks the world straight in the eye after corrective surgery.

Chapter 66
Back to Reality

Karin picks up the story...

While it may stretch credibility to suggest that a supermarket, a hot shower, and a stylish haircut are the stuff of dreams, it was these thoughts that filled my mind as the flight attendant trundled her trolley down the aisle. I was en route to Brussels, and I was on my own. After a short break in neighbouring Namibia, I left Wei behind in Luanda, to catch another flight two days later.

Not for the first time in my life, a steaming plate of innocuous food was placed before me on a plastic tray. Normally, I would sigh. Intoxicated, I tore open the plastic bag that held my knife and fork and did my best to manoeuvre the various items around the confines of the tray. I sunk my teeth into the soft bread roll, closed my eyes and tasted what seemed like warm marshmallow. In greedy rapture I peeled open the foil that hid some monochromatic culinary delight smothered in congealed gravy. My taste buds captivated, I savoured every tantalizing mouthful.

Immensely satisfied I anaesthetised my mind with a glass of red wine. Lulled by the drone of the aircraft, I drifted in and out of a fitful sleep. At some stage, my eyelids flung open and I struggled to focus on Tom Cruise parading across the screen in some inane action movie. The more the mindless drama unfolded, the more wretched I felt and the more resentful I became about being cheated of sleep. A feeling of dread grew with each passing hour. My emotional battle pitted guilt against longing. Guilt for leaving. Longing for familial surroundings. Fear of confronting a world of detached indifference with my burning passion to reach out and do more. Sensing that our homecoming was to be almost as confronting as the situation we had left behind, I sunk back into the insufferably uncomfortable airline seat feeling thoroughly dispirited.

How simple it was. I had jumped on a plane as if on a business trip or vacation, just as I had done countless times before. Soon I would land in oh-so-civilized Brussels, where my mobile phone would rapidly remind me of my transformation. I would phone home and announce more convincingly that I was safe and sound. In a sense there was comfort in that.

Yet my mood stayed sombre as we edged closer to Belgium. The grey Brussels sky unloaded gentle tears in harmony with my sentiment. The cold granite and stainless steel of the airport clashed with thoughts of mud and slush; the harried business travellers morphed into humble homeless refugees. I had simply wrenched myself away from misery and taken a jet back to a world where no one noticed. I was back where I started, as if by some strange *Back to the Future* phenomenon. Had we never been absent or was the place where we had gone just a chimera?

I settled in to a characterless inn in an equally bland suburb of Brussels, each day dank and colourless. I feasted on stodgy food and filled the dull hours until Wei's arrival, blindly mesmerized by the television. I wondered where life would take us from there.

Two days later Wei flew in to Paris. It was only as he stepped out onto the railway platform at Brussels that I realized for the first time just how thin and angular his face had become. Months of demanding surgery had exacted their toll. He yearned for nothing more than a warm shower and a good sleep, but there was little time for that. We rushed over to the MSF headquarters to debrief them on the outcome of our mission. Wei had prepared an informative presentation on the work of the surgical team, which he delivered before we flew to Istanbul that evening. I was ecstatic about seeing my sister Ingrid again.

The next morning we lounged in the warm Mediterranean sunshine, enchanted by sounds from the minarets. At the edge of my sister's garden we watched ships ply the sparkling Bosphorus once more. And it was here, drifting in and out of that strange state of disbelief, where we learned that six aid workers from the Red Cross had been shot and brutally hacked to death in the Congo. It happened just a few hundred kilometres from Angola's northern border. The atrocity occurred on April 27, just days after our departure from Luanda. The aid workers had been in an area not considered particularly dangerous, going about their business. They were administering medication and helping to repatriate the displaced from the conflict there. It shocked us to think that they were doing things that we now knew to be just a normal part of an ordinary day in the life of aid workers everywhere.

Feeling somewhat rested, although still bewildered, we left

Ingrid's and pushed eastward. We popped into Singapore for a short visit to see my sister Sandra and my growing nephew before returning to Hong Kong in early May 2001. We arrived less than twenty-four hours before Wei's brother's wedding, a celebration that had been postponed twice to accommodate our return. From somewhere we mustered the jet-lagged energy to be charmed by Clara, our new sister-in-law, and to enjoy the Chinese banquet, festooned with red and gold. The evening was warm and familial and we were glad to be home to share their happiness.

From there we spent weeks talking publicly about MSF's work in Angola before travelling the world once more to catch up on lost time with family and friends. And we did more of those things that we had always said we would do "one day." It was during these months of travel that many often asked: "What was it like in Angola?" Or challenged us with deep and meaningful questions like: "How has it changed you and your perception of the world?" Intelligent questions that begged intelligent answers. Surprisingly we found this difficult to do. Emotions churned. We felt the need for succinct one-line answers to satisfy the equally succinct questions. Yet, we had none. Each answer differed from the last, as we tried to gauge the real level of interest and match it with the most appropriate answer. We often opted for dinner-party style conversation: general patter that filled the void and satisfied the curiosity in a few words. In short, we undersold. We reduced real life stories to simplistic one-liners. For two relatively intelligent individuals, we dragged our inability to articulate our experiences around like apolio-ravaged limbs.

"So why don't Angolans just do something? Why don't they rise up and overthrow the government?" proclaimed an equally inquisitive soul, in a melodramatic tone. Sounds simple, doesn't it? Yet how could one explain the reality? That the majority of people in rural Angola were malnourished, exhausted, impoverished, brutalized, and in poor health. How could one explain this to someone of our modern age where mobile phones, satellites, and computers are the norm? How could Angolans organize such an uprising and with what? They lived in conditions where simple communication was near impossible. And how could they have mustered the finances or the energy? Subjugated, Angolans had been pulverized by a tireless war that had dragged on for as long as most could remember. Any energy they had left went into their daily struggle to survive.

Another popular question, one that we have even asked ourselves, was: "Did we make a difference?" In the end all we know is that we helped people at a moment when they needed help. We often wonder what happened after they recovered sufficiently for us to send them on their way so that we could fill their beds with others in need. Wei still lives with his ghosts, the ones he lost. Each death impacted us in some way. But at the same time we have learned to "live for another, if you wish to live for yourself."[49] It was our privilege to have served the people of Kuito.

Epilogue

Karin writes...

One day the rain did stop. On February 23, 2002, our newspaper reported that Dr. Jonas Malheiro Savimbi, the leader of UNITA, was dead.

Nowadays we read articles about Africa with more zeal than ever before. However, it is surprisingly difficult to find out what is really happening in Africa today. News is rarely reported, and, when it is, it appears insignificantly in a tiny summary in a column towards the middle of the newspaper.

But one day in the *Globe & Mail* there it was. We could hardly believe our eyes:

"UNITA's Savimbi killed, Angolan army says."

Savimbi, the man who led UNITA in an endless fight for power for over thirty years, who had dodged death for so long, had his own mortality reported in two short sentences. He was assassinated in Luena, Moxico province, 400 kilometres east of Kuito. Having flown there when I had first arrived, I knew exactly where it was. Curled up on the sofa in our Toronto home, the news seemed remote, but the images came rushing back. The commandos stationed in Kuito, the troop movements, the *limpezas*...it was all too confusing at the time, but the army had been closing in on their elusive opponent.

With reports of his death fuelling hope for an end to Africa's longest-running war, we were keen to see what would transpire. We scanned the papers for weeks looking for snippets of news and corresponded eagerly with our friends in Kuito.

On April 4, 2002, a peace treaty was signed and at last there was reason to hope. With Savimbi gone UNITA could no longer keep the soldier-peasantry within its thrall. UNITA troops rapidly capitulated. They were exhausted and hungry.

The war had long given the government an excuse to keep its defence budget secret, connivance to shield its contracts from scrutiny. It had also long refused to disclose what had happened to the annual income from oil receipts (estimated to be in the vicinity of $3 to $5 billion). Surely now this has to change.

The yearning for peace was like the impending rain. It finally came. Perhaps now Agostinho Neto's prophecy of freedom for all Angolans has finally been realized. And when the true spirit of ordinary *Angolanos* is harnessed then "no one can stop the rain."[50] That said, rebuilding Angola will be arduous. It will take decades of wise, benevolent leadership for prosperity to reach the rural hinterland. Graft and self-interest are sure to thwart even the best efforts. But, for the survivors, even that prospect is more promising than a futile war.

We remain connected to Angola in many ways. Another friendship evolved from a remarkable encounter made over the Internet. One particularly chilly winter evening, while researching some historical facts to support this book, I was immersed in my efforts to find out more about the Benguela Railway. The railway was once at the very centre of life for the community of Kuito, a town formerly known as Silva Porto. I was just about to give up when I came across the fascinating Web site of the Costa family.[51] The Web site, half in English and half in Portuguese, chronicles the history of this settler family. They traced their roots to the island of Madeira, Portugal and wrote of the arrival of their ancestors in southern Angola in the late 1800s. I quickly became absorbed in their photos and their struggle to build a new life in Angola's rugged hinterland. With a map sprawled out on the floor of our study, I traced the path as the narrator told of the journey by oxen cart across the interior into an area that sounded so familiar. I guessed it to be close to Kuito, but as the names had all changed after independence it was difficult to verify.

By now it was well past midnight and my eyes were heavy. I laboured to read the pages in Portuguese and I was growing impatient. Suddenly I was awestruck by several photos of buildings in Silva Porto, which matched our own photos of the ruined city. I couldn't believe it and called out to Wei, but it was late and he was already asleep. Kuito has had several names in its history. Francisco Ferreira da Silva, an explorer who was sent to open up the interior, arrived in Kuito in 1845, establishing the town on the banks of Rio Kuito. The area had first been called Belmonte, later Amarante, and then Silva Porto. The explorer Da Silva was born in Porto, Portugal, hence the town's name *Silva do Porto* (Silva from Porto) or Silva Porto. Kuito was finally renamed using its local name, following independence in 1975.

The photos on the Web site were undeniably that of Kuito's central square, the same as our own, except without the destructive effects of war. I was in awe when I found a photo of Kuito's post office and saw for the first time what it once looked like back in its heyday. It was an uncanny feeling, as if spying on a lost world. In my animated excitement I started to flick through the rest of their cyber photo album to see what else it contained and suddenly became confused. Had I clicked the wrong button? There before me were several photos of something even more familiar: Jervis Bay and the bridge over the Shoalhaven River in Nowra, Australia. This was the town of my birth! Jervis Bay was the playground of my youth and many a family sailing weekend. Puzzled, I nimbly hammered at the "Back" and "Forward" buttons until I established the link was genuine. I then looked up at the Web address and became intrigued by the service provider: shoal.net. The Shoalhaven? They live in the Shoalhaven region? Surely not?

Fernando Costa, his pregnant wife, Filomena, and their young daughter didn't leave Angola until 1979. They tried to stay on, countering the tide of émigrés who were leaving en masse. They remained defiant, unwilling to give up on the beloved country of their birth. Fernando was born in Silva Porto and grew up in Bela Vista, a smaller town along the railway line from Kuito. His family eventually bought a farm in Mavinga, in the southeast of the country, but Fernando attended school in Novo Lisboa (now the destroyed city of Huambo). He trained as an electrical engineer and after graduation married Filomena, from Huambo. They moved to Lobito, near Benguela on the coast of Angola, where their first daughter was born. Fernando was responsible for maintaining the electricity supply up along the Benguela Railway to towns such as Huambo and Kuito. He tells fascinating stories about what this was like back then. He was even involved in the establishment of an electrical substation at Kunge. Kunge is destroyed now, but the remnants of this town were within Kuito's security perimeter, out near Katala camp, and I passed it often enough. His uncle had even been the superintendent of the hospital where Wei worked.

Fernando and Filomena stayed in Lobito for as long as they could, eventually becoming concerned about the uncertain future for their young family, and ultimately deciding to move on. They went first to Portugal, a country no more "home" than any other foreign land. From Portugal, Fernando found work in Portuguese Macao, then Nauru, and finally, over the course of several years, they immigrated to Australia. They found their way to the South Coast town of Nowra, the pretty town where I was born. And, as if by some amazing coincidence, Fernando and Filomena live just a few kilometres away from the home of my youth. Theirs is the neighbourhood where I once rode my bike and hiked the rugged bush with childhood friends.

At the time the coincidence seemed all too incredible to believe, so before turning in for the night I sent an e-mail to verify my discovery. I half expected to be rebuffed. But by morning the seeds of a wonderful new friendship had been sown. What has transpired since then has been the most delightful interchange of stories and photos. Like all men of his youth, Fernando was drafted into the national army to fight the leftist-leaning insurgency and the MPLA in the years before independence. Through Fernando we have learned much about life in Angola leading up to independence and the early years thereafter.

Fernando remains patriotic and we share his passion for the country of his birth. He dreams of returning and has been keen to learn about the Kuito of today. News had been sketchy, so we were pleased to fill him in on everything we knew and we still exchange stories we hear through friends. And in the winter of 2003 we finally had the pleasure of meeting in person. In a delightful Madeira restaurant in a Sydney suburb we talked endlessly about Kuito then and now. That special bond formed with his family is yet another delightful chapter that connects us to Kuito.

Karin Moorhouse
Toronto, 2004

Whatever Happened To…

Peace came at last to Kuito and the endless stream of war casualties at the *Banco de Urgência* came to a sudden halt. The veil was also lifted on the inaccessible "grey areas" where humanitarian assistance was not possible while we were there. As such, the true extent of the human catastrophe gradually came to light, but still the world was slow to respond. MSF moved out beyond Kuito, stepping up its operations and pushing further into the interior. The organization now works in eleven of Angola's eighteen provinces, and, in 2002, Angola became MSF's largest relief operation worldwide.

Operations at the Provincial Hospital of Bié were handed back to the Angolan government as soon as doctors and a surgeon were committed to work there. Several doctors from Angola, Vietnam, and North Korea are reportedly working there now. MSF still supports the facility with medical supplies, but has moved on to focus on the nutritional emergency. MSF still employs over two hundred fifty local staff members for the nutrition and camp health programs.

Some renovation is being undertaken, and with the opening of provincial roads, vehicular traffic is returning to the streets of Kuito. But the wounds are still fresh. Residents are now exhuming the bodies of their loved ones from the makeshift graves of wartime. The dead are being reburied in formal cemeteries and the endless funerals continue. Only then can people hope to move on. The twenty-five IDP camps are fast disappearing as over one hundred thousand displaced returned home to pick up their lives or resettle elsewhere in the country.

Wavemail and e-mail still keep us in touch with many of our wonderful friends, both in Angola and around the world.

Augusto Sapalo Silivondela secured a permanent job with MSF just prior to our departure. Regrettably, Karin was forced to dismiss Armando due to various misdemeanours towards local staff, leaving his position in the administration team vacant. Augusto outclassed all candidates in the selection process and works with Julio to this day. It couldn't have happened to a more deserving man.

We were astonished to receive a phone call from him just recently, as he proudly informed us that he now owns a cell phone.

Julio Domingos Mbumba still works for the administration team. The office in Kuito has been scaled back to just seven or eight foreign volunteers, but both Julio and Augusto are central to the project.

Antonio Jacinto *Bento,* *Malaquias* **Wana Jila,** *Eduardo* **Elambo Kayangula** and **Mario de** *Jesus* **Setumba** all still live in Kuito with their families. They completed their surgical nursing training, and, following my recommendation, MSF awarded each a certificate acknowledging their surgical skills. They continue to work for the Ministry of Health and we recently learned that Eduardo and Jesus were selected by the government for formal medical training in Luanda. One day soon they will become qualified surgeons, and we are thrilled that two such talented nurses have been recognized in this way. Until the academic year started Eduardo worked in *Banco de Urgência* at the Provincial Hospital of Bié in Kuito, as did Jesus. Meanwhile, Bento is superintendent at a small hospital in Kunhinga, about thirty kilometres north of Kuito. Of more concern was the health of Malaquias who was ill with tuberculosis. However, with peace and stability, MSF has been able to initiate a program to treat TB. By all accounts, Malaquias has recuperated well and is the health delegate of Chitembo commune.

Sebastião de Melo (Loló) is the only one still working in the surgery department along with other members of the extended hospital team.

As for the team of MSF volunteers…

An returned to lead the project in Kuito and our last news of her was from Angola.

Anna returned to Kuito with the International Committee of the Red Cross. She stayed on for over a year and through her we learned much about life in Kuito after the war. She has since been on another MSF mission to Bangladesh and recently returned to Britain where she works as a training officer for the National Blood Service.

After Kuito, **Anne-Sophie** joined GOAL, another aid agency, and worked in Luena, Angola. She still writes from time to time and we love to hear her news. She met her partner on a mission in Mozambique and the couple recently had a baby.

I caught up with **Arnaud** recently on a mission in Liberia. Arnaud has volunteered with MSF for over ten years in many trouble spots throughout the world, including Afghanistan and Rwanda. We salute his dedication.

Christelle married a Zimbabwean while on a mission there and has recently settled in Belgium. The couple has a new baby.

Daniela still works for MSF and at last count was on a mission in Zimbabwe.

After visiting us in Angola **Elaine** went on a mission to Afghanistan but is back in Hong Kong, where she works as a nurse and is a board member of MSF Hong Kong.

In another of life's delightful coincidences, we were living in Canada when **Emilie and Tanguy** married in Quebec in the Spring of 2002. We attended their wedding, which was held in a tiny chapel in the Quebec countryside. It was a charming occasion in tranquil surroundings—a surreal contrast to our days in Kuito. Until recently they were still working as a nurse and a logistician on missions to Chad, Kenya, Afghanistan, and Congo. They have recently settled in Quebec City, where Tanguy is attending Laval University to requalify as a Canadian lawyer and Emilie works as a nurse. Both still volunteer with MSF on short missions. Our lives stay intertwined.

Eric continues his great work as a journalist-cameraman in Hong Kong.

Inger is working in Norway and stays in touch from time to time, as do **Helle** and **Lone** from Denmark.

Katelijn has spent the last three years on a mission with MSF working with AIDS patients in Peru's worst prison. She remains in Peru as medical coordinator for MSF's AIDS and TB programs. Her continued commitment to MSF's work is admirable.

Monica returned to Italy to wed her African boyfriend and continues her medical career. She is now a board member of MSF Italy.

Olivier and Emmanuelle recently married and set up home in Brussels. Most recently they worked in the Belgium headquarters, however, I recently encountered them both during a short mission to Liberia.

Peter returned to the hospital in Kuito for a brief visit after the war and marvelled at the wondrous sight: no more war casualties. They once comprised over one-third of the surgical workload. He still consults for MSF Belgium on matters of anaesthesia and works in the Netherlands.

Roberto, our Italian logistician, returned to Kuito. He was evacuated due to poor health and was gravely ill for many months with an unknown virus. However, he slowly recuperated and immediately returned to Angola. There was no stopping him!

The team from Kuito still stays connected.

Wei Cheng
Toronto, 2004

Glossary

Administradora de finanças: Portuguese for financial administrator.

Africare: US-based private, charitable organization assisting African nations in developmental projects.

Angolanos: Portuguese for Angolans.

Ascaris (lumbricoides): A genus of large intestinal parasites. A roundworm resembling the earthworm commonly found in the small intestine, causing diarrhea, pain, and bowel perforation.

Abscess: A collection of pus in a body cavity usually caused by bacteria, which results in swelling and inflammation.

Anastomosis: Rejoining of the two parts of the resected bowel.

Ano Novo: Portuguese for New Year.

Aorta: The main artery for the body.

AZT: A drug that slows the reproduction of HIV by interfering with reverse transcriptase. Known as Zidovudine, it is also called ZDV or Retrovir.

Banco de Urgência: Portuguese for the Accident and Emergency Department of a hospital.

BBC: British Broadcasting Corporation

Billabong: Australian Aboriginal word meaning a waterhole formed in an anabranch of a river or creek that is replenished only in flood time. Also a well-known Australian brand name for a range of surf and casual wear.

Bowel resection: Removal of part of the intestine.

Caritas Internationalis: A confederation of Catholic relief, development, and social service organizations, primarily helping the poor. In Hong Kong Caritas Medical Centre is managed by the Department of Health as part of the public health network.

Chook: Colloquial Australian word for chicken.

CIA: Central Intelligence Agency of the United States of America

CNS: Centre Nutritionel Supplementaire (Supplementary Nutrition Centre)

CSUSC: Coalition to Stop the Use of Child Soldiers, London.

Dermatitis: Inflammation of the skin.

Ectopic pregnancy: A potentially life-threatening condition characterized by the fetus being in locations outside the uterus, such as the fallopian tubes.

Elephantiasis: A chronic disease caused by parasites, affecting the lymphatic channels and leading to swelling of the limbs, principally the legs and feet

FAA: Forças Armadas Angolanas (Angolan Armed Forces)

FAO: Food and Agriculture Organization of the United Nations

FNLA: Frente Nacional de Libertação de Angola (National Liberation Front of Angola)

GDP: Gross Domestic Product. The total market value of all final goods and services produced in a country in a given year, equal to total consumer, investment, and government spending, plus the value of exports and minus the value of imports.

GOAL: An international humanitarian organization and NGO based in Dublin, Ireland

Haematocolpos: An accumulation of menstrual blood in the vagina (usually due to an imperforate hymen).

Hemoglobin: Protein responsible for the red colour of blood, which carries oxygen to the tissue.

HALO Trust: An acronym for Hazardous Area Life-Support Organization. A charitable organization involved in de-mining.

Hernia: A protrusion of an organ or tissue through an opening in the surrounding area, especially in the abdomen; a rupture.

Home monitors: Refugee or IDP camp residents who report the cases of ill health, births, deaths, etc. among their neighbours.

Humerus: Single, long bone in the arm that extends from the shoulder to the elbow.

ICRC: International Committee of the Red Cross (based in Geneva)

IDP: Internally Displaced Person; a national forced to move within their own country due to war, ongoing insecurity, or famine, but who has not crossed an international border to be classified as a refugee.

Intussusception: The prolapse of one part of the intestine into the cavity of an immediately adjoining part.

KZR: Kwanza, national currency of Angola

Laparotomy: An incision into the abdominal wall, sometimes conducted to establish a diagnosis.

Limpeza: In Portuguese it refers to a systematic military engagement to "cleanse" an area of guerrillas.

Mastitis: Infection and inflammation of a breast occurring in women who are breastfeeding their babies.

M*A*S*H: Mobile Army Surgical Hospital, US Army. Also a television comedy series by the same name.

Mestiço: Mixed race; used when referring to the population of Angolans of Portuguese and African decent.

MINSA: Ministry of Health of Angola

MONUA: United Nations Mission of Observers in Angola, June 1997–February 1999

MPLA: Movimento Popular de Libertação de Angola (Popular Movement for the Liberation of Angola)

MSF: Médecins Sans Frontières, also known as Doctors Without Borders

MUAC: Mid-upper arm circumference measurement used to quickly screen the malnourished.

NGO: Non-governmental organization

OCHA: United Nations Office for the Coordination of Humanitarian Affairs

Peritonitis: Inflammation of the membrane lining the abdominal cavity and its internal organs; this membrane is referred to as the peritoneum.

Post-partum haemorrhage: Heavy bleeding following childbirth

PNA: Polícia Nacional de Angola (National Police of Angola)

PR: Public relations

RTHK: Radio Television Hong Kong

SFC: Supplementary Feeding Centre

Sonangol: Sociedade Nacional de Combustíveis (National Fuels Company of Angola)

SWAPO: South West Africa People's Organization

TAAG: Linhas Aéreas Angolanas (Angolan Airlines)

TFC: Therapeutic Feeding Centre

Tibia: Shinbone, shin; the inner and thicker of the two bones of the human leg between the knee and ankle

UHF: Ultra high frequency radio

UN: United Nations

UNESCO: United Nations Educational, Scientific, and Cultural Organization

UNFPA: United Nations Population Fund

UNHCR: United Nations High Commission for Refugees

UNICEF: United Nations Children's Fund

UNITA: União Nacional para a Independência Total de Angola (National Union for the Total Independence of Angola)

USSR: Union of Soviet Socialist Republics

Utero-vesical fistula: An abnormal communication between the urinary bladder and the vagina resulting in continuous involuntary discharge of urine into the vagina, usually the result of a prolonged and obstructed labour. This condition is more common in developing countries where obstetric care is limited. In West Africa three to four cases per 1,000 deliveries have been reported (Margolis, T., Mercer, L.J. "Vesicovaginal fistula." *Obstetrics Gynecology Survey*, 49(12) (December 1994): 840-7.

UXO: Unexploded ordnance
WFP: United Nations World Food Programme
WHO: World Health Organization

References

1 Shah, A. *Conflicts in Africa*. "Geopolitics." www.globalissues.org/geopolitics/africa.asp. 1999.

2 MSF reluctantly withdrew from Afghanistan after twenty-four years, following the brutal killing of five colleagues on June 2, 2004. The Land Cruiser they were travelling in was ambushed. They were Besmillah (driver), Egil Tynaes (doctor), Fazil Ahmad (translator), Hélène de Beir (project coordinator), and Willem Kwint (logistician).

3 Socrates, Greek philosopher (469–399 B.C.). From Plato. *Dialogues*. "Apology."

4 Pelton, R.Y, *The World's Most Dangerous Places*, 4th editon (New York: HarperResource, 2000).

5 Doctors Without Borders/Médecins Sans Frontières. "The Ten Most Under-Reported Humanitarian Crises of 2000." Third Annual Report, Doctors Without Borders USA. www.doctorswithoutborders.org/publications/reports/2001/top10.htm.

6 Poem by Marshall Peng Dehuai, a highly decorated Red Army General who led troops during the Korean War. In 1959, he submitted a lengthy essay to the Chinese Communist Party urging it to take immediate action to avert the impending famine disaster, which was a direct result of the policies of the Great Leap Forward. He was denounced for his honesty and imprisoned. He died in prison.

7 From *Sacred Hope* (1974), a book of collected poetry, by Antonio Agostinho Neto. Republished in 1988 by Journeyman Press and UNESCO.

8 As reported by the National Ultramarine Bank from 1872, cited on the Web site of ANIP (Agência Nacional de Investimento Privado), www.iie-angola-us.org/luanda.htm.

9 Statistics collated by the UN Population Fund, published on UNICEF's Web site, www.unicef.org/infobycountry/angola_statistics.html.

10 United Nations Development Report 1999. A composite measure of GDP, life expectancy, and literacy rate. In the 2004 report, Angola ranks 166th out of 177 nations. http://hdr.undp.org/.

11 "Provincial Emergency Action Plan for Resettlement and Return," June 4, 2002, by João Baptista Kussumua, Minister of Social Welfare, Government of Angola.

12 As of 2000, Angola was rated as the sixth most corrupt nation according to Internet Centre for Corruption Research, a joint initiative of Goettingen University, Sweden and Transparency International.

13 In Transparency International's 2002 Corruption Perceptions Index, Angola ranked third lowest out of 102 countries surveyed, with a score of 1.7 out of 10, making it the world's third most corrupt nation. www.transparency.org/pressreleases_archive/2002/ 2002.10.18.angola.html.

14 British Broadcasting Corporation Web site (2002), www.bbc.co.uk

15 Médecins Sans Frontières, "Voices from the Silence: Testimonies from Angola" (Toronto: Médecins Sans Frontières, 2004).

16 Médecins Sans Frontières, "Voices from the Silence: Testimonies from Angola" (Toronto: Médecins Sans Frontières, 2004).

17 Food and Agriculture Organization of the United Nations (FAO), 2000, www.fao.org/News/2000/000801-e.htm.

18 UNICEF, 2000, "Angola at a Glance," www.unicef.org/infoby-country/angola_502.html.

19 In Canada there is approximately one doctor per 500 people, while in Australia the doctor-patient ratio is approximately one doctor per 400 people.

20 UNICEF, 2005, "Angola at a Glance," www.unicef.org/infoby-country/angola_502.html.

21 UNICEF, 2005, "Angola at a Glance," www.unicef.org/infoby-country/angola_502.html.

22 UNICEF, 2000, 1,854 per 10,000 births. Also, "Maternal Mortality in 2000," Estimates developed by WHO, UNICEF, and UNFPA, (Geneva: Department of Reproductive Health and Research, WHO, 2004), 17.

23 WHO, 1997, www.who.int/reproductive-health/global_monitoring/skilled_attendant.html.

24 Donnay, F., and L. Weil, "Obstetric Fistula: The International Reponse," *The Lancet* (2004), 363 (9402): 71-72.

25 Lancaster, Carol, *Aid to Africa* (Chicago: University of Chicago Press, 1999).

26 UN Report by the Representative of the Secretary-General, Mr. Francis Deng, on internally displaced persons, submitted pursuant to Commission on Human Rights resolution 2000/53 (November 2000).

27 Chung, Cheuk Ming, *Crying Angola* (Hong Kong: Hong Kong

Arts Development Council, 2002), www.angelfire/blues/cry-ing-angola.

28 UNICEF, 2000. "Angola at a Glance," www.unicef.org/infoby-country/angola_502.html. Under 5 mortality rate (U5MR) was 292 per 1,000 live births. Angola was ranked second highest in the world. In 2002, Angola improved its ranking to fourth. It is now estimated that one in four children die before their fifth birthday (U5MR = 260/1,000).

29 World Food Programme (WFP), 2001. www.wfp.org.

30 Oxfam International, 2001, Oxfam Briefing Paper 2, "Angola's Wealth: Stories of War and Neglect," cited in "Global Survey on Education in Emergencies: Angola Country Report," by Women's Commission for Refugee Women and Children, p. 15. www.schoolnetafrica.net/fileadmin/resources/ed_Angol.pdf.

31 UN IDP Network, Senior Inter-Agency Network on Internal Displacement, "Mission to Angola: Findings and Recommendations," March 23, 2001.

32 UNICEF, 2004, www.unicef.org/infobycountry/angola.

33 UNICEF, 2004, www.unicef.org/infobycountry/angola.

34 From CSUCS (Coalition to Stop the Use of Child Soldiers), London, "Global Report on Child Soldiers," Cited by Rory Mungoven of CSUCS in an interview with Reuters on May 10, 2000.

35 The Portuguese first docked in Macao in 1535, some forty-three years after establishing contact with the Kongo kingdom (close to present-day Angola). In 1553, a settlement was established in Macao and, by 1557, Portugal took possession. It remained a colony until December 20, 1999, some four hundred forty-two years.

36 Heywood, Linda. *Central Africans and Cultural Transformations in the American Diaspora*. (Cambridge, UK: Cambridge University Press, 1999).

37 Source unknown, sometimes attributed to George Bernard Shaw's remarks on dancing: "Vertical expression of a horizontal desire legalized by music."

38 George Bernard Shaw (1856–1950), Irish-born playwright and dramatist.

39 Cilliers, J., and Dietrich, C., *Angola's War Economy: The Role of Oil and Diamonds* (South Africa: Institute for Security Studies, 2000).

40 Bureau of Intelligence and Research, USA, 1999, "Arms and

Conflict in Africa," http://www.state.gov/s/inr/rls/fs/ 2001/4004.htm.

41 Under Article 41 of the UN Charter, the Security Council may call upon Member States to apply measures not involving the use of armed forces in order to maintain or restore international peace and security. The Security Council invoked Chapter VII of the UN Charter to impose sanctions in the following countries: Afghanistan, Angola, Ethiopia, Eritrea, Federal Republic of Yugoslavia/Kosovo, Haiti, Iraq, Liberia, Libya, Rwanda, Sierra Leone, Somalia, South Africa, Southern Rhodesia, Sudan, and former Yugoslavia. http://ochaonline.un.org/webpage.asp? Page-901.

42 Ministry of Health, Republic of Angola, "National Strategic Plan Against STD/HIV/AIDS in Angola," p. 10, July 15, 1999. http://unpan1.um.org/intradoc/groups/public/documents/CAFRAD/UNPAN004729.pdf.

43 Ministry of Health, Republic of Angola, "National Strategic Plan Against STD/HIV/AIDS in Angola," p. 10, July 15, 1999. http://unpan1.um.org/intradoc/groups/public/documents/CAFRAD/UNPAN004729.pdf.

44 UN Survey, 2000.

45 Global malnutrition varied. In December 1999 there was 16.1% global malnutrition in the camps and 7.9% in the town. From a November 9, 2000, MSF report on Angola, "Behind the Façade of 'Normalization': Manipulation, Violence and Abandoned Populations," www.doctorswithoutborders.org /publications/ reports/2000/angola_11-2000.html.

46 CSUCS (Coaltion to Stop the Use of Child Soldiers), London, "Global Report on Child Soldiers, 2001," June 11, 2001.

47 Official Web site of the Government of the Republic of Angola, maintained by the Embassy of the Republic of Angola in Washington, D.C., www.angola.org/business/sector/rehab/ agrehab.html.

48 *The Economist*, May 2004, Economist Intelligence Unit statistic.

49 Seneca (4 BC–AD 65), Roman philosopher.

50 From *Sacred Hope* (1974), a book of collected poetry, by Antonio Agostinho Neto. Republished in 1988 by Journeyman Press and UNESCO.

51 www.shoal.net.au/~fcosta now moved to www.nhamalanda. com.

Index

Acknowledgements

At the end of our book-writing odyssey, we have a deep appreciation for the impact of others on the evolution of this book. However, in listing some here, we fear we may undervalue the contribution of others, as so many people supported and inspired us in ways they wouldn't have been aware. We thank them all from the bottom of our hearts. That said, there are some who undeniably deserve special mention for their contributions.

We are particularly indebted to our friend Lincoln Siliakus, whose contributions at a critical stage enabled us to reach the finish line. Lincoln dedicated months of his own valuable time to refine and edit the first manuscript. This was a mammoth and altruistic undertaking. His friendship and command of the English language continue to inspire.

To our families: Muriel Moorhouse, for the courage, compassion, and sense of conviction she instilled; Owen Moorhouse, for the spirit of adventure he imparted; Cheng Sui Feng and Yeh Lu Yun, for their wisdom and understanding; Ingrid Aysu (formerly Uğurlu), whose sisterly love was a constant every step of the way; Mehmet Uğurlu, in whose memory we changed our lives. He inspired us to make every day special and to get more out of life; Lloyd Moorhouse, who spurred us on from start to finish; Sandra Moorhouse, for her insightful critique of our early draft; and lastly, Cheng Xie, Clara Zhou Ying Xia, Sebastien Chin, Richard Chin, and Haluk Aysu, all of who supported us their own special ways.

We thank our friends to whom we are especially grateful: Bill Bowman and Olivia Yan Lai Ping, who looked after our affairs while we were away; Linda Peach and Elizabeth Foley, who also provided candid feedback on the book's first draft; Geneviève Le Caër; Anne Froger; Alyson and Nigel; Nicholas and Felicity Myer, especially for Nicholas' musings, which continue as his "Letter from England." All provided immeasurable support and encouragement.

We would also like to acknowledge Nathália Haas and her husband, Tuğhan Uludağ. Nathália's teachings in the basics of Portuguese were both invaluable and entertaining. She continued as our Portuguese coach from afar until the book's completion, and we thank her for her kind contributions. Thanks also to Heather and Tim Young, whose hospitality we soaked up in Durban, during our short, but therapeutic, break from Kuito. New friends emerged through our book writing and include Fernando and Filomena Costa. We share their passion for Angola and thank them for furthering our understanding of the country of their birth.

There are many whose e-mails, words of encouragement, and support in the field or along the way, meant so much to us. They include Aurea Arce, Sanjay and Shalini Bahadur, Simon and Roxane Berkowicz, Julie Bowman, Hélène and Richard De Vries, Bronwyn Evans, Chris Guinery, Winnie Har and Philip Kung, Jarka and Ivan Hybs, Mike Irwin, Christiane and Rolf Kuehne, Marian and Bill Leadbitter, Sandie Legg, Sally Lockhart, Lourdes Mayora and Peter Sargent, Frank Moorhouse, Kathy and Chris Morris, Irène Pianetti, Margarita Quevedo and Juan Escobar, Anna-Marie and Mehmet Sağ iroğlu, Margaret and Mike Sprague, Matthew and Margaret Tam, Ernest and Lonneke Van Heurn, Nadine Vincenc and Robert Bozek, Greg Wallace, Betty Wong, Bonnie Wong, Sarah Wong, Sherry Wu and Doug C. Lee, and hundreds of Hong Kong donors who sent messages to us in Kuito, notably the students of St. Patrick's School. Our friends from Nestlé China Limited deserve mention, especially Chan Man Sang, Cherry Chan Yuet Hing, Choo May Ling, Hermus Fok, Tobie Gordon, Grace Ho, Ron Houston, and Heidi Nam. Thanks also to the teams from Beijing Children's Hospital, especially Zhou Hong and Guo Weihong; Queen Mary Hospital; and the University of Hong Kong. We also acknowledge the more recent encouragement of our colleagues and friends at Nestlé Canada Inc. and the Hospital for Sick Children in Toronto.

The terrific team of volunteers, staff, and friends in Kuito were our inspiration. This is as much their story, too. We acknowledge the MSF volunteers in Kuito during that period: An Verwulgen, Anna Hardy, Anne-Sophie Gérin, Arnaud Cabal, Bérengère Leurquin, Bert Corijn, Bertrand Draguez Tripels De Hault, Berit Syversen Aamild, Brook Deres, Carina Johansson, Christelle François, Daniela Stone, Elisabeth Attner, Emilie Chagnon, Emmanuelle Lurquin, Felicitas Ibanez Llado, Francis Coteur, Helle Borg, Inger Haug, Katelijn Deknopper, Laurence Remacle, Lone Lund, Mieke Ponnet, Monica Minardi, Olivier Hubert, Patrick Depienne, Peter Rosseel, Rakel Ludviksen, Roberto Pizzorni, Rosemarie Lopez Sterup, Stephane Heymans, and Tanguy Paquot, as well as our special Kuito guests from Hong Kong, Chung Cheuk Ming, Elaine Lau, and Eric Poon Tat-Pui.

Thanks to the extraordinary team at the Provincial Hospital at Bié, without exception, but especially to Antonio Jacinto Bento, Malaquias Wana Jila, Eduardo Elambo Kayangula, Mario de Jesus Setumba, and Sebastião de Melo. We are also indebted to Augusto Sapalo Silivondela and Julio Domingos Mbumba of MSF Kuito for their loyal support, rich insights, and humour. The commitment of the local MSF team in Kuito deserves special mention and includes Albino Vionga (mechanic), Ana Maria (cleaner, *Casa Um*), Antonio Pacheco de Almeida (driver), Benjamim Maquina (assistant mechanic), Bernardo Chimbiambiulo Cassoma (driver), Catarina Amelia da Fonseca (cleaner, *Casa Três*), Domingos Moisés Cabinda (driver), Frederico Samoma (hospital assistant), Gloria Angelina (cook, *Casa Dois*), Joaquim Baptista Barreira (driver), José Manuel Canjungo (driver), Leontino Lelemba Quintino (driver), Luisa Fernanda Machado (cook, *Casa Um*), Madalena Chiconde Sunga (office janitor), Maria de Fatima Kalumbo (cleaner, *Casa Quatro*), Maria do Ceu Marques (nutrition assistant), Mario Gama (logistician), Mario Laurindo Natumbo Piriquito (radio operator), Sandro Sebastião (driver), Teodoro Jacinto (driver), and the others too numerous to mention individually.

The MSF support team in Luanda at that time included volunteers Céline Remy, Christian Criboom, Christopher Stokes, Geneviève Kaponda-Kilufya, Frédéric Jamar, Laetitia Liebert, Mourad Gumusboga, Nadine De Lamotte, and numerous national staff. We thank each of them for sharing such a meaningful part of our lives.

Our friends at various MSF offices in Hong Kong, Brussels, and Toronto are to be acknowledged, especially Olivier Bonnet and Anne Lung, who were first to encourage us to write this book; Chan Fung Kit, who inspired us with her noble dedication to the book's Chinese translation; Dick Van Der Tak and Tommi Laulajainen, who helped us push the project along; and many others including Nancy Forgrave, Anita Kwok, June Kashio, and Vivien Pun.

Lastly, our hearty thanks to Mike O'Connor of Insomniac Press for taking us on as first-time authors. Also thanks to Emily Schultz and our editor, Maria Bruk Aupérin, for their encouragement and guidance.

About the Authors

Karin Moorhouse was born in the Australian coastal town of Nowra. She studied marketing at University of New South Wales in Sydney, where she met her husband, Wei Cheng. She rose through the corporate ranks, working in Australia, Britain, China, and Hong Kong. She became head of marketing and sales for a leading division of Nestlé in Hong Kong, where the couple lived for eleven years. She resigned to join Médecins Sans Frontières and worked as financial administrator in Angola. She is now vice president, marketing for the ice cream division of Nestlé Canada Inc.

Wei Cheng was born in Beijing, China and grew up during the futile years of Mao's Cultural Revolution. At the age of fifteen he became a refugee when he left China for Hong Kong in the hope of obtaining an education. He went on to study medicine in Australia, before returning to Hong Kong. He trained as a general surgeon, specializing further to become a pediatric surgeon and an assistant professor of surgery at University of Hong Kong. In 2000 he and his wife left Hong Kong to volunteer for Médecins Sans Frontières in Angola. He is now a medical researcher at The Hospital for Sick Children, Toronto and is completing a Ph.D. at University of Toronto. Wei also volunteered for a short emergency mission to Monrovia, Liberia.

No One Can Stop the Rain is the couple's first book.

Kuito, April 1, 2001.